Interfaces of the Word

STUDIES IN THE EVOLUTION OF
CONSCIOUSNESS AND CULTURE

Also by Walter J. Ong, S.J.

Frontiers in American Catholicism (1957)
Ramus, Method, and the Decay of Dialogue (1958)
Ramus and Talon Inventory (1958)
American Catholic Crossroads (1959)
Darwin's Vision and Christian Perspectives (1960)
  (Editor and Contributor)
The Barbarian Within (1962)
In the Human Grain (1967)
The Presence of the Word (1967)
Knowledge and the Future of Man (1968)
  (Editor and Contributor)
Petrus Ramus and Audomarus Talaeus, *Collectaneae praefationes, epistolae, orationes* (1969) (Editor)
Petrus Ramus, *Scholae in liberales artes* (1970) (Editor)
Rhetoric, Romance, and Technology (1971)
Why Talk? (1973)

Interfaces of the Word

STUDIES IN THE EVOLUTION OF
CONSCIOUSNESS AND CULTURE

Walter J. Ong, S. J.

Cornell University Press ITHACA AND LONDON

First published 1977 by Cornell University Press.
Published in the United Kingdom by Cornell University Press Ltd., 2-4 Brook Street, London W1Y 1AA.

International Standard Book Number 0-8014-1105-X
Library of Congress Catalog Card Number 77-3124
Printed in the United States of America by York Composition Co., Inc.
Librarians: Library of Congress cataloging information
appears on the last page of the book.

To the memory of
William Kurtz Wimsatt, Jr.,
who once told me, "I am a space man,
you are a time man,"
and of
Alexander Wimsatt
and for Margaret and James

Quoniam Deus creavit hominem inexterminabilem
et ad imaginem similitudinis suae fecit illum.

Iustorum autem animae in manu Dei sunt,
et non tanget illos tormentum mortis.
—Lib. Sap. 2:23, 3:1

Contents

Preface

The present volume carries forward work in two earlier volumes by the same author, *The Presence of the Word* (1967) and *Rhetoric, Romance, and Technology* (1971). The first of these describes and interprets the evolution of modes of thought and verbal expression from primary oral culture, before the invention of script, through the subsequent technological transformations of the word—through writing, print, and the electronic devices of recent times (the so-called media)—and the resulting evolution of consciousness, of man's sense of presence in the human lifeworld, including the physical world and what man senses beyond. The second undertakes to show how the history of rhetoric in the West has mirrored the evolution of society, variously ordering knowledge, guiding thought, focusing perception, and shaping culture for over two thousand years until the ancient rhetorical economy of thought and expression was finally swamped by the effects of print and the advent of the Age of Romanticism.

The thesis of these two earlier works is sweeping, but it is not reductionist, as reviewers and commentators, so far as I know, have all generously recognized: the works do not maintain that the evolution from primary orality through writing and print to an electronic culture, which produces secondary orality, causes or explains everything in human culture and consciousness. Rather, the thesis is relationist: major developments, and very likely even all major developments, in culture and consciousness are related, often in unexpected intimacy, to the evolution of the word from primary orality to its present state. But the relationships are varied and complex, with cause and effect often difficult to distinguish.

This book undertakes to develop lines of investigation that connect with those in the two earlier books. Some of the new findings reported here have been made possible by comparative studies, particularly studies involving the Occident (Europe and the Americas) and Central and West Africa. All of the new studies have been grouped around the dialectically related themes of change or alienation on the one hand and growth or integration on the other. The technological history of the word has apparently moved in such dialectical patterns: the world of primary orality was torn to pieces by writing and print, which then created, agonizingly, a new kind of noetic and a new kind of culture based on analysis and self-conscious unification that has itself been fragmenting and re-forming today in new constellations.

At a few points I refer in passing to the work of French and other European structuralists—variously psychoanalytic, phenomenological, linguistic, or anthropological in cast—such as Jacques Derrida, Michel Foucault, Jacques Lacan, Roland Barthes, and Tzvetan Todorov, not to mention Claude Lévi-Strauss and certain cisatlantic critics such as Paul de Man, Geoffrey Hartman, J. Hillis Miller, and Harold Bloom, who are more or less in dialogue with these Europeans. Many readers will doubtless note that the works of these scholars and the present volume share common themes and perhaps even a kind of common excitement. In particular, as I am well aware, my treatment of discourse and thought as rooted ineradicably in orality contrasts with Derrida's chirographic and typographic focus in his *De la grammatologie* and other works.

But this book has its own history, traceable through my earlier works and the references embedded in them; it has also, I hope, its own intelligibility. From the time of my studies of Peter Ramus and Ramism, my work has grown into its own kind of phenomenological history of culture and consciousness, so I have often been assured by others, elaborated in terms of noetic operations as these interrelate with primary oral verbalization and later with chirographic and typographic and electronic technologies that reorganize verbalization and thought. In treating the transit from orality to typographic cultures, the present volume, like its immediate predecessors, ingests and variously nuances or adapts a great deal of the germinal American scholarship represented by Milman Parry, Albert B. Lord, Eric A. Havelock, and other scholars and field workers, all of which appears virtually unknown to Continental Europeans, at least up to the immediate present. For discussion of the shift from chirographic culture to typographic, certain academic and para-academic and literary phenomena from the later fifteenth century through the eighteenth have been compared, and for the shift to electronic operations, besides academic and para-academic and literary phenomena, other phenomena in the so-called mass media have been attended to. To relate lines of thought worked out of such data to the structuralist and other developments mentioned above, impressive and fecund though these developments are, would result in endless complications which could only obscure my own presentation, or so I believe. So, too, would discussion with Marxist critics, who in fact have touched very little if at all on these subject matters. It has seemed best therefore to say here what I have to say and to leave to others the establishment of affinities or disparities.

Some of the studies in this volume are published here for the first time. Others have appeared in journals and collections and are printed here, slightly revised, with the permission of the publishers. All were written after *The Presence of the Word* and *Rhetoric, Romance, and Technology,* although one actually preceded the latter book into print. "The Writer's Audience Is Always a Fiction" first appeared in *PMLA: Publications of the Modern Language Association of America,* 90 (1975), 9–22. It was developed from a much briefer paper read at Cambridge University, August 24, 1972, at the Twelfth International Congress of the International Federation for Modern Languages and Literatures. At the Center for Advanced Study in the Behavioral

Sciences at Stanford, California, in 1973–74, I profited much from conversations with Albert Cook of the State University of New York, Buffalo, and with Robert Darnton of Princeton University concerning matters in this final version. "Media Transformation: The Talked Book" appeared in *College English,* 34 (1972), 405–410, as an adaptation of a talk given at the Annual Meeting of the National Council of Teachers of English in November, 1970. "African Talking Drums and Oral Noetics" was published in *New Literary History,* 8 (1977), 411–429, and " 'I See What You Say': Sense Analogues for Intellect" in *Human Inquiries: Review of Existential Psychology and Psychiatry,* Nos. 1–3 (1970), pp. 22–42, after it had been presented as a paper at the First International Lonergan Congress held at St. Leo College, St. Leo, Florida, in March, 1970. "Typographic Rhapsody: Ravisius Textor, Zwinger, and Shakespeare" appeared as "Commonplace Rhapsody: Ravisius Textor, Zwinger, and Shakespeare" in *Classical Influences on European Culture A.D. 1500–1700,* edited by R. R. Bolgar (Cambridge, England: Cambridge University Press, 1976). "From Epithet to Logic: Miltonic Epic and the Closure of Existence" was published in the *Proceedings of the American Philosophical Society,* 120 (1976), 295–305, as "Milton's Logical Epic and Evolving Consciousness." In abridged form, this study was presented as a paper at the Autumn General Meeting of the American Philosophical Society in Philadelphia, November 18, 1975. "The Poem as a Closed Field: The Once New Criticism and the Nature of Literature" appeared in *The Possibilities of Order: Cleanth Brooks and His Work,* edited by Lewis P. Simpson (Baton Rouge: Louisiana State University Press, 1976) under the title "From Rhetorical Culture to New Criticism: The Poem as a Closed Field." "From Mimesis to Irony: Writing and Print as Integuments of Voice" is reprinted from *The Bulletin of the Midwest Modern Language Association,* 9 (1976), 1–24. In much abridged form, this paper was read as a keynote address at the opening session of the Seventeenth Annual Meeting of the Midwest Modern Language Association in Chicago, November 6, 1976.

Some of these studies were worked out during a wonderful year, 1973–74, when I was a Fellow at the Center for Advanced Study in the Behavioral Sciences at Stanford, California. Here, from my fellow Fellow Sydney Shoemaker, I learned the term "disambiguate," indispensable in discussing African talking drums, and labored to disambiguate my own utterances or mutterings under challenge from various other Fellows, particularly those duly footnoted at specific points in this book—all under the benign incitation of the Center's director, O. Meredith Wilson, who told us, "You have been invited here as Fellows to do your own work as you please, with the understanding that the only pressure on you is what comes from within each of you." He did not add, though he might have, that he had brought together at the Center the forty-four most inner-driven characters he could find at that moment across the face of the earth. I am grateful to all at the Center and to those responsible for its existence. I have also been helped immeasurably in these studies by many at Saint Louis University, colleagues on the faculty, librarians, and members of the Jesuit community, particularly by Fathers Bert Akers, S.J., Marcus A. Haworth, S.J., and John F. Kavanaugh, S.J., Professors Charles K. Hofling, M.D., Clarence Harvey Miller, and Wolfgang Karrer, by Miss Catherine Weidle, by many of my students, by Miss Viola C. C. Liu of Washington University in Saint Louis, and by members of the Jesuit community at the University of Santa Clara, notably Father James Torrens, S.J., and Father Frederick P. Tollini, S.J. The others to whom I am indebted are simply too numerous to be enumerated, but they have my sincere thanks.

W. J. O.

Saint Louis, Missouri

I

CLEAVAGE AND GROWTH

1

Transformations of the Word and Alienation

Orality, Writing, and Disjuncture

Alienation, a favorite diagnosis variously applied to modern man's plight since at least Hegel and Feuerbach, has not been commonly thought of in terms of the technological history of the word, although some attention, more analytic than historical or clinical, has been given by structuralists to certain tensions attendant on writing.[1] Yet it would appear that the technological inventions of writings, print, and electronic verbalization, in their historical effects, are connected with and have helped bring about a certain kind of alienation within the human lifeworld. This is not at all to say that these inventions have been simply destructive, but rather that they have restructured consciousness, affecting men's and women's presence to the world and to themselves and creating new interior distances within the psyche.

1. See, for example, Jacques Derrida, *De la grammatologie* (Paris: Editions de Minuit, 1967), Pt. II, Ch. 1, "La Violence de la lettre: de Lévi-Strauss à Rousseau." With work such as Derrida's, philosophy, which as a formal discipline depends on a certain interiorization of writing, becomes acutely and exquisitely aware of its own chirographic framework, but has not yet much attended to the orality out of which the chirographic has developed historically and in which it is always in some way embedded. It may be worth noting that Derrida's key distinction between *différence* and *différance* (his neologism) is not phonemic, but chirographic. For the distinction, see Jacques Derrida, "La Différance," in *Théorie d'ensemble,* ed. Phillippe Sollers *et al.* (Paris: Editions du Seuil, 1968). The proliferation of such terms in the work of Derrida, Roland Barthes, and other structuralists appears to register the sensibility fostered by an electronic noetic economy, a sensibility conditioned to work with massive accumulation of detailed information and rapid exchange of ideas—even though its chief focus of attention is chirographic (and typographic).

Primary orality, the orality of a culture which has never known writing, is in some ways conspicuously integrative. The psyche in a culture innocent of writing knows by a kind of empathetic identification of knower and known, in which the object of knowledge and the total being of the knower enter into a kind of fusion,[2] in a way which literate cultures would typically find unsatisfyingly vague and garbled and somehow too intense and participatory. To personalities shaped by literacy, oral folk often appear curiously unprogramed, not set off against their physical environment, given simply to soaking up existence, unresponsive to abstract demands such as a "job" that entails commitment to routines organized in accordance with abstract clock time (as against human, or lived, "felt," duration).

This kind of reaction to "primitives" is commonplace in highly technologized cultures and hardly calls for documentation. With writing, the earlier noetic state undergoes a kind of cleavage, separating the knower from the external universe and then from himself.[3] This separation makes possible both "art" (technē) in the ancient Greek sense of detached abstract analysis of human procedures, and science, or detached abstract analysis of the cosmos, but it does so at the price of splitting up the original unity of consciousness and in this sense alienating man from himself and his original lifeworld. The original unity was not by any means totally satisfactory, of course. It was destined to crumble,

2. Eric A. Havelock, *Preface to Plato* (Cambridge, Mass.: Belknap Press of Harvard University Press, 1963), pp. 169–190. Although studies of this depth have yet to be made for cultures other than that of ancient Greece, the noetic processes examined in minute detail by Havelock can be readily recognized in the heroic poetry of other oral cultures. See, for example, Daniel P. Kunene, *Heroic Poetry of the Basotho* (Oxford: Clarendon Press, 1971); Jeff Opland, "*Imbongi Nezibongo:* The Xhosa Tribal Poet and the Contemporary Poetic Tradition," *PMLA,* 90 (1975), 185–208. All primary oral cultures are more or less "heroic." Claude Lévi-Strauss observes that "the savage mind totalizes"—*The Savage Mind* (Chicago: University of Chicago Press, 1966), p. 245: this "savage" mind is the functionally oral mind as against the literate.

3. Havelock, *Preface to Plato,* pp. 197–214, and 3–19, 254–278; Walter J. Ong, *The Presence of the Word* (New Haven: Yale University Press, 1967), pp. 22–35.

for man is programmed for alienation, more than any other being in the cosmos. Such programming gives mankind both discomfort and promise. But some original unity had been for the time real.

Oral cultures appropriate actuality in recurrent, formulaic agglomerates, communally generated and shared. Formulas are communally fixed ways of organizing simultaneously object and response-to-object. They can be typified by epithets, that is, standard, expected qualifiers or surrogates—the sturdy oak, the rosy-fingered dawn, the brave soldier, the noble chief, the hated foe, Son of Peleus (for Achilles). It should be noted, however, that to say that oral cultures use and need formulas is not to say that their verbalization processes, either in formal prose or poetry or in other discourse, consists simply of stringing together in various orders items from a catalog of fixed phrases. The use of formulas is far more complex than this. The surface actualizations in ancient Greek formulaic poetry, for example, overlie what Michael M. Nagler has well characterized as "an inheritance of habits, tendencies, and techniques rather than of completed entities," which make oral poetry "spontaneous-traditional" art in which "the oral poet . . . at the moment of performance makes spontaneous, and therefore original realizations of inherited, traditional impulses."[4] What Nagler says of poetry would apply, *mutatis mutandis,* to other forms of discourse in oral cultures, where the entire noetic economy is dominated by formulas, so that poets simply maximize, in often exquisite ways, processes of thought and discourse endemic through the entire culture. The point here is simply that the elements figuring in the discourse are basically formulary to an extent radically greater than what highly literate cultures can ordinarily tolerate.

Epithets are not merely descriptive, but also approbatory or

4. Michael M. Nagler, *Spontaneity and Tradition: A Study in the Oral Art of Homer* (Berkeley: University of California Press, 1974), pp. xxiii, xxi. Nagler's work renders obsolete many of the disputes about definitions of formulas and themes. Here, I understand formulas or formulaic elements in no arcane sense but simply as expressions which are expected or highly predictable.

depreciatory: they cue in the audience's evaluatory response, as with "brave," "noble," "hated," in the examples just given. Such formulas hold together the noetic world in units which discourage and even defy analysis. Breaking up such units, into an objective component (oak, soldier) and an evocative component eliciting a subjective response (sturdy, brave) would be too traumatic even to think about as a possibility. Sturdiness goes with oaks forever, and bravery with soldiers, at least the real ones. Moreover, since formulas are of their nature expected, nonsurprising—in terms of information theory, carrying zero new knowledge or "information"—they require no adjustment of knower to known but bind the two in familiar, unbreakable bonds. This was the world, as Havelock has shown, that Plato set himself against in expelling the poets from his republic, as it is the world of oral cultures generally, the "heroic" world. The total merger of knower and known in a holistic, formulary experience made virtually impossible any programmatic developments in abstract thought, such as Plato envisioned. This is why Plato excluded poets, "rhapsodizers" who stitched together (*rhaptein,* to sew; *rhapsōidein,* to stitch a song together) themes and formulas.

The diaeretic effects of writing and print in the developments that broke up this noetic world to establish a line of more or less disengaged, pure thought become apparent if we recall that the real word, the spoken word, in a profound sense is of itself bound to ongoing, lived human existence, and thus is of itself aggregative, or unitive, the opposite of diaeretic or disjunctive or analytic, despite the fact that without the word the disjunction necessary for abstract thinking cannot be achieved. The spoken word, however abstract its signification or however static the object it may represent, is of its very nature a sound, tied to the movement of life itself in the flow of time. Sound exists only when it is going out of existence: in uttering the word "existence," by the time I get to the "-tence," the "exis-" is gone and has to be gone.[5] A spoken word, even when it refers to a statically modeled "thing,"

5. See Ong, *The Presence of the Word,* pp. 40–45.

is itself never a thing or even a "sign" ("sign" refers primarily to something seen and thus, however subtly, reduces the aural to the visual and the static). No real word can be present all at once as the letters in a written "word" are. The real word, the spoken word, is always an event, whatever its codified associations with concepts, thought of as immobile objectifications. In this sense, the spoken word is an action, an ongoing part of ongoing existence.

Oral utterance thus encourages a sense of continuity with life, a sense of participation, because it is itself participatory. Writing and print, despite their intrinsic value, have obscured the nature of the word and of thought itself, for they have sequestered the essentially participatory word—fruitfully enough, beyond a doubt—from its natural habitat, sound, and assimilated it to a mark on a surface, where a real word cannot exist at all.

It seems offensively banal to note that written or printed "words" are only codes to enable properly informed and skilled persons to reconstruct real words in externalized sound or in their auditory imaginations. However, many if not most persons in technological cultures are strongly conditioned to think unreflectively just the opposite, to assume that the printed word is the real word, and that the spoken word is inconsequential. Permanent unreality is more plausible and comforting than reality that is transient. Until the past few decades, from their origins in the seventeenth and eighteenth centuries, dictionaries of modern European vernaculars were generally printed—for dictionaries are essentially printed constructs, their totally alphabetized reference economy being virtually inoperable in a nontypographic script culture—with this assumption: the only speakers of a language who could be trusted to use the "real" language, pure and uncorrupted, were professional writers, which is to say writers whose work got regularly into print. The usage of professional writers, and only their usage, was what dictionaries properly registered, and even this usage might itself occasionally be exceptionable if it strayed from other printed usage. Away from print, all was chaos, for away from print, "corruption" was likely or even sure to set in.[6]

Yet, to get words into writing and, a fortiori, into print has called for massive technological interventions which separate the word from man and man from the word. Writing and print are technologies, requiring reflectively prepared materials and tools. Everywhere, among all groups of human beings, the spoken word is simply a datum of life. Only some six thousand years ago, with the invention of the first script around 3500 B.C., did man begin to commit the spoken word to a visually perceived surface set off from himself. There are still millions of men and women who cannot do so. Languages, in which words originate, are commonly styled "tongues" (*langue, lingua,* tongue) and require no external technological skills at all. They are not "out there," distanced. Languages come from within and they are distinctively human in that, among other things, they require man's own kind of oral and vocal apparatus. (One of the troubles in trying to make apes shape words is that apes are not built for it.)

Identity, Mother Tongues, and Distancing Languages

Oral verbalization, unlike writing, is thus natural. The word comes to each of us first orally in our "mother" tongue. Its association with mother and early nature and nurture is why speech is so closely involved with our personal identity and with cultural identity, and why manipulation of the word entails various kinds of alienation.

Why do we think so effortlessly of the first language we learn as our "mother" tongue? Or perhaps as our "native" tongue—which is pretty much the same thing, since *natura* (adjective, *nativus;* cognate, *nativitas*) means basically "birth," and hence refers primarily to mother (cf. "Mother Nature"). In many languages—perhaps not in all—there are no "father" tongues, though a motherland can, with certain adjustments, be considered a fatherland, and vice versa.

6. See Walter J. Ong, *In the Human Grain* (New York: Macmillan, 1967), pp. 52–59.

The concept of "mother" tongue registers deeply the human feeling that the language in which we grow up, the language which introduces us as human beings to the human lifeworld, not only comes primarily from our mother but belongs to some degree intrinsically to our mother's feminine world. Our first language claims us not as a father does, with a certain distance that is bracing because it is both austere and founded in deep love, but as a mother does, immediately, from the beginning, lovingly, possessively, participatorily, and incontrovertibly. Mother is closer than father: we were carried in her womb. In her and from her we were born. Our world is a fragment of hers.

A mother's closeness is not only biological and psychological. It is linguistic as well. This is not to say that fathers do not teach speech at all, for they obviously do, or that other persons in contact with the child do not, for they obviously do also. But the father's role here is subordinate, and so is that of others in the child's ambiance—sisters, brothers, nurses, and the like—except insofar as the mother's world envelopes and validates them.[7] Normally, it is dominantly the mother or surrogate mother recognized precisely as a maternal, not a paternal, agent who by continuing contact during the lalling stage and beyond converts the infant (Latin, *infans, in-fans,* non-speaking, from the Latin *in-,* not, and *fari,* to speak) into a user of words.

The association of mother with first language learning is, moreover, not merely a matter of proximity, of her being normally more within earshot of the child. It is also physiological and psychosomatic. An infant's contact with its mother is a distinctively

7. P. Herbert Leiderman and Gloria F. Leiderman, "Affective and Cognitive Consequences of Polymatric Infant Care in the East African Highlands," *Minnesota Symposia on Child Psychology,* 8, ed. Anne D. Pick (Minneapolis: University of Minnesota Press, 1974), 81–110, have reported on some of the effects when, while mothers are working elsewhere, older sisters or brothers or other surrogate mothers take care of an infant during a great part of the day. In general, the infant receives more attention in such an arrangement than otherwise might be the case and develops faster cognitively. In the cases reported, the mother is, however, always clearly in charge, even when temporarily absent, and is of course the only one nursing the infant.

oral and lingual one in more ways than one. Tongues are used early for both suckling and for speaking, and language is usually, if not always, learned while a child is still at the breast (or bottle). Who wipes an infant's mouth, and how many times a day? First languages especially are associated with feeding, as all languages are to some extent.[8] A vast tradition from the past as well as brilliant and profound scholarly studies such as the late Marcel Jousse's *La Manducation de la parole*, treat the "eating" of the written word. It is by "eating," psychologically chewing, swallowing, digesting, assimilating from within, rather than by mere visual imaging that the written word becomes truly oral again, and thereby alive and real, entering into the human consciousness and living there.[9]

It is significant that we tend to think of language as basically an oral or mouth phenomenon. Language does indeed issue from the oral cavity, the mouth (Latin, *os, oris*). Yet the most distinctive feature of language might well seem to be not its orality or "mouthiness," the fact that it comes out of a certain area of the face, but rather its tonicity, its acoustic or sound quality. Sound has no distinctive association with mouths except for the upper reaches of the animal kingdom. There are many animal mouths from which no sounds ever issue, and many animals that are very noisy do not use their mouths at all to make their sounds—cicadas and crickets, for example. Even in man vocal sound involves much more than the mouth—the diaphram, the esophagus, the lungs and chest cavity for air pressure, various head and body

---

8. There appears to be little recent psychoanalytic literature directly relevant to connections between language and feeding. For some leads, see E. Trillat, "Oralité et langage," *Evolution psychiatrique*, 25 (1960), 383–409; Augusta Bernard, "The Primal Significance of the Tongue," *International Journal of Psycho-Analysis*, 41 (1960), 301–307; René Arpand Spitz, "The Primal Cavity," *Psychoanalytic Study of the Child*, 10 (1955), 215–240; Nandor Fodor, "Psychotherapy and Problems of Libido in the Use of Language," *American Imago*, 11 (1960), 347–381. Peter Ostwald, "The Sound System of Man," *Explorations in Communication*, 2 (1975), 31–50, provides an excellent survey of recent literature, including much about the origins of language, phylogenetic and ontogenetic, but little on connections between language and feeding.

9. Marcel Jousse, *La Manducation de la parole* (Paris: Gallimard, 1975).

cavities for resonance, and particularly the vocal cords. These are not in the mouth but in the larynx, which connects with the lungs, not with the alimentary canal. Nevertheless, we commonly think of language in terms of the mouth and refer to it not as an acoustic phenomenon but as a mouth or "oral" phenomenon, thus honoring its association with nourishment and mother.

There are, however—or have been—languages, and extraordinarily influential languages, which have existed as no one's mother tongue, languages learned by males from other males, always as second languages acquired by those who already have other mother tongues. Such languages are indeed spoken and hence are acoustic and "oral" phenomena. But they depend on writing rather than on oral speech for their existence. Writing establishes them at a distance from the immediate interpersonal human lifeworld where the word unites one human being with another, and particularly infant with mother. These sex-linked male languages have distanced their users very often from their fathers, too, for they have been acquired normally not from the learner's father at all but from some more distant male or males, such as schoolmasters or their equivalents.[10] In the West, such languages have been represented by Learned Latin, as we can designate Latin in the condition in which it existed from around A.D. 550 or so to the present. Learned Latin has not been inherited from within the family and has normally been used exclusively to deal with tribal and public affairs rather than with domestic affairs. That is, it has been used for more or less abstract, academic, philosophical, scientific subjects or for forensic or legal or administrative or liturgical matters. Father is more outward-facing than mother, and, if Learned Latin has not been exactly a father tongue, it has nevertheless been even more outward-facing than father himself has been.

Not only were all of the teachers of Learned Latin males for

10. I am treating here whole languages, not varieties of speech within a language such as expressions or styles which are the prerogatives of male groups, nor corresponding special vocabularies or styles of women, nor other special speech modes within a language.

well over a millennium, but all its learners were males as well, with exceptions so few as to be negligible. By the nineteenth century, academic education opened up more and more to girls (who earlier had often had impressive nonacademic education, particularly if they were of the aristocracy or gentry, such as enabled them to manage formidable households of sixty or seventy persons or more not only with efficiency but often also with grace and charm).[11] As girls and women came into academia, Latin declined. The decline was not exactly planned, and some female students did study Latin, but, overall, the admission of women to academic education and the decline of Latin moved *pari passu.* Girls and women who learned Latin seldom if ever used it for practical purposes, academic, literary, diplomatic, or other, as millions of males did over the centuries. Women religious chanted the Church's office in Latin, devoutly and effectively, but they had not composed the text and seldom understood its exact meaning. By the present day, many distinguished women scholars have studied Latin poetry and prose literature and have written about Latin literature sensitively and expertly—but in the vernaculars. In contrast, over the past thousand years hundreds of thousands of boys and men have written about Latin as well as about everything else under the sun in Learned Latin, which was the mother tongue of none of them. Communication in Latin for the programmatically agonistic, disputatious, Latin-writing and Latin-speaking world of the West, from Cassiodorus through Erasmus and Milton and beyond, the only academic world the West had

11. Ann Harrison, Lady Fanshawe, "flung" away her "childishnesses" at the age of fifteen years and three months, when her mother died, and took up managing the household. This and other here useful instances of some effects of women's education in the past, with a bibliography, are given by Patricia A. Sullivan, "Education and the Styles of Seventeenth Century Women Writers: The Case of Margaret Cavendish" (M.A. thesis, Saint Louis University, 1975, pp. 26–45). Works on women's education which are otherwise invaluable, such as Dorothy Gardiner's *English Girlhood at School* (London: Oxford University Press, 1929) or Doris Mary Stenton's *The English Woman in History* (London: Allen & Unwin, 1957), seldom provide the kind of information relating women's education to the linguistic or social forces discussed in the present work.

ever known at all until three centuries ago, was never anything other than an all-male enterprise.[12]

But even so male-dominated a language as Learned Latin had itself been a mother tongue originally, for all languages come into being as mother tongues or from mother tongues.[13] Latin found itself converted from a mother tongue into an extrafamilial medium when in the sixth and seventh centuries of the Christian era, the Latin that mothers in Latin-speaking cultures had been talking to their children had in the course of normal linguistic development evolved away from the earlier Latin always found in schoolbooks and had shaped itself into one or another of the modern Romance tongues such as Italian or Spanish or French or Roumanian. When children whose mother tongue was thus evolving further and further from an original Latin base could no longer understand at all the Latin in the schoolbooks that their great-grandfathers had understood with little difficulty, Learned Latin found itself in existence. It was the old Latin destitute of any native speakers.

By around A.D. 550–700, Latin was settling down as a chirographically controlled language, thereafter fated normally to be acquired extradomestically in all-male schools by boys previously acquainted with speech in at least one other tongue. Latin was never more learned by *in-fantes*, non-speakers. Latin was still widely spoken, all through the academic world, known to far more persons than were many or even most vernaculars, but it was always learned with the assistance of pen and ink. The way it developed henceforth depended on the way it was written, not the way it was uttered. This is a strange situation for a language. Latin was distanced—alienated—not from day-to-day life, for it was of the substance of daily life for lawyers, physicians, academic

12. Walter J. Ong, *Rhetoric, Romance, and Technology* (Ithaca, N.Y.: Cornell University Press, 1971), pp. 113–141; Walter J. Ong, "Agonistic Structures in Academia: Past to Present," *Interchange: A Journal of Educational Studies* (Toronto), 5 (1974), 1–12.

13. Artificial languages, such as Esperanto, inevitably reveal the linguistic connections of their inventors. There is no way to invent a language that is not based, directly or indirectly, on the ones you know.

educators, and clergymen, but from the psychological and psycho-somatic roots of consciousness. It no longer in any sense belonged to mother. It did not come from where you came from.

Learned Latin was not an isolated phenomenon. Other learned languages appeared elsewhere at roughly the same stage in the history of consciousness. This fact has seldom if ever been ad-verted to by historians or linguists. The establishment of special languages through chirographic distancing has been fairly wide-spread across the globe in highly literate cultures, always occur-ring in the period after writing was interiorized enough to affect thought processes but before print had further affected thought processes. Putting aside chirographically controlled languages used exclusively for liturgical purposes, such as Old Church Slavonic, and other less than definite developments such as post-classical or Byzantine Greek, as examples of other learned lan-guages somewhat like Learned Latin one thinks especially of Sanskrit, Classical Chinese, Classical Arabic, and Rabbinic Hebrew.[14] These languages have been of the utmost importance for the development of thought and of civilization—during their ascendancy much more important than any mother tongues.

The fact that at a crucial stage in its development the most advanced thought of mankind in widely separated parts of the globe has been worked out in linguistic economies far removed from the hearth and from the entire world of infancy would seem to deserve far more attention than it has received, if only because it has received almost no attention whatsoever. The causes for the development and use of these nonmaternal, chiro-

14. For the commonly known features here noted in Latin, Sanskrit, Chinese, Arabic, and Hebrew during various stages of their development, the best immediate sources are the respective articles on these languages in the *Encyclopaedia Britannica* (1965), with the references there cited. In addi-tion, the following works provide invaluable information: Mario Pei, *One Language for the World* (New York: Devin-Adair, 1958); H. A. Gleason, Jr., *An Introduction to Descriptive Linguistics,* rev. ed. (New York: Holt, Rinehart, & Winston, 1961); John P. Hughes, *The Science of Language: An Introduction to Linguistics* (New York: Random House, 1962). See also Robert A. D. Forrest, *The Chinese Language,* 2d ed. rev. (London: Faber & Faber, 1965), and for certain aspects of developments in Learned Latin, Ong, *The Presence of the Word,* pp. 76–87, 208–22, 241–55, and *passim.*

graphically controlled languages are of course varied. Although the matter needs further study before any definitive statements can be made, it appears obvious that geographical, political, economic, and various sociological causes would come into play. These cannot be gone into here. The present discussion concerns itself principally with certain psychocultural causes and implications.

The learned languages just named do not relate all the same way to the mother tongues from which they respectively derive or to the mother tongues which surround them. But they have certain features in common. Three just have been noted. First, they have never been learned as mother tongues but always after a mother tongue has been learned. Second, they have been learned always with the help of writing, for, despite widespread oral use, they have been sustained and controlled by script. Third, they came into being between the period when writing was interiorized in the psyche sufficiently to affect thought processes and personality structures and the period when print and print technology appeared and further affected thought processes and personality structures.[15] Fourth, they were all sex-linked languages, used only by males with mostly negligible exceptions (the few women writers in Classical Chinese appear to have been perhaps slightly less negligible than women writers in the other learned languages). Fifth, these learned languages are all, in one way or another, either disappearing from use or regaining status as mother tongues: the age of chirographically distanced, exclusively learned languages is over with, across the globe.

Two of these influential learned languages are Indo-European, Sanskrit and Learned Latin. The relationship of Sanskrit to a mother tongue remains uncertain: it is not certain exactly how close the literary language we know as Sanskrit was to the Indo-Asian language which was its oral antecedent. In any event, if there was a spoken Sanskrit close to the literary language, it long ago ceased to function as a medium for living communication,

15. Ong, *The Presence of the Word*, pp. 130–140.

though it may be artificially cultivated as such a medium even today in isolated special groups in India.[16] Sanskrit in India and elsewhere is and has long been a subject to study, not a medium for widespread use in the study of other subjects.

Latin, the other Indo-European learned language, is in the last stages of slipping into this same state. It was still being used for such things as medical books in the early 1800s and for doctoral dissertations in some European universities (such as those in Hungary) to the middle of the present century, but its most recent use has been more and more restricted to service as an administrative language in the Roman Catholic Church, as a liturgical language in the Latin rite of the Roman Catholic Church, and as a language of instruction in many, though not all, professional courses for Roman Catholic clergy of the Latin rite (for there are Roman Catholic rites other than Latin). Here, moreover, the changes in the past two decades have been drastic, so that Mario Pei's account of the status of Latin, which was a thoroughly up-to-date account in 1958, is now completely out of date so far as it treats the Roman Catholic milieu.[17]

Until the 1960s, for example, houses of study for members of the Society of Jesus preparing for the priesthood across the world provided three years of philosophical studies and four years of theology in which textbooks and the lectures in the core subjects and all examinations in these subjects were in Latin (the examinations oral, the major ones of two hours' duration). This was the course that the present writer followed. Within the past ten

---

16. An Indian friend of mine reports having not long ago visited a Hindu temple where children in the school were all taught to use Sanskrit as their ordinary tongue (much as in Shakespeare's day, schoolboys were supposed to use Latin in school, not only during all classes but during recreation as well—a rule certainly not always honored, or honored more in the breach than in the observance). This use of Sanskrit seemed to my Indian friend incredibly quaint. The non–mother tongue quality of the language was enhanced by the fact that these children were all orphans, their hold on their mothers and their mother tongues precarious. There was very likely no true baby talk in this Sanskrit, any more than there had been in Learned Latin.

17. Pei, *One Language for the World*, pp. 99–101.

years or so, this regimen has changed. Few books or learned articles appear anymore in Latin, although some still do.[18]

Latin is retained in many Roman Catholic administrative documents for practical reasons (continuity of terminology with the past, for example) but in other sectors of administration within the Church, it is being abandoned. Latin had been the language of all oral discussions as well as of documents at the General Congregations of the Society of Jesus since its foundation over four hundred years ago, through the Thirtieth General Congregation in 1957, but it was abandoned at the Thirty-First (1965–66) and the Thirty-Second (1974–75) General Congregations in favor of vernaculars, accompanied by simultaneous translation. And this despite the fact that members of these Congregations, coming from across the world, were far more comprehensively international and interracial and linguistically diversified than ever before, many of them being Indian, African, and Far Eastern Jesuits. Latin is no longer used as the language of instruction even by the totally international faculty and student body of the Gregorian University in Rome or other comparable Catholic institutions in Rome or elsewhere around the world. By and large, at the "Greg" and similar Roman institutions, Italian is becoming the most common language of instruction, although English, French, and Spanish are also widely used, so I am informed by professors active there today.

Two of the influential classical languages are Semitic, Classical Arabic and Hebrew. Classical Arabic, though no longer a mother tongue, has in some ways not been so distanced as have the other learned languages. It is the language not only of the Koran but

18. E.g., a 374-page textbook on sacramental theology, by William A. Van Roo, S.J., *De sacramentis in genre* (Rome: apud aedes Universitatis Gregorianae, 1957), was not an unusual production two decades ago; today it would certainly be. But scholarly articles in Latin still appear in many periodicals, such as *Collectanea Franciscana* (Rome) or *Periodica de re morali, canonica, liturgica* (Rome). Most learned journals published out of the ecclesiastical milieu in Rome, however, now present their articles in major Western European languages, French, English, Spanish, German, or Italian: some are pretty solidly in Italian.

also of most ordinary written and printed discourse today. However, it differs considerably from the various Arabic "dialects" (so-called traditionally, though some "dialects" have split away from all others so much as to constitute several separate Arabic languages, mutually unintelligible, each with its own subset of dialects). But in the case of Arabic, as in the cases of other learned languages, there are movements to collapse the distance between the Classical language and the mother-tongue languages with their dialects, either by reestablishing Classical Arabic as a mother tongue or by making the oral language a "middle language" intermediate between Classical Arabic and the other Arabic languages with their dialects.

By comparison with Classical Arabic, Rabbinic Hebrew, both in its classical and its modified Mishnaic and other forms, was for centuries far more disparate from the vernaculars which most of its users possessed as mother tongues. In the Arab world, most of those who were to learn Classical Arabic came to it from mother tongues closely related to it, for most were Arabs, whose mother-tongue dialects were some form of Arabic (exceptions would be Moslems whose mother tongue was one or another of the many African languages other than Arabic, or Persian, or a Southeast Asian language). However, for centuries those who were to learn Hebrew came to it from mother tongues which were not even of the same language family as Hebrew. The most widespread mother tongues of Hebrew scholars for many centuries were either Yiddish, which is a high German dialect, or Ladino, a form of Spanish, and various Hebrew scholars from Western Europe and the Americas as well as from the Near East and India had many other non-Semitic mother tongues. Today, Hebrew provides a rare, perhaps unique, instance of a learned language reconverted, in modern Israel, into a mother tongue, with a real, deliberately established, oral base. In Hebrew, what was once a learned language is today no longer under chirographic control and no longer extradomestic, and thus no longer simply a learned language. You can buy canned goods and automobiles in the language of the Bible (somewhat adapted, of course).

Classical Chinese is a very special case because of its non-alphabetic character system of writing. Chinese is conventionally spoken of as a language of various "dialects" but is in fact a group of mutually unintelligible languages, each with its own subset of dialects, all of which languages and dialects use a system of writing consisting of tens of thousands of the same highly stylized pictures or "characters," allusively nuanced with an exquisite sophistication developed over the centuries. The K'anghsi dictionary of A.D. 1716 lists 40,545 characters. If two persons speaking "dialects" of "Chinese" so different that they cannot understand one another at all when they talk (thus really speaking different languages), will only write in Chinese characters what they are saying, each will be able to understand what the writer means, although when the reader reads it off in his own Chinese, the writer will not be able to understand what is being said. Of course, since every word has a different character, most Chinese writers can normally write only a certain percentage of the words they understand, often a fairly small percentage.

This situation is destined to be altered drastically when all the speakers of Chinese learn Mandarin Chinese, which is now being taught, more or less satisfactorily, as obligatory to everyone in the People's Republic of China, and being taught in Taiwan as well. Mandarin is the most widespread of the Chinese "dialects" (that is, languages). Even before the present program to spread it, Mandarin alone was the mother tongue of more people than English is, and it can now become the mother tongue for millions more. But Mandarin is not Classical Chinese, *wênyen,* the learned language, which today can be and is recited or quoted orally but which is never used by any group for conversation or practical purposes and is no one's mother tongue. Though even illiterates can and do quote *wênyen,* this Classical Chinese, like the other learned languages noted here, is essentially controlled by writing. It has not even any standard pronunciation: each user gives the words the modern pronunciation of his own Chinese "dialect" (language) so that a speaker of Cantonese and a speaker of Mandarin cannot understand one another when they read the same Classical Chinese from exactly the same page of Confucius' *Analects* or of the poems of Li Po.

Once Mandarin is known to speakers of all varieties of Chinese, the step to alphabetization will be short and, in this writer's considered opinion, inevitable and rapid, however sad and disastrous. For with everyone using the same spoken words and thus able to understand one another's speech, it will no longer be so advantageous to keep drawing pictures. The step will be sad and disastrous because it is quite impossible to put Classical Chinese, including that of a present-day story, into alphabetic writing, even alphabetized written Chinese, since visual characters and spoken words interact in Chinese and, with the characters gone, the reader cannot get all that is being said.[19] But in the uses of language there are other things at stake besides the preservation of the classics. Sad though it may be, it is difficult to see how in any way Chinese character writing could long continue to survive in a technological society dependent upon typewriters, elaborate indexes, and quantified knowledge retrieval systems.

The status of these various chirographically controlled languages has been summarized here to bring out the fact that Learned Latin is not the only language especially contoured by the technological inventions of writing and, later, print so that it imposes on its users a certain alienation and also to suggest that the existence of learned languages across the globe at certain specific times in mankind's history deserves consideration as a phenomenon related to the evolution of states of consciousness and to the various kinds of psychological distancing more or less involved with the growth of consciousness out of the unconscious. At a certain stage in the history of consciousness, a stage defined by the technological transformations of the word that we know as writing and print, learned languages, non–mother tongues, develop, flourish, and then disappear fairly well across the northern half of the Eastern Hemisphere.

19. See below, Ch. 4, n. 6.

Chirographic Control and Abstraction

Alienation can at times be serviceable. Learned Latin had certain advantages in keeping the human lifeworld at a distance. As a male-polarized language developed with the aid of writing and always controlled by writing, for centuries the most widely used language in the West, but a foreign tongue, never a mother tongue, to absolutely all the millions who used it, Learned Latin provided a special instance of the sometimes devious role of writing in the emergence of the modern scientific and technological world and of the modern consciousness.

An affinity seems to exist between early modern science, in its need to hold at arm's length the human lifeworld with its passionate, rhetorical, practical concerns, and Learned Latin as a tongue which had been isolated from infant development and thus from the physiological and psychosomatic roots of consciousness and which had been given instead an artificial base in writing. In Learned Latin, even the most impassioned invective operated at a kind of formalized distance from the human lifeworld.[20] There was available no slang, no current gutter-talk for exploitation, and formal rhetorical devices dominated even the most scurrilously insulting and savage exchanges, as, for example, in John Milton's *Pro se defensio contra Alexandrum Morum* (1655).

Modern science and much of modern technology (although technology has other roots, too, besides those connecting it with science[21]) developed out of an intellectual world which shaped its concepts and vocabulary and its cognitive style on Learned Latin, that is, out of the intellectual world of the medieval universities in the West and their continuators, and out of the subsequent and closely related humanist enterprise of the Renaissance

20. See John G. Rechtien, *Thought Patterns: The Commonplace Book as Literary Form in Theological Controversy during the English Renaissance,* (Diss. Saint Louis University 1973; Ann Arbor, Mich.: University Microfilms, 1975, No. 75–26306).

21. See R. Hooykaas, *Humanisme, science, et réforme: Pierre de la Ramée (1515–1572)* (Leiden: J. Brill, 1958), for connections between the intellectual world of the universities and of humanism and the world of artisans and technology during the sixteenth century.

and subsequent ages. Modern science only gradually became viable in the vernacular atmosphere as it transformed this atmosphere by injecting it with Latin terms and forms of thought. Copernicus' *De revolutionibus* appeared in 1543 in Latin, and so did the other scientific works of the time. In Shakespeare's age there was still no easy way to explain science effectively in the vernaculars or to think about science in the vernaculars, which had no widely current terms for scientific matters. Only with great effort, which included inventing new vernacular words wholesale, could an elementary explanation even of grammar be worked out in any European vernacular in the mid-sixteenth century. By 1687, the situation was better in the vernaculars, but that year Isaac Newton still published his *Philosophiae naturalis principia mathematica* in Latin rather than in English. In doing so, he only followed common practice and assured himself of an immediate maximum audience.

Studies of the matter are nonexistent, but one could argue as an initial hypothesis that the modern intellectual world and the modern state of consciousness could never have come into being without Learned Latin or something like it.[22] As noted earlier, Havelock has shown in his seminal work *Preface to Plato* that writing made possible the separation of the knower and the known, the substitution of knowledge-by-analysis for knowledge-by-empathy, that lay at the base of abstract Greek thought. Modern science and technology need even greater large-scale abstraction than Plato imagined, a strongly developed feel for highly artificial intellectual constructs. If writing initially helped thought to separate itself from the human lifeworld so as to help establish and manipulate abstract constructs, Learned Latin would seemingly have helped at a crucial period with special efficiency, for its commitment to writing is in a way total, as has been seen: it

22. On the persistence of Latin in the face of growing vernacularism, see Paul Oskar Kristeller, *Renaissance Thought II: Papers on Humanism and the Arts* (New York: Harper Torchbooks, Harper & Row, 1965), Ch. 7, "The Origin and Development of the Language of Italian Prose."

does not merely use writing but is controlled by writing. Such a chirographically controlled language would appear to reduce to a new minimum connections with sound and thereby connections with the intimate human lifeworld in its interiority and darkness. Print aided further, for it committed the evanescent spoken word to neutral space even more totally than writing had done and did so at the very time that modern science was emerging within the Learned Latin world.

Learned Latin was of course not merely a scientific medium, servicing the kind of noninvolvement that science demands. It was also a literary language, and to that extent concerned with the relatively unfiltered human lifeworld. Hundreds of new literary works in Learned Latin, poetry and prose, poured from presses well through the nineteenth century. In many editions, Newman's *Idea of a University* includes a section on the development of a Latin *style* by university students, and Latin poetry continued to be written in the nineteenth century by major writers such as Gerard Manley Hopkins and Walter Savage Landor. Earlier, Milton had come close to writing his *Paradise Lost* in Latin, and with reason, since almost all of the scores of comparable epics written in his age were in that tongue.[23] But Learned Latin remained always distanced even in its literary use. It was always insulated from the writer's infancy. As noted before, it knew no baby talk. There was no way to conceive of anything such as Swift's *Journal to Stella* in Learned Latin. This sounds trivial, but it also means that the areas of consciousness and of the unconscious surfaced in *Finnegans Wake* were unreachable in Learned Latin, as were the areas of experience which figure in Virginia Woolf's novels. Learned Latin was a literary medium in a specialized, distanced sense. Moreover, its use as a literary medium was, until the nineteenth century, much less widespread

23. See John Clark, *A History of Epic Poetry: Post Virgilian* (Edinburgh: Oliver and Boyd, 1900). *The Latin Poetry of English Poets,* ed. J. W. Binns (London and Boston: Routledge & Kegan Paul, 1974), includes a study of Landor's Latin poems.

than its use for formally academic, administrative, or liturgical purposes.

Scientific abstractions had of course been in use before Learned Latin came into being. Latin users in antiquity had been more or less adept at such abstractions at least from the time that Greek philosophical thought had in part been put into Latin by Cicero and other Latin writers. And scientific abstractions continue to become more exquisite and ethereal since Learned Latin has been eclipsed by the vernaculars. But it would be legitimate to hypothesize that the Learned Latin of the Middle Ages and the Renaissance and even somewhat later periods was a better medium for the scientific needs of the crucial times which bred the modern world. The hypothesis remains to be tested by thoughtful research.

Whatever the deeper psychological connections between the Learned Latin and the beginnings of modern science, their alliance has broken up. Few persons today are even aware that such an alliance existed, and those who are aware of the fact that it did, such as historians of science and of thought, commonly do not reflect upon it directly at all. The fact that the entire academic enterprise out of which modern science emerged had been conducted in an international no man's language would appear on the face of it to have implications which would be at the very least bizarre and possibly profound. But the implications are yet to be seriously investigated, and this is no place to push the question any farther. It will suffice to have suggested some likely lines of connection and some of the forces at work in alienating the psyche from its linguistic motherland.

Mass Vernaculars, Magnavocabularies

Today the distancing effected by learned languages is gone or soon to go. Mother tongues are carrying the field. The learned languages, academic or scientific-technological, are now all living mother tongues or, as in the case of Classical Arabic, are being assimilated to mother tongues, even though they may not be the mother tongues of all their users.[24] It is often said that a mass language such as English, with hundreds of millions of speakers, is really a group of languages that distance their users from each other—the languages of relatively unschooled rural populations, of the fans of various sports (fly fishermen cannot talk to hockey fans, or either of these to drag racers), that of the psychiatrist, that of the theologian, that of the lawyer, that of the solid state physicist, that of the Citizen's Band radio buff, and so on. Such a statement, however, means little more than that various groups of people put the English language to quite diverse uses, largely by having highly specialized vocabularies or lexical repertoires. The language in its basic lexicon and structure remains totally English throughout all of these uses, which are utterly transparent to one another and can modulate into one another.

What is more significant is the effect of a language of the enormous size and weight of English upon the consciousness of its users, particularly those for whom it is a mother tongue. With a mother tongue of this virtuosity one can get closer to more things than earlier man ever dreamed of. There is no way to say exactly how many words there are in English or, for that matter, in any other language. The 1969 *World Almanac* estimates 800,000, noting that many well-educated persons manage with a speaking vocabulary of around five thousand (virtually everyone understands far more words than he or she uses). But this ball-park figure of 800,000 seems excessively modest. *Webster's Third New*

24. Some mother tongues or mother dialects are crowding out others. In the countries of Europe where several different dialects, mostly not so divergent as to constitute different languages, are used in domestic circles of different regions, the favored dialect—the one which is written, used in schools, and now on radio and television—is always a mother tongue for at least some of the speakers, used by them for domestic as well as public purposes. Thus it is with High German in German-speaking Europe, Tuscan Italian in Italy, and so on. Many of these favored mother tongues (dialects) are today, under the influence of schooling, radio, and television, crowding out the other mother tongues (dialects): German children who speak Platdeutsch with their parents at home are more and more using Hochdeutsch for their own domestic purposes so that it will probably become the mother tongue or dialect of their own children. There are other special cases, such as Swahili, which is primarily not a mother tongue but a lingua franca spoken by nonnative speakers.

International Dictionary states that it could have included "many times" the number of entries that it does include, which total some 450,000, and this doubtless means that Merriam Webster has actually in its files instances of the use in print of the additional words. Besides these, there are all the words used by English speakers that never get into print or into Merriam Webster's files. No one can find them all. This is the way live languages are.

What does it mean to grow up in a language which has hundreds of millions of native speakers and, let us say, well over a million words? The question may sound jejune to those who have grown up in such a language. To sense its urgency, let us ask the complementary question, What does it mean to grow up in a language which has only five thousand speakers or less, and has never had more so far as we know? This is the experience of hundreds of thousands of persons today, and in the past has been the experience of most of the human race. What is the "shape" of English in consciousness and its effect on consciousness as compared to that of a less exfoliated language? No one really knows. Who is more alienated, the native English speaker, overwhelmed with lexical and noetic possibilities, or the village dweller in an isolated culture embracing only a few thousand persons, or even less, within its linguistic world? Each appears isolated in his or her own way. But it would appear that their ways of experiencing themselves in the universe differ radically.

The mass languages with magnavocabularies relate to the spoken word with utmost complexity. They could not sustain themselves at all without writing and print. They need writing and print to steady them synchronically in dictionaries that record what hundreds of thousands of words mean now, but they need writing and print also to orient them diachronically, to inform them what these words used to mean and how they came to their present meanings. Mass spoken languages not anchored to writing and print would in the course of time splinter into dialects which would soon evolve into separate languages. And they could not even have come into existence without the kind of diversified thinking and of visual control which only writing and print make possible. But the mass languages with magnavocabularies are all also living mother tongues. And now they far surpass any of the purely learned languages in linguistic and noetic resources. No learned language ever developed its lexicon so far.

The triumph of mother tongues in the displacement of learned languages and the development of mass mother-tongues such as English has been followed in very recent years by a further development, the programmatic cultivation of mother tongues among even the smallest cultural groups across the globe, from Ireland through the native Indian cultures of the Americas into the Philippines. In places such as Central and West Africa, where the hundreds upon hundreds of different languages (not dialects, but mutually unintelligible languages) cannot indefinitely survive national unification, linguistic scholars, Africans mostly but also many others, are taping and transcribing the hundreds upon hundreds of African mother tongues as fast as they can bring their electronic equipment into the farthest flung villages.

This apotheosis of mother tongues is one manifestation of the identity crises making themselves felt among human beings across the globe at present. In terms of what has been discussed above, it calls attention to the intensity of the present-day return to mother, the strong antialienation drive that marks technological cultures—which are romantic in their deepest roots[25] and more self-consciously integrating than other cultures. How successful the return will be remains to be seen. But it does relate to mankind's renewed interest both in women's liberation and in the spoken word.[26] This renewed interest is of course different from the earlier involvement of purely oral cultures: it is self-consciously programed, as movements in a typographically active age are likely, or indeed almost sure, to be.

Technology, Alienation, and the Evolution of Consciousness

The transformations of the word attended to here have all been intimately involved with technology, for writing and print, as well as electronic devices, are technologies, as has been seen. Technology has implemented not merely the distancing of the word

25. See Ong, *Rhetoric, Romance, and Technology,* pp. 1–22, 255–283.
26. See Ong, "Agonistic Structures in Academia."

by writing and print, but also more particularly the emergence of learned languages isolated from mother tongues. It has further implemented the resurgent interest in mother tongues, for nativist movements promoting mother tongues today are involved with writing and print. Often the complaint of promoters of neglected native languages is that writing and print technologies used for mass languages are not applied to languages of minority groups. The aim of nativists is not merely to have such a language spoken, but to teach it in school. And the problem is often technological: native languages have little or no literature (technologically processed speech) to teach. The revival of Gaelic in Ireland, for example, has this problem to contend with. There are some medieval Gaelic texts to teach, but few first-rate modern Irish writers are willing to write in a language with only a few thousand regular readers when they can write in one with hundreds of millions. The language best served by technology has the human advantage.

Technology is important in the history of the word not merely exteriorly, as a kind of circulator of pre-existing materials, but interiorly, for it transforms what can be said and what is said. Since writing came into existence, the evolution of the word and the evolution of consciousness have been intimately tied in with technologies and technological developments. Indeed, all major advances in consciousness depend on technological transformations and implementations of the word.

The evolution of consciousness as it is being considered here can be understood with reference to the interior, psychic world and with reference to the exterior world. Interiorly, consciousness grows through time. This is true ontogenetically, with regard to the individual person, and phylogenetically, with regard to the human race. Ontogenetically, consciousness grows in individual human beings in the sense that for a normal adult more of life is under conscious reflective control than for a child. A child's reactions are governed more by the unconscious and the subconscious. The consciousness of the individual can be said to grow out of the unconscious and gradually to supersede the unconscious as a base of response to existence in more and more areas, without ever, of course, eliminating the unconscious.

This ontogenetic or individual growth of consciousness is meshed with phylogenetic growth. Through the development of culture, a store of experience and knowledge that human beings can accumulate and hand on to succeeding generations, mankind as a whole gains more and more conscious access to and control over the cosmos and itself. Early man had to relate in one way or another to the cosmos around him, psychologically as well as physically, not to selected parts he chose, but to all parts of it which impinged upon him, if not with full consciousness, then unconsciously or subconsciously. Though his conscious awareness of what the sun, the moon, and the stars were remained vague at best, he had to integrate them into his lifeworld. So he generated myths, which were consciously narrated but provided a pattern of integration deriving more from unconscious psychic structures than from the external phenomena themselves. Early myths tell more about their proponents than about the universe. Over the ages, as consciousness gains more and more of a beachhead in the psyche through the growth and processing of experience, more and more of myth is displaced by science: astrology becomes astronomy, alchemy becomes chemistry, magic becomes physics and medicine, tales of the gods become philosophy and theology.

Science is knowledge, a psychic phenomenon, an interior actuality. But the evolution of consciousness can also be thought of in terms of its exterior effects. As I look out of my twelfth-story room over metropolitan St. Louis, virtually everything I see on the surface of the earth to the horizon above the limestone Illinois bluffs across the Mississippi River to the north and east and the low rolling hills of Missouri to the west is, directly or indirectly, under the conscious control of human beings, men and women: thousands of buildings, homes and commercial and manufacturing units, bridges, marvelously coded traffic lights, thousands of miles of pavement, acres of lawns and trees and shrubs, (not growing where nature would have had them, but placed and tended by men and women), the clothes on the people in the streets, the thousands of automobiles, Saint Louis University's Pius XII Memorial Library with its hundreds of thousands of books carefully indexed in its card catalogs and with its millions of microfilmed pages of manuscripts from the Vatican Library and elsewhere, many of which are over one thousand or fifteen hundred years old—all this witnesses not just to man's physical presence but also to the omnipresence of conscious human activity. So do other things under the surface of the landscape that I cannot see—tunnels, basements, subbasements, sewers, electric and gas conduits—and above the surface, where the atmosphere is being worked on to free it from the fumes man pours into it and is streaked with the vapor trails of planes in which and between which human consciousness has established incredibly complex controls and information patterns.

It appears evident that the human psyche in the kind of exterior setting I have just described feels its relationship with the surrounding world, to time, and to space in a way immeasurably different from that of the psyche of 30,000 years ago. And the individual human being's relationship to his or her own self is correspondingly altered. The experience of being human has undergone a kind of sea-change. These changes have been studied by psychoanalysts and anthropologists and others in a vast literature to which Erich Neumann's *The Origins and History of Consciousness* still serves as an invaluable introduction.[27] The generation coming to maturity today has always known the moon as something that men who have been there have reported on.

The exterior effects of the evolution of consciousness play back into the interior evolution. They do so in countless ways and, in terms of our concerns here, particularly through the exterior technological devices that affect the word, the inventions which enable man to do new things with his noetic world, to shape, store, retrieve, and communicate knowledge in new ways and thus to think in new ways. Such inventions, treated in this volume, are

27. Erich Neumann, *The Origins and History of Consciousness*, with a forward by C. G. Jung, trans. R. F. C. Hull, Bollingen Series, 42 (New York: Pantheon Books, 1954); originally published in German in 1949.

writing, print, and electronic devices, as well as, in another line of development, the talking drums of Central and West Africa.

The terms just used, "shape, store, retrieve, and communicate" (this last in the sense of "circulate," "distribute," "move around"), are diagrammatic terms, applicable directly to mechanical operations. Used to refer to the human mind, such terms, it must be remembered, are reductionist: they provide a model— knowledge is a commodity, and noetic activities move it around— and in providing a model inevitably leave out part of the actuality they propose to deal with. For knowledge is much more than a commodity. Corresponding terms closer to the real lifeworld or to experienced reality might be, respectively, "generate, remember, recall, share" (or "communicate" if this is taken in its deeper sense as expressive of sharing or psychological need).

The technological operations which the mind finds helpful have this vast and irreducible difference (among other differences) from human noetic operations themselves: technological operations are like the conscious side of human operations in being "logical" in structure, but they are unlike human operations in that they have no unconscious that underlies the consciousness. Machines have no hunches. This is why computers cannot really think. Human thinking always and of necessity involves unconscious and conscious components. Total explicitness is impossible. The effort of formal logic to make thought entirely explicit, while an admirable and in many ways indispensable and fantastically productive effort, is ultimately doomed to failure and entails deep psychological strain because of its unreality. Thought can only be made more and more explicit, never totally so.[28]

28. Mathematical thinking is popularly considered to be fully explicit, fully conscious, but like all real thought, it involves the unconscious, too. Typically the connections of mathematics to the unconscious are isolated in postulates and definitions, where they are kept in confinement, but not eliminated. Thus, a straight line may be defined (I am aware that there are better definitions, but this one is not bad and is familiar and serviceable here) as the shortest distance between two points. This may be quite satisfactory as a postulate, but it does not make matters entirely explicit by any means. What is meant by "shortest," by "distance," by "between"? Can you define these terms nontautologically? These concepts are not defined in the definition or postulate, which simply assumes that we are in agreement

Unreflective reliance on models has generated the term "media" to designate new technological ways of managing the word, such as writing, print, and the electronic devices. The term is useful and I use it regularly here. But it can be misleading, encouraging us to think of writing, print, and electronic devices simply as ways of "moving information" over some sort of space intermediate between one person and another. In fact, each of the so-called "media" does far more than this: it makes possible thought processes inconceivable before.[29] The "media" are more significantly within the mind than outside it. With the use of writing or print or the computer, the mind does not become a machine, reducing its generation of thought ("concepts") to "shaping," its memory to "storage," its recalling to "retrieval," its sharing to "circulation." But writing and print and the computer enable the mind to constitute within itself—not just on the inscribed surface or on the computer programs—new ways of thinking, previously inconceivable questions, and new ways of searching for responses.

---

as to what they are, even though we do not and cannot define them. Like other concepts, directly or reductively referring to "inside" or "outside," the concept "between," for example, is an existential formation based on experience of one's own body and its inwardness and outwardness. I feel myself inside my own body and everything else as outside of it. *That* is what "in" and "out" mean—these terms point out this situation which I experience and enable me to use it as an analogue for other situations. "In" situates the meaning of "between." "Between" is a kind of inwardness—we say "in between" these two points, and there is no way to manage "out between."

The agreement, as in mathematical postulates and definitions, that we know what we mean when we are pointing somehow to a situation that we share but that we cannot or need not further define or otherwise make more explicit, is what Michael Polanyi refers to in terms of "tacit thinking," "tacit knowledge," "tacit agreement." It is obviously based on unconscious and subconscious elements in our thinking as much as upon conscious elements. It is possible to push back further and define such agreed-upon terms in many instances, but further definitions must themselves be couched in similar agreed-upon terms, if not immediately, at least eventually. Making more and more explicit these relatively implicit agreements is one part of mathematics, notably in work concerned with set theory and other "foundations" (note the metaphor) of mathematics. See Michael Polanyi, *Personal Knowledge* (Chicago: University of Chicago Press, 1958), and *The Tacit Dimension* (Garden City, N.Y.: Doubleday, 1966).

29. Ong, *The Presence of the Word*, pp. 111–138 and *passim*.

The mind does not enter into the alphabet or the printed book or the computer so much as the alphabet or print or the computer enters the mind, producing new states of awareness there. Relieving the mind of its onus of conscious but routine operations (such as computing, sorting, matching patterns, and so on), the computer, for example, actually releases more energy for new kinds of exploratory operations by the human mind itself, in which the unconscious is deeply involved and which the computer, lacking an unconscious, cannot carry forward. Earlier, writing and print had effected comparable energy releases.

Thus technological development, from writing on, has made for a massive exfoliation of noetic activity, sometimes referred to as a knowledge explosion, not only in the physical sciences (where its effects are most conspicuous) but also, we sometimes forget, in the humanities.[30] This growth in noetic activity is also referred to as growth or intensification of the noosphere, to use Pierre Teilhard de Chardin's term for the shared consciousness of man now covering the earth. Yet, at the same time that they humanize by increasing knowledge, technological transformations of the word also alienate man from the real word, the living spoken word, and thus from himself.

Alienation, cleavage, is not all bad. To understand other things and themselves, to grow, human beings need not only proximity but also distance, even from themselves. Out of alienation, and only out of alienation, certain greater unities can come. Persons at ease with their origins and with their own unconscious welcome certain alienations, for they can put them to good use. The evolution of human consciousness would be impossible—unthinkable—without the alienations introduced by writing, print, and the electronic transformations of the word.

The studies in this volume have to do with the alienation and subsequent transformations which have come about in the technological development of the word and the concomitant evolution of consciousness.

30. See Ong, *In the Human Grain*, pp. 41–51.

The first few chapters treat artificially controlled distances between writers and their "audience" of readers, the mixtures of oral proximity and printed distance in today's new kind of "talked" books, made by editing and printing electronically recorded exchanges of thought, the contrasting hypertrophy of oral modes of thought found in the drum languages of Central and West Africa, and the drive in highly technologized cultures to divorce understanding from hearing and to wed it to sight, a distancing sense.

The second group of studies examines the tendency of print to establish closed-off economies of thought and utterance. Shakespeare lived at the end of the pretypographic script world, a residually oral world devoted to retooling the wisdom of the past through the new invention of print, which in codifying the oral world for visual retrieval was actually destroying it. Milton was unable to use techniques essential to the epic because the noetic structures of his day were based deeply on writing and print and thus hardly depended at all any longer upon the oral techniques of processing knowledge which had brought the epic into existence and given it its early beauty and appeal. Partly consciously and partly unconsciously, Milton turned to Ramist logic as a principle of organization and thereby through Ramist "method" projected his material largely in closed-field patterns. The once New Criticism exhibits not exactly the same drive but a similar one, sequestering the poem as a unit from life and from all else. The next study in this section takes up directly the indissoluble alliance which writing and print have with death, the great separator, and the anomalous and unique situation of the Bible because of its future-oriented textuality. Finally in this section, a lengthy study investigates the shift from mimesis (imitation or copying, a unitive activity) to irony (a diaeretic, separating tactic) evident if one contrasts poetic and literary theory through the mid-eighteenth century with the poetics and literary theory of the romantic and postromantic age. The earlier interpretations of literature and of art generally are typically mimetic: art imitates nature. The later interpretations are generally ironic: art fends off nature and thus itself becomes suspect, even to itself. As José Ortega y Gasset notes, "All peculiarities of modern art can be summed up in this one feature of its renouncing its [own] importance."[31] The shift from mimesis to irony is brought about by the use of writing and print and by interiorization of the separations they imply.

The single chapter in the final section undertakes to show how, and to what extent, today's trend to an open-system mind-set, conspicuously exemplified in television and in the recent surge of ecological concern across the globe, counters the closed-system mind-set fostered by writing and print but also depends on the continued use of writing and print. In its evolution, consciousness does not slough off its earlier stages but incorporates them in transmuted form into its later stages. The various more or less closed systems for managing the word are interfaced with one another in our present opening state of consciousness.

31. *The Dehumanization of Art and Other Writings on Art and Culture* (New York: Doubleday, 1956), p. 48.

II

THE SEQUESTRATION OF VOICE

2

The Writer's Audience
Is Always a Fiction

Epistola . . . non erubescit.
—Cicero *Epistolae ad familiares* 5.12.1.

Ubi nihil erit quae scribas, id ipsum scribes.
—Cicero *Epistolae ad Atticum* 4.8.4.

I

Although there is a large and growing literature on the differences between oral and written verbalization, many aspects of the differences have not been looked into at all, and many others, although well known, have not been examined in their full implications. Among these latter is the relationship of the so-called "audience" to writing as such, to the situation that inscribed communication establishes and to the roles that readers as readers are consequently called on to play. Some studies in literary history and criticism at times touch near this subject, but none, it appears, take it up in any historical detail.

The standard locus in Western intellectual tradition for study of audience responses has been rhetoric. But rhetoric originally concerned oral communication, as is indicated by its name, which comes from the Greek word for public speaking. Over two millennia, rhetoric has been gradually extended to include writing more and more, until today, in highly technological cultures, this is its principal concern. But the extension has come gradually and has advanced *pari passu* with the slow and largely unnoticed emergence of markedly chirographic and typographic styles out of those originating in oral performance, with the result that the differentiation between speech and writing has never become a matter of urgent concern for the rhetoric of any given age: when orality was in the ascendancy, rhetoric was oral-focused; as orality yielded to writing, the focus of rhetoric was slowly shifted, unreflectively for the most part, and without notice.

Histories of the relationship between literature and culture have something to say about the status and behavior of readers, before and after reading given materials, as do mass media studies, readership surveys, liberation programs for minorities or various other classes of persons, books on reading skills, works of literary criticism, and works on linguistics, especially those addressing differences between hearing and reading. But most of these studies, except perhaps literary criticism and linguistic studies, treat only perfunctorily, if at all, the roles imposed on the reader by a written or printed text not imposed by spoken utterance. Formalist or structuralist critics, including French theorists such as Paul Ricoeur as well as Roland Barthes, Jacques Derrida, Michel Foucault, Philippe Sollers, and Tzvetan Todorov, variously advert to the immediacy of the oral as against writing and print and occasionally study differences between speech and writing, as Louis Lavelle did much earlier in *La Parole et l'écriture* (1942). In treating of masks and "shadows" in his *Sociologie du théâtre* (1965), Jean Duvignaud brilliantly discusses the projections of a kind of collective consciousness on the part of theater audiences. But none of these appear to broach directly the question of readers' roles called for by a written text, either synchronically as such roles stand at present or diachronically as they have developed through history. Linguistic theorists such as John R. Searle and John L. Austin treat "illocutionary acts" (denoted by "warn," "command," "state," etc.), but these regard the speaker's or writer's need in certain instances to secure a special hold on those he addresses,[1] not any special role imposed by writing.

1. See, e.g., J. R. Searle, *The Philosophy of Language* (London: Oxford University Press, 1971), pp. 24–28, where Austin is cited, and Searle's bibliography, pp. 146–48.

Wayne Booth in *The Rhetoric of Fiction* and Walker Gibson, whom Booth quotes, come quite close to the concerns of the present study in their treatment of the "mock reader," as does Henry James, whom Booth also cites, in his discussion of the way an author makes "his reader very much as he makes his character."[2] But this hint of James is not developed—there is no reason why it should be—and neither Booth nor Gibson discusses in any detail the history of the ways in which readers have been called on to relate to texts before them. Neither do Robert Scholes and Robert Kellogg in their invaluable work, *The Nature of Narrative:* they skirt the subject in their chapter on "The Oral Heritage of Written Narrative,"[3] but remain chiefly concerned with the oral performer, the writer, and techniques, rather than with the recipient of the message. Yet a great many of the studies noted here as well as many others, among which might be mentioned some by Georges Poulet or Jacques Derrida or Paul Ricoeur as well as Norman N. Holland's *The Dynamics of Literary Response* (1968), suggest the time is ripe for a study

2. *The Rhetoric of Fiction* (Chicago: University of Chicago Press, 1961), pp. 49–52, 138, 363–64.

3. *The Nature of Narrative* (New York: Oxford University Press, 1966), pp. 17–56. Among recent short studies exhibiting concerns tangent to but not the same as those of the present article might be mentioned three from *New Literary History:* Georges Poulet, "Phenomenology of Reading," 1 (1969–70), 53–68; Geoffrey H. Hartman, "History-Writing as Answerable Style," 2 (1970–71), 73–84; and J. Hillis Miller, "The Still Heart: Poetic Form in Wordsworth," 2 (1970–71), 297–310, esp. p. 310; as well as Gerald Prince, "Introduction à l'étude du narrataire," *Poétique,* No. 14 (1973), pp. 178–96, which is concerned with the "narrataire" only in novels ("narratee" in a related English-language study by the same author as noted by him here) and with literary taxonomy more than history. See also Paul Ricoeur, "What Is a Text? Explanation and Interpretation," Appendix, pp. 135–50, in David Rasmussen, *Mythic-Symbolic Language and Philosophical Anthropology: A Constructive Interpretation of the Thought of Paul Ricoeur* (The Hague: Martinus Nijhoff, 1971). Since this study was first worked out, new treatments of related, though far from identical, material have appeared. These include Wolfgang Iser, *The Implied Reader* (Baltimore: Johns Hopkins University Press, 1972—the same year as the German original); Stanley E. Fish, *Self-Consuming Artifacts* (Berkeley and Los Angeles: University of California Press, 1972); Harold Bloom, *A Map of Misreading* (New York: Oxford University Press, 1975); and Geoffrey Hartman, *The Fate of Reading* (Chicago: University of Chicago Press, 1975).

of the history of readers and their enforced roles, for they show that we have ample phenomenological and literary sophistication to manage many of the complications involved.

So long as verbal communication is reduced to a simplistic mechanistic model which supposedly moves corpuscular units of something labeled "information" back and forth along tracks between two termini, there is of course no special problem with those who assimilate the written or printed word. For the speaker, the audience is in front of him. For the writer, the audience is simply further away, in time or space or both. A surface inscribed with information can neutralize time by preserving the information and conquer space by moving the information to its recipient over distances that sound cannot traverse. If, however, we put aside this alluring but deceptively neat and mechanistic mock-up and look at verbal communication in its human actuality, noting that words consist not of corpuscular units but of evanescent sound and that, as Maurice Merleau-Ponty has pointed out,[4] words are never fully determined in their abstract signification but have meaning only with relation to man's body and to its interaction with its surroundings, problems with the writer's audience begin to show themselves. Writing calls for difficult, and often quite mysterious, skills. Except for a small corps of highly trained writers, most persons could get into written form few if any of the complicated and nuanced meanings they regularly convey orally. One reason is evident: the spoken word is part of present actuality and has its meaning established by the total situation in which it comes into being. Context for the spoken word is simply present, centered in the person speaking and the one or ones to whom he addresses himself and to whom he is related existentially in terms of the circumambient actuality.[5] But the meaning caught in writing comes provided with no such present circumambient actuality, at least normally. (One might except special cases of written exchanges between

4. *Phenomenology of Perception,* trans. Colin Smith (London: Routledge, 1962), pp. 181–84.
5. See my *The Presence of the Word* (New Haven: Yale University Press, 1967), pp. 116–17.

persons present to one another physically but with oral channels blocked: two deaf persons, for example, or two persons who use different variants of Chinese and are orally incomprehensible to one another but can communicate through the same written characters, which carry virtually the same meanings though they are sounded differently in the different varieties of Chinese.)

Such special cases apart, the person to whom the writer addresses himself normally is not present at all. Moreover, with certain special exceptions such as those just suggested, he must not be present. I am writing a book which will be read by thousands, or, I modestly hope, by tens of thousands. So, please, get out of the room. I want to be alone. Writing normally calls for some kind of withdrawal.

How does the writer give body to the audience for whom he writes? It would be fatuous to think that the writer addressing a so-called general audience tries to imagine his readers individually. A well-known novelist friend of mine only laughed when I asked him if, as he was writing a novel, he imagined his real readers—the woman on the subway deep in the book, the student in his room, the businessman on a vacation, the scholar in his study. There is no need for a novelist to feel his "audience" this way at all. It may be, of course, that at one time or another he imagines himself addressing one or another real person. But not all his readers in their particularities. Practically speaking, of course, and under the insistent urging of editors and publishers, he does have to take into consideration the real social, economic, and psychological state of possible readers. He has to write a book that real persons will buy and read. But I am speaking—or writing—here of the "audience" that fires the writer's imagination. If it consists of the real persons who he hopes will buy his book, they are not these persons in an untransmuted state.[6]

6. T. S. Eliot suggests some of the complexities of the writer-and-audience problem in his essay on "The Three Voices of Poetry," by which he means (1) "the voice of the poet talking to himself—or to nobody," (2) "the voice of the poet addressing an audience," and (3) "the voice of the poet when he attempts to create a dramatic character speaking" (*On Poetry and Poets*, New York: Noonday Press, 1961, p. 96). Eliot, in the same work, states that these voices often mingle and indeed, for him, "are

Although I have thus far followed the common practice in using the term "audience," it is really quite misleading to think of a writer as dealing with an "audience," even though certain considerations may at times oblige us to think this way. More properly, a writer addresses readers—only, he does not quite "address" them either: he writes to or for them. The orator has before him an audience which is a true audience, a collectivity. "Audience" is a collective noun. There is no such collective noun for readers, nor, so far as I am able to puzzle out, can there be. "Readers" is a plural. Readers do not form a collectivity, acting here and now on one another and on the speaker as members of an audience do. We can devise a singularized concept for them, it is true, such as "readership." We can say that the *Reader's Digest* has a readership of I don't know how many millions—more than it is comfortable to think about, at any rate. But "readership" is not a collective noun. It is an abstraction in a way that "audience" is not.

The contrast between hearing and reading (running the eye over signals that encode sound) can be caught if we imagine a speaker addressing an audience equipped with texts. At one point, the speaker asks the members of the audience all to read silently a paragraph out of the text. The audience immediately fragments. It is no longer a unit. Each individual retires into his own microcosm. When the readers look up again, the speaker has to gather them into a collectivity once more. This is true even if he is the author of the text they are reading.

To sense more fully the writer's problem with his so-called audience let us envision a class of students asked to write on the

---

most often found together" (p. 108). The approach I am here taking cuts across Eliot's way of enunciating the problem and, I believe, brings out some of the built-in relationships among the three voices which help account for their intermingling. The "audience" addressed by Eliot's second voice not only is elusively constituted but also, even in its elusiveness, can determine the voice of the poet talking to himself or to nobody (Eliot's first sense of "voice"), because in talking to oneself one has to objectify oneself, and one does so in ways learned from addressing others. A practiced writer talking "to himself" in a poem has a quite different feeling for "himself" than does a complete illiterate.

subject to which schoolteachers, jaded by summer, return com-
pulsively every autumn: "How I Spent My Summer Vacation."
The teacher makes the easy assumption, inviting and plausible
but false, that the chief problem of a boy or a girl in writing is
finding a subject actually part of his or her real life. In-close subject matter is supposed to solve the problem of invention. Of
course it does not. The problem is not simply what to say but
also whom to say it to. Say? The student is not talking. He is
writing. No one is listening. There is no feedback. Where does he
find his "audience"? He has to make his readers up, fictionalize
them.

If the student knew what he was up against better than the
teacher giving the assignment seemingly does, he might ask,
"Who wants to know?" The answer is not easy. Grandmother?
He never tells grandmother. His father or mother? There's a lot
he would not want to tell them, that's sure. His classmates?
Imagine the reception if he suggested they sit down and listen
quietly while he told them how he spent his summer vacation.
The teacher? There is no conceivable setting in which he could
imagine telling his teacher how he spent his summer vacation
other than in writing this paper, so that writing for the teacher
does not solve his problems but only restates them. In fact, most
young people do not tell anybody how they spent their summer
vacation, much less write down how they spent it. The subject
may be in-close; the use it is to be put to remains unfamiliar,
strained, bizarre.

How does the student solve the problem? In many cases, in a
way somewhat like the following. He has read, let us say, *The
Adventures of Tom Sawyer*. He knows what this book felt like,
how the voice in it addressed its readers, how the narrator hinted
to his readers that they were related to him and he to them, whoever they may actually have been or may be. Why not pick up
that voice and, with it, its audience? Why not make like Samuel
Clemens and write for whomever Samuel Clemens was writing
for? This even makes it possible to write for his teacher—itself
likely to be a productive ploy—whom he certainly has never been

quite able to figure out. But he knows his teacher has read *Tom Sawyer*, has heard the voice in the book, and could therefore obviously make like a *Tom Sawyer* reader. His problem is solved, and he goes ahead. The subject matter now makes little difference, provided that it is something like Mark Twain's and that it interests him on some grounds or other. Material in-close to his real life is not essential, though, of course, it might be welcome now that he has a way to process it.

If the writer succeeds in writing, it is generally because he can fictionalize in his imagination an audience he has learned to know not from daily life but from earlier writers who were fictionalizing in their imagination audiences they had learned to know in still earlier writers, and so on back to the dawn of written narrative. If and when he becomes truly adept, an "original writer," he can do more than project the earlier audience, he can alter it. Thus it was that Samuel Clemens in *Life on the Mississippi* could not merely project the audience that the many journalistic writers about the Midwestern rivers had brought into being, but could also shape it to his own demands. If you had read Isaiah Sellers, you could read Mark Twain, but with a difference. You had to assume a part in a less owlish, more boisterous setting, in which Clemens' caustic humor masks the uncertainty of his seriousness. Mark Twain's reader is asked to take a special kind of hold on himself and on life.

II

These reflections suggest, or are meant to suggest, that there exists a tradition in fictionalizing audiences that is a component part of literary tradition in the sense in which literary tradition is discussed in T. S. Eliot's "Tradition and the Individual Talent." A history of the ways audiences have been called on to fictionalize themselves would be a correlative of the history of literary genres and literary works, and indeed of culture itself.

What do we mean by saying the audience is a fiction? Two things at least. First, that the writer must construct in his imagination, clearly or vaguely, an audience cast in some sort of role—entertainment seekers, reflective sharers of experience (as those who listen to Conrad's Marlow), inhabitants of a lost and remembered world of prepubertal latency (readers of Tolkien's hobbit stories), and so on. Second, we mean that the audience must correspondingly fictionalize itself. A reader has to play the role in which the author has cast him, which seldom coincides with his role in the rest of actual life. An office worker on a bus reading a novel of Thomas Hardy is listening to a voice which is not that of any real person in the real setting around him. He is playing the role demanded of him by this person speaking in a quite special way from the book, which is not the subway and is not quite "Wessex" either, though it speaks of Wessex. Readers over the ages have had to learn this game of literacy, how to conform themselves to the projections of the writers they read, or at least how to operate in terms of these projections. They have to know how to play the game of being a member of an audience that "really" does not exist. And they have to adjust when the rules change, even though no rules thus far have ever been published and even though the changes in the unpublished rules are themselves for the most part only implied.

A history of literature could be written in terms of the ways in which audiences have successively been fictionalized from the time when writing broke away from oral performance, for, just as each genre grows out of what went before it, so each new role that readers are made to assume is related to previous roles. Putting aside for the moment the question of what fictionalizing may be called for in the case of the audience for oral performance, we can note that when script first came on the scene, the fictionalizing of readers was relatively simple. Written narrative at first was merely a transcription of oral narrative, or what was imagined as oral narrative, and it assumed some kind of oral singer's audience, even when being read. The transcribers of the *Iliad* and the *Odyssey* presumably imagined an audience of real listeners in attendance on an oral singer, and readers of those works to this day do well if they can imagine themselves hearing a singer of tales.[7] How these texts and other oral performances were in fact originally set down in writing remains puzzling, but the transcribers certainly were not composing in writing, but rather recording with minimal alteration what a singer was singing or was imagined to be singing.

Even so, a scribe had to fictionalize in a way a singer did not, for a real audience was not really present before the scribe, so it would seem, although it is just possible that at times one may have been (Lord, pp. 125–128). But, as transcription of oral performance or imagined oral performance gave way gradually to composition in writing, the situation changed. No reader today imagines *Second Skin* as a work that John Hawkes is reciting extempore to a group of auditors, even though passages from it may be impressive when read aloud.

III

We have noted that the roles readers are called on to play evolve without any explicit rules or directives. How readers pick up the implicit signals and how writers change the rules can be illustrated by examining a passage from a specialist in unpublished directives for readers, Ernest Hemingway. The passage is the opening of *A Farewell to Arms*. At the start of my comment on the passage, it will be clear that I am borrowing a good deal from Walker Gibson's highly discerning book on modern American prose styles, *Tough, Sweet, and Stuffy*.[8] The Hemingway passage follows:

In the late summer of that year we lived in a house in a village that looked across the river and the plain to the mountains. In the bed of the river there were pebbles and boulders, dry and white in the sun, and the water was clear and swiftly moving and blue in the channels.

7. See Albert B. Lord, *The Singer of Tales,* Harvard Studies in Comparative Literature, 24 (Cambridge, Mass.: Harvard University Press, 1964), pp. 124–138.

8. *Tough, Sweet, and Stuffy* (Bloomington: Indiana University Press, 1966), pp. 28–54. In these pages, Gibson gets very close to the concern of the present article with readers' roles.

Hemingway's style is often characterized as straightforward, unadorned, terse, lacking in qualifiers, close-lipped; and it is all these things. But none of them were peculiar to Hemingway when his writing began to command attention. A feature more distinctive of Hemingway here and elsewhere is the way he fictionalizes the reader, and this fictionalizing is often signaled largely by his use of the definite article as a special kind of qualifier or of the demonstrative pronoun "that," of which the definite article is simply an attenuation.

"The late summer of that year," the reader begins. What year? The reader gathers that there is no need to say. "Across the river." What river? The reader apparently is supposed to know. "And the plain." What plain? "*The* plain"—remember? "To the mountains." What mountains? Do I have to tell you? Of course not. *The* mountains—*those* mountains we know. We have somehow been there together. Who? You, my reader, and I. The reader—every reader—is being cast in the role of a close companion of the writer. This is the game he must play here with Hemingway, not always exclusively or totally, but generally, to a greater or lesser extent. It is one reason why the writer is tight-lipped. Description as such would bore a boon companion. What description there is comes in the guise of pointing, in verbal gestures, recalling humdrum, familiar details. "In the bed of the river there were pebbles and boulders, dry and white in the sun." The known world, accepted and accepting. Not presentation, but recall. The writer needs only to point, for what he wants to tell you about is not the scene at all but his feelings. These, too, he treats as something you really had somehow shared, though you might not have been quite aware of it at the time. He can tell you what was going on inside him and count on sympathy, for you were there. You *know*. The reader here has a well-marked role assigned him. He is a companion-in-arms, somewhat later become a confidant. It is a flattering role. Hemingway readers are encouraged to cultivate high self-esteem.

The effect of the definite article in Hemingway here is quite standard and readily explicable. Normally, in English, we are likely to make an initial reference to an individual object by means of the indefinite article and to bring in the definite only subsequently. "Yesterday on the street *a* man came up to me, and when I stopped in my stride *the* man said. . . ." "A" is a modified form of the term "one," a kind of singular of "some." "A man" means "one man" (of many real or possible men). The indefinite article tacitly acknowledges the existence or possibility of a number of individuals beyond the immediate range of reference and indicates that from among them one is selected. Once we have indicated that we are concerned not with all but with one-out-of-many, we train the definite article or pointer article on the object of our attention.[9] The definite article thus commonly signals some previous, less definite acquaintanceship. Hemingway's exclusion of indefinite in favor of definite articles signals the reader that he is from the first on familiar ground. He shares the author's familiarity with the subject matter. The reader must pretend he has known much of it before.

Hemingway's concomitant use of the demonstrative distancing pronoun "that" parallels his use of "the." For "the" is only an attenuated "that." It is a modified form of the demonstrative pronoun that replaced the original Old English definite article "seo." Both hold their referents at a distance, "that" typically at a somewhat greater distance than "the." *That* mountain you see ten miles away is indicated there on *the* map on *the* wall. If we wish to think of the map as close, we would say, "*This* map on

9. The present inclination to begin a story without the initial indefinite article, which tacitly acknowledges a range of existence beyond that of the immediate reference, and to substitute for the indefinite article a demonstrative pronoun of proximity, "this," is one of many indications of the tendency of present-day man to feel his lifeworld—which is now more than ever the whole world—as in-close to him, and to mute any references to distance. It is not uncommon to hear a conversation begin, "Yesterday on the street this man came up to me, and. . . . " A few decades ago, the equivalent would very likely have been, "Yesterday on the street a man came up to me, and. . . . " This widespread preference, which Hemingway probably influenced little if at all, does show that Hemingway's imposition of fellowship on the reader was an indication, perhaps moderately precocious, of a sweeping trend.

this wall." In distancing their objects, both "that" and "the" can tend to bring together the speaker and the one spoken to. "That" commonly means that-over-there at a distance from you-and-me here, and "the" commonly means much the same. These terms thus can easily implement the Hemingway relationship: you-and-me.

This you-and-me effect of the distancing demonstrative pronoun and the definite article can be seen perhaps more spectacularly in romance etymology. The words for "the" in the romance languages come from the Latin word *ille, illa, illud,* which yields in various romance tongues *il, le, la, el, lo,* and their cognates. *Ille* is a distancing demonstrative in Latin: it means "that-over-there-away-from-you-and-me" and stands in contrastive opposition to another Latin demonstrative which has no counterpart in English, *iste, ista, istud,* which means "that-over-there-by-you" (and thus can readily become pejorative—"that-little-no-account-thing-of-yours"). *Ille* brings together the speaker and the one spoken to by contrast with the distanced object; *iste* distances from the speaker the one spoken to as well as the object. *Ille* yields the romance definite articles, which correspond quite closely in function to the English "the," and thus advertises the close tie between "the" and "that."

Could readers of an earlier age have managed the Hemingway relationship, the you-and-me relationship, marked by tight-lipped empathy based on shared experience? Certainly from antiquity the reader or hearer of an epic was plunged *in medias res*. But this does not mean he was cast as the author's boon companion. It means rather that he was plunged into the middle of a narrative sequence and told about antecedent events only later. A feeling of camaraderie between companions-in-arms is conveyed in epics, but the companions-in-arms are fictional characters who are not the reader or hearer and the narrator. *"Forsan et haec olim meminisse iuvabit"*—these words in the *Aeneid,* "perhaps some day it will help to recall these very things," are spoken by Aeneas to his companions when they are undergoing a period of hardships. They are one character's words to other characters, not Virgil's words to his hearer or reader. One might urge further that, like Hemingway's reader, the reader or hearer of an epic—most typically, of an oral folk epic—was hearing stories with which he was already acquainted, that he was thus on familiar ground. He was, but not in the sense that he was forced to pretend he had somehow lived as an alter ego of the narrator. His familiarity with the material was not a pretense at all, not a role, but a simple fact. Typically, the epic audience had heard the story, or something very much like it, before.

The role in which Hemingway casts the reader is somewhat different not only from anything these situations in early literature demand but also from anything in the time immediately before Hemingway. This is what makes Hemingway's writing interesting to literary historians. But Hemingway's demands on the reader are by no means entirely without antecedents. The existence of antecedents is indicated by the fact that Hemingway was assimilated by relatively unskilled readers with very little fuss. He does not recast the reader in a disturbingly novel role. By contrast, the role in which Faulkner casts the reader is a far greater departure from preceding roles than is Hemingway's. Faulkner demands more skilled and daring readers, and consequently had far fewer at first, and has relatively fewer even today when the Faulkner role for readers is actually taught in school. (Perhaps we should say the Faulkner roles.)

No one, so far as I know, has worked up a history of the readers' roles that prepared for that prescribed by Hemingway. But one can discern significantly similar demands on readers beginning as early as Addison and Steele, who assume a new fashionable intimacy among readers themselves and between all readers and the writer, achieved largely by casting readers as well as writer in the role of coffeehouse habitués. Defoe develops in his own way comparable author-reader intimacy. The roots of these eighteenth-century intimacies are journalistic, and from earlier journalism they push out later in Hemingway's own day into the world of sportswriters and war correspondents, of whom Hem-

ingway himself was one. With the help of print and the near in-
stantaneousness implemented by electronic media (the telegraph
first, later radio teletype and electronic transmission of photography), the newspaper writer could bring his reader into his
own on-the-spot experience, availing himself in both sports and
war of the male's strong sense of camaraderie based on shared
hardships. Virgil's *forsan et haec olim meminisse iuvabit* once
more. But Virgil was telling a story of the days of old and, as has
been seen, the camaraderie was among characters in the story,
Aeneas and his men. Sports and war journalism are about the
here and now, and, if the story can be got to the reader quickly,
the camaraderie can be easily projected between the narrator
and the reader. The reader is close enough temporally and
photographically to the event for him to feel like a vicarious
participant. In journalism Hemingway had an established foundation on which to build, if not one highly esteemed in snobbish
literary circles. And he in turn has been built upon by those who
have come later. Gibson has shown how much the style of *Time*
magazine is an adaptation of Hemingway (pp. 48–54). To
Hemingway's writer-reader camaraderie *Time* adds omniscience,
solemnly "reporting," for example, in eyewitness style, the behavior and feelings of a chief of state in his own bedroom as he
answers an emergency night telephone call and afterward returns
to sleep. Hemingway encouraged his readers in high self-esteem.
Time provides its readers, on a regular weekly basis, companion-
ship with the all-knowing gods.

When we look the other way down the corridors of time to the
period before the coffeehouses and the beginnings of intimate
journalism, we find that readers have had to be trained gradually
to play the game Hemingway engages them in. What if, *per im-
possibile,* a Hemingway story projecting the reader's role we have
attended to here had turned up in Elizabethan England? It
would probably have been laughed out of court by readers totally
unable to adapt to its demands upon them. It would certainly
have collided with representative literary theory, as propounded
for example by Sir Philip Sidney in *The Defense of Poesie.* For

Sidney and most of his age, poetry—that is to say, literature generally—has as its aim to please, but even more basically to teach, at least in the sense that it gave the reader to know what he did not know before. The Hemingway convention that the reader had somehow been through it all before with the writer would have been to Sidney's age at best confusing and at worst wrongheaded. One could argue that the Hemingway narrator would be telling the reader at least something he did not know before—that is, largely, the feelings of the narrator. But even this revelation, as we have seen, implies in Hemingway a covert awareness on the part of the reader, a deep sympathy or empathy of a basically romantic, nonpublic sort, grounded in intimacy. Sidney would have sent Hemingway back to his writing table to find something newer to write about, or to find a way of casting his material in a fresher-sounding form.

Another, and related, feature of the Hemingway style would have repelled sixteenth-century readers: the addiction to the "the" and "that" to the calculated exclusion of most descriptive qualifiers. There is a deep irony here. For in the rhetorical world that persisted from prehistoric times to the age of romanticism, descriptive qualifiers were commonly epithetic, expected qualifiers. The first chapter of Sidney's *Arcadia* (1590) presents the reader with "the hopeless shepheard," the "friendly rival," "the necessary food," "natural rest," "flowery fields," "the extreme heat of summer," and countless other souvenirs of a country every rhetorician had trod many times before. Is this not making the reader a recaller of shared experience much as Hemingway's use of "the" and "that" does? Not at all in the same way. The sixteenth-century reader recalls the familiar accouterments of literature, which are the familiar accouterments or commonplaces also of sculpture, painting, and all art. These are matters of shared public acquaintanceship, not of private experience. The sixteenth-century reader is walking through land all educated men know. He is not made to pretend he knows these familiar objects because he once shared their presence with this particular author, as a Hemingway reader is made to pretend. In Sidney, there is none of the you-and-I-know-even-if-others-don't ploy.

IV

To say that earlier readers would have been nonplussed at Hemingway's demands on them is not to say that earlier readers did not have special roles to play or that authors did not have their own problems in devising and signaling what the roles were. A few cases might be instanced here.

First of all, it is only honest to admit that even an oral narrator calls on his audience to fictionalize itself to some extent. The invocation to the Muse is a signal to the audience to put on the epic-listener's cap. No Greek, after all, ever talked the kind of language that Homer sang, although Homer's contemporaries could understand it well enough. Even today we do not talk in other contexts quite the kind of language in which we tell fairy stories to children. "Once upon a time," we begin. The phrase lifts you out of the real world. Homer's language is "once upon a time" language. It establishes a fictional world. But the fictionalizing in oral epic is directly limited by live interaction, as real conversation is. A real audience controls the narrator's behavior immediately. Students of mine from Ghana and from western Ireland have reported to me what I have read and heard from many other sources: a given story may take a skilled or "professional" storyteller anywhere from ten minutes to an hour and a half, depending on how he finds the audience relates to him on a given occasion. "You always knew ahead of time what he was going to say, but you never knew how long it would take him to say it," my Irish informant reported. The teller reacts directly to audience response. Oral storytelling is a two-way street.

Written or printed narrative is not two-way, at least in the short run. Readers' reactions are remote and initially conjectural, however great their ultimate effects on sales. We should think more about the problems that the need to fictionalize audiences creates for writers. Chaucer, for example, had a problem with the conjectural readers of the *Canterbury Tales*. There was no established tradition in English for many of the stories, and certainly none at all for a collection of such stories. What does Chaucer do? He sets the stories in what, from a literary-structural point of view, is styled a frame. A group of pilgrims going to Canterbury tell stories to one another: the pilgrimage frames the individual narratives. In terms of signals to his readers, we could put it another way: Chaucer simply tells his readers how they are to fictionalize themselves. He starts by telling them that there is a group of pilgrims doing what real people do, going to a real place, Canterbury. The reader is to imagine himself in their company and join the fun. Of course this means fictionalizing himself as a member of a nonexistent group. But the fictionalizing is facilitated by Chaucer's clear frame-story directives. And to minimize the fiction by maximizing real life, Chaucer installs himself, the narrator, as one of the pilgrims. His reader-role problem is effectively solved. Of course, he got the idea pretty much from antecedent writers faced with similar problems, notably Boccaccio. But he naturalizes the frame in the geography of southeast England.

The frame story was in fact quite common around Europe at this period. Audience readjustment was a major feature of mature medieval culture, a culture more focused on reading than any earlier culture had been. Would it not be helpful to discuss the frame device as a contrivance all but demanded by the literary economy of the time rather than to expatiate on it as a singular stroke of genius? For this it certainly was not, unless we define genius as the ability to make the most of an awkward situation. The frame is really a rather clumsy gambit, although a good narrator can bring it off pretty well when he has to. It hardly has widespread immediate appeal for ordinary readers today.

In the next period of major audience readjustment, John Lyly's *Euphues* and even more Thomas Nashe's *The Unfortunate Traveler* can be viewed as attempts to work out a credible role in which Elizabethan readers could cast themselves for the new medium of print. Script culture had preserved a heavy oral residue signaled by its continued fascination with rhetoric, which had always been orally grounded, a fascination that script culture passed on to early print culture. But the new medium was changing the noetic economy, and, while rhetoric remained strong in the curriculum, strain was developing. Lyly reacts by hyper-rhetoricizing his text, tongue-in-cheek, drowning the audience and himself in the highly controlled gush being purveyed by the schools. The signals to the reader are unmistakable, if unconsciously conveyed: play the role of the rhetorician's listener for all you are worth (*Euphues* is mostly speeches), remembering that the response the rhetorician commands is a serious and difficult one—it takes hard work to assimilate the baroque complexity of Lyly's text—but also that there is something awry in all the isocola, apophonemata, and antisagogai, now that the reader is so very much more a reader than a listener. Such aural iconographic equipment had been functional in oral management of knowledge, implementing storage and recall, but with print it was becoming incidental—which is, paradoxically, why it could be so fantastically elaborated.

Nashe shows the same uneasiness, and more, regarding the reader's role. For in the phantasmagoria of styles in *The Unfortunate Traveler* he tries out his reader in every role he can think of: whoever takes on Nashe's story must become a listener bending his ear to political orations, a participant in scholastic disputations, a hanger-on at goliardic Woodstocks, a camp follower fascinated by merry tales, a simpering reader of Italian revenge stories and sixteenth-century true confessions, a fellow conspirator in a world of picaresque cheats, and much more.

Nashe gives a foretaste of other trial-and-error procedures by which recipes were to be developed for the reader of the narrative prose works we now call novels. Such recipes were being worked out in other languages, too: in French notably by Rabelais, whose calls for strenuous shifts in the reader's stance Nashe emulated, and in Spanish by Cervantes, who explores all sorts of ironic possibilities in the reader's relationship to the text, incorporating into the second part of *Don Quixote* the purported reactions of readers and of the tale's characters to the first part of the work. Picaresque travels, well known at least since Apuleius' *Golden Ass,* multiplied, with major audience adjustments, in English down through *Tom Jones:* the unsettled role of the reader was mirrored and made acceptable by keeping the hero himself on the move. Samuel Richardson has his readers pretend they have access to other persons' letters, out of which a story emerges. Journals and diaries also multiplied as narrative devices, the reader becoming a snooper or a collector of seeming trivia that turn out not to be trivia at all. Ultimately, Laurence Sterne is able to involve his reader not only in the procreation of his hero Tristram Shandy but also in the hero's writing of his autobiography, in which pages are left blank for the reader to put his "own fancy in." The audience-speaker interaction of oral narrative here shows the reader in a new ironic guise—somewhat destructive of the printed book, toward which, as an object obtruding in the person-to-person world of human communication, the eighteenth century was feeling some ambiguous hostilities, as Swift's work also shows.

The problem of reader adjustment in prose narrative was in great part due to the difficulty that narrators long had in feeling themselves as other than oral performers. It is significant that, although the drama had been tightly plotted from classical antiquity (the drama is the first genre controlled by writing, and by the same token, paradoxically, the first to make deliberate use of colloquial speech), until the late eighteenth century there is in the whole Western world (and I suspect in the East as well) no sizable prose narrative, so far as I know, with a tidy structure comparable to that known for two millennia in the drama, moving through closely controlled tensions to a climax, with reversal and denouement. This is not to say that until the modern novel emerged narrative was not organized, or that earlier narrators were trying to write modern novels but regularly fell short of their aims. (Scholes and Kellogg have warned in *The Nature of Narrative* against this retroactive analysis of literary history.)

But it is to say that narrative had not fully accommodated itself to print or, for that matter, to writing, which drama had long before learned to exploit. *Tom Jones* is highly programed, but in plot it is still episodic, as all prose narrative had been all the way back through the Hellenic romances. With Jane Austen we are over the hurdle: but Jane Austen was a woman, and women were not normally trained in the Latin-based, academic, rhetorical, oral tradition. They were not trained speechmakers who had turned belatedly to chirography and print.

Even by Jane Austen's time, however, the problem of the reader's role in prose narrative was by no means entirely solved. Nervousness regarding the role of the reader registers everywhere in the "dear reader" regularly invoked in fiction well through the nineteenth century. The reader had to be reminded (and the narrator, too) that the recipient of the story was indeed a reader—not a listener, not one of the crowd, but an individual isolated with a text. The relationship of audience-fictionalizing to modern narrative prose is very mysterious, and I do not pretend to explain it all here, but only to point to some of the strange problems often so largely overlooked in the relationship. Tightly plotted prose narrative is the correlative of the audiences fictionalized for the first time with the aid of print, and the demands of such narrative on readers were new.

V

The present reflections have focused on written fictional narrative as a kind of paradigm for the fictionalizing of writers' "audiences" or readers. But what has been said about fictional narrative applies ceteris paribus to all writing. With the possible[10] exception noted above of persons in the presence of one another communicating by writing because of inability to communicate

10. "Possible," because there is probably a trace of fictionalizing even when notes are being exchanged by persons in one another's presence. It appears unlikely that what is written in such script "conversations" is exactly the same as what it would be were voices used. The interlocutors are, after all, to some extent pretending to be talking, when in fact they are not talking but writing.

orally, the writer's audience is always a fiction. The historian, the scholar or scientist, and the simple letter writer all fictionalize their audiences, casting them in a made-up role and calling on them to play the role assigned.

Because history is always a selection and interpretation of those incidents the individual historian believes will account better than other incidents for some explanation of a totality, history partakes quite evidently of the nature of poetry. It is a making. The historian does not make the elements out of which he constructs history, in the sense that he must build with events that have come about independently of him, but his selection of events and his way of verbalizing them so that they can be dealt with as "facts," and consequently the overall pattern he reports, are all his own creation, a making. No two historians say exactly the same thing about the same given events, even though they are both telling the truth. There is no *one* thing to say about anything; there are many things that can be said.

The oral "historian" captures events in terms of themes (the challenge, the duel, the arming of the hero, the battle, and so on), and formulas (the brave soldier, the faithful wife, the courageous people, the suffering people), which are provided to him by tradition and are the only ways he knows to talk about what is going on among men. Processed through these conventions, events become assimilable by his auditors and "interesting" to them. The writer of history is less reliant on formulas (or it may be he has such a variety of them that it is hard to tell that is what they are). But he comes to his material laden with themes in much vaster quantity than can be available to any oral culture. Without themes, there would be no way to deal with events. It is impossible to tell everything that went on in the Pentagon even in one day: how many stenographers dropped how many sheets of paper into how many wastebaskets when and where, what they all said to each other, and so on ad infinitum. These are not the themes historians normally use to write what really "happened." They write about material by exploiting it in terms of themes that are "significant" or "interesting." But what is "significant" depends on what kind of history you are writing—national political history, military history, social history, economic history, personal biography, global history. What is significant and, perhaps even more, what is "interesting" also depends on the readers and their interaction with the historian. This interaction in turn depends on the role in which the historian casts his readers. Although so far as I know we have no history of readers of history, we do know enough about historiography to be aware that one could well be worked out. The open-faced way the reader figures in Samuel Eliot Morison's writings is different from the more conspiratorial way he figures in Perry Miller's and both are quite different from the way the reader figures in Herodotus.

Scholarly works show comparable evolution in the roles they enforce on their readers. Aristotle's works, as has often been pointed out, are an agglomerate of texts whose relationships to his own holographs, to his students' notes, and to the work of later editors will remain always more or less a puzzle. Much of Aristotle consists of school logia or sayings, comparable to the logia or sayings of Jesus to his followers of which the Gospels chiefly consist. Aristotle's logia were addressed to specific individuals whom he knew, rather than simply to the wide world. Even his more patently written compositions retain a personal orientation: his work on ethics is the *Nicomachean Ethics,* named for his son. This means that the reader of Aristotle, if he wants to understand his text, will do well to cast himself in the role of one of Aristotle's actual listeners.

The practice of orienting a work, and thereby its readers, by writing it at least purportedly for a specific person or persons continues well through the Renaissance. The first edition of Peter Ramus' *Dialectic* was the French *Dialectique de Pierre de la Ramée à Charles de Lorraine Cardinal, son Mécène* (Paris, 1555), and the first edition of the far more widely used Latin version preserved the same personal address: *Dialectici Libri Duo . . . ad Carolum Lotharingum Cardinalem* (Paris, 1556).

Sidney's famous romance or epic is *The Countess of Pembroke's Arcadia*. Often in Renaissance printed editions a galaxy of prefaces and dedicatory epistles and poems establishes a whole cosmos of discourse which, among other things, signals the reader what roles he is to assume. Sidney's, Spenser's, and Milton's works, for example, are heavily laden with introductory material—whole books have been devoted to the study of Sidney's introductory matter alone.

Until recent times the rhetorical tradition, which, with the allied dialectical or logical tradition, dominated most written as well as oral expression, helped in the fictionalizing of the audience of learned works in a generic but quite real way. Rhetoric fixed knowledge in agonistic structures.

For this reason, the roles of the reader of learned works until fairly recent times were regularly more polemic than those demanded of the reader today. Until the age of romanticism reconstituted psychological structures, academic teaching of all subjects had been more or less polemic, dominated by the ubiquitous rhetorical culture, and proceeding typically by proposing and attacking theses in highly partisan fashion. (The academic world today preserves much of the nomenclature, such as "thesis" and "defense" of theses, but less of the programed fighting spirit, which its members let loose on the social order more than on their subject matter or colleagues.) From Augustine through Thomas Aquinas and Christian Wolff, writers of treatises generally proceeded in adversary fashion, their readers being cast as participants in rhetorical contests or in dialectical scholastic disputations.

Today the academic reader's role is harder to describe. Some of its complexities can be hinted at by attending to certain fictions which writers of learned articles and books generally observe and which have to do with reader status. There are some things the writer must assume that every reader knows because virtually every reader does. It would be intolerable to write, "Shakespeare, a well-known Elizabethan playwright," not only in a study on Renaissance drama but even in one on marine ecology. Otherwise the reader's role would be confused. There are other things that established fiction holds all readers must know, even though everyone is sure all readers do not know them: these are handled by writing, "as everyone knows," and then inserting what it is that not quite everyone really does know. Other things the reader can safely be assumed not to know without threatening the role he is playing. These gradations of admissible ignorance vary from one level of scholarly writing to another, and since individual readers vary in knowledge and competence, the degree to which they must fictionalize themselves to match the level of this or that reading will vary. Knowledge of the degrees of admissible ignorance for readers is absolutely essential if one is to publish successfully. This knowledge is one of the things that separates the beginning graduate student or even the brilliant undergraduate from the mature scholar. It takes time to get a feel for the roles that readers can be expected comfortably to play in the modern academic world.

Other kinds of writing without end could be examined in our reflections here on the fictionalizing of readers' roles. For want of time and, frankly, for want of wider reflection, I shall mention only two others. These are genres that do not seem to fall under the rule that the writer's audience is always a fiction since the "audience" appears to be simply one clearly determined person, who hardly need fictionalize himself. The first of the genres is the personal letter and the second the diary.

The case of the letter reader is really simple enough. Although by writing a letter you are somehow pretending the reader is present while you are writing, you cannot address him as you do in oral speech. You must fictionalize him, make him into a special construct. Whoever saluted a friend on the street with "Dear John"? And if you try the informal horrors, "Hi!" or "Greetings!" or whatever else, the effect is not less but more artificial. You are reminding him that you wish you were not writing him a letter, but, then, why are you? There is no way out. The writer has to set up another relationship to the reader and has to set the reader in a relationship to the writer different from that of non-chirographical personal contact.

The dimensions of fiction in a letter are many. First, you have no way of adjusting to the friend's real mood as you would be able to adjust in oral conversation. You have to conjecture or confect a mood that he is likely to be in or can assume when the letter comes. And, when it does come, he has to put on the mood that you have fictionalized for him. Some of this sort of adjustment goes on in oral communication, too, but it develops in a series of exchanges: a tentative guess at another's mood, a reaction from him, another from yourself, another from him, and you know about where you are. Letters do not have this normal give-and-take: they are one-way movements. Moreover, the precise relationships of writer to reader in letters vary tremendously from age to age even in intensively role-playing correspondence. No one today can capture exactly the fiction in Swift's *Journal to Stella,* though it is informative to try to reconstruct it as fully as possible, for the relationships of children to oldsters and even of man to woman have subtly altered, as have also a vast mesh of other social relationships which the *Journal to Stella* involves.

The epistolary situation is made tolerable by conventions, and learning to write letters is largely a matter of learning what the writer-reader conventions are. The paradoxes they involve were well caught some years ago in a Marx Brothers movie—if I recall correctly where the incident occurred. Letters start with "Dear Sir." An owlish, bemused businessman calls his secretary in. "Take this letter to Joseph Smithers," he directs. "You know his address. 'Dear Sir: You dirty rat. . . .' " The fiction of the exordium designed to create the *lector benevolens* is first honored and then immediately wiped out.

The audience of the diarist is even more encased in fictions. What is easier, one might argue, than addressing oneself? As those who first begin a diary often find out, a great many things are easier. The reasons why are not hard to unearth. First of all, we do not normally talk to ourselves—certainly not in long, in-

volved sentences and paragraphs. Second, the diarist pretending
to be talking to himself has also, since he is writing, to pretend
he is somehow not there. And to what self is he talking? To the
self he imagines he is? Or would like to be? Or really thinks he is?
Or thinks other people think he is? To himself as he is now? Or
as he will probably or ideally be twenty years hence? If he addresses not himself but "Dear Diary," who in the world is "Dear
Diary"? What role does this imply? And why do more women
than men keep diaries? Or if they don't (they really do—or did),
why do people think they do? When did the diary start? The history of diaries, I believe, has yet to be written. Possibly more than
the history of any other genre, it will have to be a history of the
fictionalizing of readers.

The case of the diary, which at first blush would seem to
fictionalize the reader least but in many ways probably fictionalizes him or her most, brings into full view the fundamental deep
paradox of the activity we call writing, at least when writing
moves from its initial account-keeping purposes to other more
elaborate concerns more directly and complexly involving human persons in their manifold dealings with one another. We are
familiar enough today with talk about masks—in literary criticism,
psychology, phenomenology, and elsewhere. Personae, earlier
generally thought of as applying to characters in a play or other
fiction (dramatis personae), are imputed with full justification
to narrators and, since all discourse has roots in narrative, to
everyone who uses language. Often in the complexities of present-
day fiction, with its "unreliable narrator" encased in layer after
layer of persiflage and irony, the masks within masks defy complete identification. This is a game fiction writers play, harder
now than ever.

But the masks of the narrator are matched, if not one-for-one,
in equally complex fashion by the masks that readers must learn
to wear. To whom is *Finnegans Wake* addressed? Who is the
reader supposed to be? We hesitate to say—certainly I hesitate to
say—because we have thought so little about the reader's role as

such, about his or her masks, which are as manifold in their own way as those of the writer.

Masks are inevitable in all human communication, even oral. Role playing is both different from actuality and an entry into actuality: play and actuality (the world of "work") are dialectically related to one another. From the very beginning, an infant becomes an actual speaker by playing at being a speaker, much as a person who cannot swim, after developing some ancillary skills, one day plays at swimming and finds that he is swimming in truth. But oral communication, which is built into existential actuality more directly than written, has within it a momentum that works for the removal of masks. Lovers try to strip off all masks. And in all communication, insofar as it is related to actual experience, there must be a movement of love. Those who have loved over many years may reach a point where almost all masks are gone. But never all. The lover's plight is tied to the fact that every one of us puts on a mask to address himself, too. Such masks to relate ourselves to ourselves we also try to put aside, and with wisdom and grace we to some extent succeed in casting them off. When the last mask comes off, sainthood is achieved, and the vision of God. But this can only be with death.

No matter what pitch of frankness, directness, or authenticity he may strive for, the writer's mask and the reader's are less removable than those of the oral communicator and his hearer. For writing is itself an indirection. Direct communication by script is impossible. This makes writing not less but more interesting, although perhaps less noble than speech. For man lives largely by indirection, and only beneath the indirections that sustain him is his true nature to be found. Writing, alone, however, will never bring us truly beneath to the actuality. Present-day confessional writing—and it is characteristic of our present age that virtually all serious writing tends to the confessional, even drama—likes to make an issue of stripping off all masks. Observant literary critics and psychiatrists, however, do not need to be told that confessional literature is likely to wear the most masks of all. It is hard to bare your soul in any literary genre. And it is hard to write outside a genre. T. S. Eliot has made the point that so far as he knows, great love poetry is never written solely for the ear of the beloved (p. 97), although what a lover speaks with his lips is often indeed for the ear of the beloved and of no other. The point is well made, even though it was made in writing.

3

Media Transformation:
The Talked Book

When you talk about the media today, one question constantly recurs: Do the new media wipe out the old? Or, more particularly, has television wiped out books? Since no moderately alert person who notices bookstalls or the habits of persons around him could possibly believe that books have disappeared, the asking of the question becomes itself interesting. Something besides the facts is disturbing him. Television and the whole of electronics must be doing something, he feels. What is it that they are doing?

Two different and indeed polarized answers are often given to this question. One answer is that electronics is wiping out books and print generally, whether you like it or not. The other is that books are books, and they are here to stay—or, with a slight variation, books are books, and we had better help them to stay, to remain as they are, for we cannot live without them (despite the fact that our ancestors lived for tens of thousands of years without any script whatsoever—all but the last six thousand years of human existence).

Any more considered answer which takes cognizance of the facts of history and of technological activity will have to be more complex than either of these. A survey of what has gone on in the past development of verbal communication and what is going on now suggests the operation of some paradoxical laws. A new medium of verbal communication not only does not wipe out the old, but actually reinforces the older medium or media. However, in doing so it transforms the old, so that the old is no longer

what is used to be. Applied to books, this means that in the fore-
seeable future there will be more books than ever before but that
books will no longer be what books used to be. If you think of
books even today as working the way books worked for Aristotle
or St. Thomas Aquinas or Chaucer or Milton or Sir Arthur
Quiller-Couch, you are out of touch with the way things are.

We are producing books already which are not written by anybody. They are talked books. Of course, we have had talked
books before. Oral epics which in the past somehow got themselves transcribed are books not written by anybody—they are
transcriptions of something someone said or sang. But our talked
books work differently from these. They are superimpositions of
electronic orality, writing, and print on or through one another.
The new kind of book, once it is printed, may look like older
books, may not have a recording or tape in a cover pocket, but
it does not sound or work the same way.

I was recently interviewed for such a talked book. The supervisor of the book, as we might style him, or the production manager—he is not the author nor am I; there is no author in any
earlier sense of this word—called me first in St. Louis by telephone from New York to arrange an interview with me in
Bethlehem, Pennsylvania. He brought a tape recorder to the
interview and taped my answers to questions which he put to me.
Then he slept on the tape in a Bethlehem hotel and came back
the next morning with supplementary questions for a fill-in interview, which he also taped. He took all the tape back to Brooklyn
and had it transcribed. Of course the stenographer edited the
tape a bit in transcribing it. The supervisor or production manager edited the transcription some more, after which he sent it to
me for further editing. When I had reworked it and sent it back
to him, he called me in St. Louis by long distance telephone from
New York and once again, this time over the telephone, taped
my answers to additional questions which had occurred to him
after the two or three revisions. Then he had these additional
questions transcribed, edited them, fed them back into the revised
manuscript, and sent the whole to me for further revisions. When

the book comes out, what do we have? The "book" is presented as an interview, with his questions and my responses. But in fact the total is something that neither of us said and that neither of us ever wrote. We have no term or readily available concept for this sort of thing. Perhaps we could call the end-result a "presentation" or a "production." More and more books are "productions" of this sort. So are more and more magazine and newspaper "articles."

History books are a good example. History in our sense of the word has been made possible by writing. But now historians of all periods after about A.D. 1900 will have to reckon with oral history. Interviewing to secure historical information or something as near like it as possible from those who can recall events in their own past has become a major academic enterprise since around 1948, when Allan Nevins began serious work with it at Columbia University. Oral history is of course no more accurate than written history. Neither is it quite like written history. It has a whole new set of problems with new kinds of inaccuracies as well as accuracies. It has been suggested that what the oral memoir gives the scholar is mostly not incontestable "facts" but simply an "incredible sense of immediacy." History written with an "incredible sense of immediacy" is certainly going to be a special kind of thing—perhaps it will be even incredibly true. One thing is certain however, namely, that oral history is also going to interact vigorously with writing (typewriting) and print. The Oral History Association is not sure what this interaction ought to be or how to control it, as they clearly show in their notes on their Fourth National Colloquium held November 7–10, 1969, at Warrenton, Virginia.[1]

The interaction, then, is intense between the media. Not only is there talking, writing, and printing going on but each one of these is being carried on with a conscious reference to the other. When the "production manager" was asking questions of me as

1. See William B. Pickett, "The Fourth National Colloquium on Oral History," *Historical Methods Newsletter* (University of Pittsburgh), 3, No. 3 (1970), 24–27.

reported above and I was responding, both of us knew that what we said was going to be taped, edited, worked over in writing, and finally printed. Electronic orality was aimed at the typewriter, blue pencil, and linotype. What we had in mind as we talked was not simply good talk but good printed matter. However, paradoxically, we wanted the final printing to sound as though the production were not printing at all but informal talk. We were talking to make edited printed matter sound as though it were not edited or printed, knowing that the only way to do this was to edit it very carefully before printing it.

To make the situation even more involuted, we commented on this state of affairs in the interview itself. The production manager remarked to me while we were being taped that we did not seem to be just talking informally to one another. "Why should we seem to be?" I returned. "We aren't." How was I supposed to believe that I was communicating with only one man when both he and I hoped that I was communicating with tens of thousands? Moreover, I was communicating with tens of thousands by making like I was communicating with only one. This was the effective way to do it. It all sounded like Catch 23. In fact, it was Catch 24, for this exchange was not left as it actually occurred but was retouched to appear in the final printed book.

One might argue that the paradoxes are no greater than those involved in all writing, for in writing you communicate with an audience who ordinarily *must* be absent while you are communicating with them (and thereby pretending that they are present). For writers, the audience is always a fiction and must be. Nevertheless the new admixture of orality, writing, and print made possible by electronics has complicated all paradoxes here. No literary form or thought processes of the crisscross sort we had been using could have been possible before it was possible to record the spoken voice directly for sound production.

The electronic media are here working not at all to destroy books but to produce more books faster. But by the same token they are producing different books, books which are not "books" in the old sense of the word. This sort of nonauthored, nonwritten book has a quite different ring from other books because, as we have just seen, the voices of those in the books are being refracted through all kinds of new conventions.

Moreover, the existence of this new kind of book is sure to affect the book which, in accordance with earlier practice, is composed by one author with pen in hand or with typewriter before him. For once the old-style author has read this other kind of orally tooled production, the ring of it will be in his ear. And he will be sure on occasion to match, consciously or unconsciously, some of its special effects.

Here we see the full complexity of the interaction of the media as successive media evolve. We have already seen that a new medium reinforces the earlier media by radically transforming them or, if you wish, radically transforms them by reinforcing them. Now we can see that part of the transformation is effected because the new medium feeds back into the old medium or media and makes them redolent of the new. The conventionally produced book can now sound to some degree like the orally programed book.

Patterns of reinforcement and transformation have existed from the very beginning in the verbal media—for we are restricting ourselves to the verbal media here. When writing began, it certainly did not wipe out talk. Writing is the product of urbanization. It was produced by those in compact settlements who certainly talked more than scattered folk in the countryside did. Once they had writing they were encouraged to talk more, if only because they had more to talk about.

But writing not only encouraged talk, it also remade talk. Once writing had established itself, talk was no longer what is used to be. Once you had writing, you could compose a scientific treatise—something, for example, such as Aristotle's *Art of Rhetoric,* a scientific tract on the art of persuasion. Before writing, many persons were skilled in persuasion but there was no scientific treatment of the subject. How could you have had anything like Aristotle's *Art of Rhetoric* in a completely oral culture? Or to focus the question on a subject matter other than discourse, how could you have had any systematic treatise such as, let us say, a treatise on hunting in a completely oral culture? No one could possibly put his mind through the series of thoughts which such books marshal.

The only way these thoughts could have been generated in an oral culture would be by having someone with no knowledge of writing or even of the possibility of such a thing as writing, recite the entire *Art of Rhetoric* or a treatise on hunting chapter after chapter from beginning to end, composing it as he went along. Such a feat is impossible. The closest an oral culture can come to a systematic treatise is through stringing together series of aphorisms: *The early bird gets the worm. All that glitters is not gold. He who hesitates is lost.*

This means that although oratory was tens of thousands of years old, the kind of thinking about oratory you have in Aristotle's *Art of Rhetoric* had never been done before writing. The human mind had never gone through this series of maneuvers, never traced this kind of trajectory of thought. But once you had produced, with the help of writing, treatises such as Aristotle's *Art of Rhetoric* or Plato's *Republic,* this kind of thinking and expression would ring in your ears. Now when you spoke you could echo to some limited degree the way it sounded when you read aloud something which could be composed, as a whole, only in writing. Moreover, you now were obliged to sound a little bit like writing quite regularly or perhaps even always, or you would not sound educated. You were expected—as we are expected today—to let your speech be colored by the way writing was or could be done. Talk, after writing, had to sound literate—and "literate," we must remind ourselves, means "lettered," or post-oral.

After writing, in other words, oral speech was never the same. In one way it was better off. For in speaking, the mind could now go through motions of the kind men had learned from using writing. Moreover, you could—and did—use writing to make notes to help your speech. But in another way oral speech was worse off. It was now regularly competing with writing. It was no longer itself—no longer self-contained. Men were aware that there were many things that writing could do verbally which oral performance could not do at all. Oral performance no longer monopolized the verbal field.

A comparable situation arose with the invention of print, and particularly of printing from movable alphabetic type. Print reinforced writing. It made universal literacy imperative—that is, print made it necessary for virtually everyone to be able to write, to work in the older medium. But print also transformed writing. With print, writers wrote about other things, and in different ways. Print made possible tight positional control such as could not be achieved with writing. With print, for the first time, a teacher could stand before a class and say, "Everybody turn to page 84, fifth line from the top, third word from the left," and everyone could find the word. In a manuscript culture the students might all have had manuscripts, but you would have had to pronounce the word and wait for them to locate it because it would be in a different position on a different page in virtually every manuscript.

With print, books literally line things up more drastically and indexes become important. It is hardly worthwhile spending time indexing manuscripts, for generally each manuscript would demand a separate index, but when you have 5000 copies of a book with everything in exactly the same place on exactly the same page, one index will do for all. Under such conditions the index becomes a highly effective and widespread retrieval device. A book is now felt as a container in which "things" are neatly ordered rather than as a voice which speaks to the reader. The medieval and early Renaissance collections of sayings give way gradually to the new kind of encyclopedia listing "facts" which tend to be regarded as physical objects available without any reference to verbalization—as "facts" in fact never are.

Subtly but irresistibly, with print what one wrote tended more and more to be thought of as lodging eventually in a fixed place. This fact appears to have affected what we call plot "structure." All the forces at work are not clear, but it appears certain that

until print there were no lengthy prose stories which were organized as tightly in plot as drama had been from the time of the
ancient Greeks. Drama had long freed itself from being a story
"told." First, it was not narration but action. And second, it had
been controlled by writing from ancient Greek times—the first
verbal genre to be so controlled (not excluding the epistle, often
orally formulated for subsequent transcription). Hence drama
long preceded lengthy prose narrative in developing tight linear
structure, building up to a climax resolved in a dénouement.
Prose narration, until around the romantic age, even in so highly
organized and late a production as *Tom Jones,* always remained
largely episodic—by contrast, for example, with the short story as
developed by Edgar Allan Poe or with a Thomas Hardy novel.
This means that prose stories were still thought of as "told" even
in a manuscript culture, not as strictly composed in writing. The
frequently recurring "dear reader" shows that even the nineteenth
century was hyperconscious regarding adjustment away from an
audience hearing a story to readers assimilating it through the
mediation of sight. Somewhere deep in the subconscious the fixity
suggested by print was at odds with the more loosely discursive,
fluid narrator-audience situation in which "tales" had normally
been "told." "Dear reader" eases the tension, or is thought to
do so.

The fixity of print underlies Joyce's composition of *Finnegans
Wake.* It is virtually impossible to produce two fully accurate
handwritten copies of *Finnegans Wake.* In a work with thousands
of portmanteau words and other idiosyncratic creations, every
single letter calls for individual supervision such as could hardly
be achieved in multiple manuscript copies. This means, of course,
that the final composition of the work—as of most works in print
today—is done on the printer's proofs.

Once you know the kind of control over discourse which print
makes possible, the feeling for such control influences your writing even in such things as your personal correspondence. You
can tell that Alexander Pope's letters were written by a man who
knew the printed book and that Cicero's were not. Cicero's sound

far more oratorical, for one thing: the reader is felt in a more oral-aural way. You can tell that my talk and yours is profoundly influenced not just by writing but also by print. The Venerable Bede or Geoffrey Chaucer could not possibly have given a talk that sounds like this one does. Neither, for that matter, could St. Thomas More or John Milton or Senator Everett Dirksen—print had not had its full effect on these people yet.

And so in the present and future, as we live with the electronic media, we are finding and will find that these have not wiped out anything but simply complicated everything endlessly. We still talk face to face, as we still write and print. The electronic media have reinforced print. One principle product of the computer is the print-out. And if you associate print with localization and space, with "linearity" or "sequentiality," there is no more linear or sequential instrument in the world than the computer, digital or analogue. It seems to be near-instantaneous only because it moves through sequences with lightning speed and thereby moves through more sequences than were ever before possible. Second, just as when you moved beyond writing to print it became urgent that nearly everyone learn to write, so now that we have moved beyond print to electronics it becomes urgent that nearly everyone know how to print, that is, to use the typewriter, which is a form of printing (making letters out of preexisting types). Moreover, electronics are even giving new forms to what used to be, we thought, "ordinary" typography. Photosetting is replacing linotyping.

A new medium, finally, transforms not only the one which immediately precedes it but often all of those which preceded it all the way back to the beginning. Thus, we still orate as did the orators before writing and print, but our oratory is completely transformed not only by writing and print but also by our new electronic orality. On television we use public address to reach millions of persons, but to reach each one as though we were having a face-to-face conversation with him or her. Our public speaking is private speaking now. Senator Dirksen was one of the last of a dying race.

With regard to the media as to so much else, we live in an age when everything is going on at once. This means that all the old media are still around us. They are working harder than ever. But they are also producing kinds of things they never produced before. We need to reinterpret the old as well as the new. No one will ever understand what print is today if he thinks of it only in terms of Gutenberg or Addison and Steele or Matthew Arnold.

To make sure you get the point, how do you think this text was composed?

4

African Talking Drums
and Oral Noetics

The primary orality in which human thought and verbal expression is initially and fundamentally lodged undergoes other metamorphoses besides those which lead through writing and print to the electronic management of thought and expression. Most of these metamorphoses have not been studied in detail. What effect, for example, did the Morse code have on the way news is formulated by journalists? Or how did use of the semaphore alphabet curtail normal oral redundancies or otherwise affect the way marine and military directives were formulated? How did nonalphabetic signaling, such as the use of varicolored flags, each the equivalent of a particular word or phrase displayed in accord with an explicitly devised "grammar," affect thought and expression where such signaling was operative? What did the sign language of the American Plains Indians do to their normal oral verbalization? How did its effects on verbalization compare with those of various sign languages for the deaf? Many other metamorphoses of primary orality could be enumerated, but in virtually every case, except for that of sign languages for the deaf, little or nothing is known of their effects on noetic processes.

The talking drums of Subsaharan Africa metamorphose primary oral processes in ways which are unique, at least in their sophistication and cultural importance. The last word has certainly not been said about all the ways the drum languages function in the hundreds of different cultures across the lower half of Africa—a vast area, since Africa is a continent some four times the size of the pre-Alaskan United States. But we do know enough to be able to compare some typical features of drum talk at least in certain African cultures with some of the features of primary oral verbalization. The present study undertakes such a comparison, in a limited, preliminary fashion. The comparison would appear to throw light not only upon the drumming processes but also upon the primary oral processes themselves out of which the drum languages have been developed.

I

For some time African talking drums or slit-gongs have been of considerable interest to anthropologists, linguists, and others, for on these instruments Africans have produced probably the most highly developed acoustic speech surrogates known anywhere in the world.[1] Various cultures have developed acoustic surrogates or sound substitutes for ordinary spoken words, using gongs or drums or whistles or bells or other instruments, as well as special sounds produced by the human voice itself, to communicate verbalized messages, often at a distance greater than that which articulate speech itself can cover. (Writing systems or scripts are also speech surrogates, but visual rather than acoustic, and we are concerned only with acoustic surrogates here.) Sometimes an acoustic speech surrogate is a code, that is to say, a system of sounds which essentially have no similarity to the sounds of the speech they represent: the Morse code used on an old-style telegraph is a standard example here, for the clicking buzz of a telegraph does not sound at all like speech and is not

---

1. In "Drum and Whistle 'Languages': An Analysis of Speech Surrogates," *American Anthropologist,* 59 (1957), 487–506, Theodore Stern has provided a permanently helpful generalized analysis of various ways in which human speech has been converted into surrogate sounds for transmission by means other than normal vocal articulation of speech itself. The article provides an extensive bibliography on drum languages. For an example of a recent technical linguistic study of drum language, see Pierre Alexandre, "Langages tambourinés," *Semiotica,* 1 (1969), 273–281. See also Thomas A. Sebeok and Donna Jean Umiker-Sebeok (eds.), *Speech Surrogates,* Vol. I (The Hague: Mouton, 1976), Vol. II in preparation.

intended to. An African drum language is not such an abstract signaling code, but rather is a way of reproducing in a specially stylized form the sounds of the words of a given spoken language.

Only recently have knowledgeable descriptions of various drum languages been worked out, and our knowledge of most such languages is still somewhat defective. To arrive at an understanding of how drums operate, one must first have a command in depth of the normal spoken language which the drums adapt, and then discover the principles governing the adaptation. That is to say, to understand African drum talk one must know the spoken language being used—for one drummer will drum his native Duala, another Yaounde, another Lokele—and, in addition, one must discover the way in which the language is adapted or styled for the drums. A drum language is not understood *ipso facto* when one knows the spoken language it reproduces: drum language has to be specially learned even when the drums speak one's own mother tongue.

To the not inconsiderable literature about the drums, much of it highly technical, there has just been added an invaluable small book (121 pages) in French, partly a translation but also an updating and magisterial streamlining of an earlier book in English by the same author.[2] Although it honors existing linguistic, anthropological, musicological, and other scientific work, this new little book is not in itself highly technical. But its author, John F. Carrington, now professor of botany at the Kisangani campus of the National University of Zaire, has qualifications, technical and other, hard to top. He has been in Africa, with only brief interruptions, since 1938 and has been writing about the drums for at least twenty-five years—an article of his on the subject appeared in the *Scientific American* in 1971,[3] and he is cited regularly in anthropological and linguistic studies. Most

2. *La Voix des tambours: Comment comprendre le langage tambouriné d'Afrique* (Kinshasa: Centre Protestant d'Editions et de Diffusion, 1974). References in parentheses in the text of the present article are to this book and the translations are my own. The earlier volume in English is *The Talking Drums of Africa* (London: Carey Kingsgate Press, 1949).

3. "The Talking Drums of Africa," *Scientific American,* December 1971, pp. 90–94.

significantly, however, he writes as one who talks on the drums himself. The title of his little volume bespeaks the confident expertise of one completely at home in his subject: *La Voix des tambours: Comment comprendre le langage tambouriné d'Afrique.*

Carrington drums chiefly in Lokele, a Bantu language which, with more meticulous regard for Bantu grammar, may also be called Kele, the language of the people known as Lokele. (I follow Carrington's later practice and English idiom in using the same form for people and language). Carrington speaks Lokele, of course. Not all who know an African language are so advantageously equipped, for of the many hundreds of African languages (not dialects but mutually incomprehensible languages) in active use today, by no means all can readily be put onto drums—Swahili, for example, lends itself to drum talk only with great difficulty, Carrington notes (p. 21).

Carrington has the in-depth knowledge of his subject which comes from having lived for over twenty-five years as a Christian missionary in intimate association with the Lokele people in upper Zaire near Kisangani, in effect as one of the Lokele themselves. He drums often for practical purposes: for example, to have a boat come from the opposite bank of a river to ferry him across. "He is not really a European," one African explained to others (pp. 65–66) on an occasion when Carrington was at the drums, "despite the color of skin. He used to be from our village, one of us. After he died, the spirits made a mistake and sent him off far away to a village of whites to enter into the body of a little baby who was born of a white woman instead of one of ours. But because he belongs to us, he could not forget where he came from and so he came back. If he is a bit awkward on the drums, this is because of the poor education the whites gave him." It is clear—at least to his fellow Africans—that Carrington has enviable credentials. He is twice a native son.

II

The sophisticated drum languages of Africa have been developed within an oral economy of thought and expression.

Recent studies have shown how oral noetic processes—ways of acquiring, formulating, storing, and retrieving knowledge in cultures unfamiliar with writing or print—have certain distinctive features as compared to the noetic processes of cultures possessed of writing and, a fortiori, of print, and how these distinctive features are related to what can be called an oral lifestyle. Because Carrington's book recreates, informally but quite substantially and circumstantially, the drum language world as a whole, a reader of the book who is familiar with oral noetics can hardly avoid being struck by the way in which the drums exemplify and often informingly exaggerate the characteristics of the oral lifeworld, or of primary orality (oral culture untouched by writing or print, as contrasted with secondary orality, the electronic orality of present-day technological cultures, implemented by telephone, radio, television, and other instruments dependent for their existence and use on writing and print). My intent here is to bring together what we know about oral noetics and about concomitant oral lifestyles on the one hand, and on the other hand what is now known about the talking drums as explained by Carrington.

The latter subject is by no means so familiar to me as the former, which I have treated and documented elsewhere at length, most notably in *The Presence of the Word*.[4] Yet the alliance between drums and an oral economy of thought and expression kept asserting itself vigorously over and over again in the course of my recent month-long visit as Lincoln Lecturer in Equatorial and West African republics, where I spoke on some thirty occasions about orality, literacy, print, and electronics to and with African anthropologists, linguists, folklorists, literary scholars, journalists and other communications specialists, novelists, poets, and others, including many students—in Zaire, Cameroun, Nigeria, and Senegal, all in the heart of the drum country. The relationship of drums to orality came up always as a familiar close-to-home subject badly needing explanatory de-

4. New Haven: Yale University Press, 1967.

velopment rather than as a subject already well fitted with explanation. But there is ample explanation in Carrington's handbook to document the conclusion already forcing itself on me in Africa before his book appeared: the talking drum is not merely an element in some primary oral cultures but is also in fact a kind of paradigm of primary orality. Because African talking drums amplify and exaggerate—sometimes almost caricature—the most basic techniques of oral noetics as we have recently come to know these, they open new depths to our understanding of orality.

Carrington's work does not treat all talking drums but primarily those of the Lokele, with some reference to other Central and West African peoples. He does not discuss every aspect of drum talk treated by other scholars, such as special ways of securing emphasis or the use of more than two tones for some languages. But the Lokele drumming is at least typical and Carrington discusses it not only in its essentials but also in rich human detail. This is all the present study requires, for it undertakes to establish merely some landmarks.

III

Not all drums that transmit information are talking drums. The Jibaro Indians, for example, as reported on by Rafael Karsten, have certain drum rhythms for signaling narcotic ceremonies, others for manioc beer ceremonies, still others for deaths and attacks by enemies, the rhythms being differentiated much as those of a dirge and of wedding music might be in Western culture.[5] Many cultures, including that of the present-day United States, use drum beats or gong beats or church bells in this way. African talking drums work differently. To make subsequent discussion here intelligible, it will be well to highlight certain points in Carrington's account of the drums.

As explained by Carrington, talking drums among the Lokele

5. Rafael Karsten, *The Head-Hunters of Western Amazonas: The Life and Culture of the Jibaro Indians of Eastern Ecuador and Peru,* Commentationes Humanarum Litterarum, 7 (Helsingfors: Societas Scientiarum Fennica, 1935), pp. 109–113.

and generally through Africa imitate words by imitating their tones. Hence, for these talking drums a tonal language is needed. A tonal language uses pitch to distinguish words. Many African languages are tonal. English is not a tonal language. It is true that English uses tone or pitch to distinguish between the several possible senses in which a word or a group or words may be used in a given case. For example, in the following group of words the speaker raises the pitch of the word "good" to identify a question: "It is good?" If he wishes the same words to be understood as a declaration, he can lower the pitch of "good:" "It is good." Or, to counter a denial, he can raise the pitch of "is": "It *is* good." But English does not normally use pitch to distinguish from each other words otherwise homonymic. Lokele does. In one of Carrington's instances (p. 19), the syllables represented in writing or print as *lisaka* can have three meanings: if the syllables are pronounced all on the same pitch (...) the resulting word means pond; if the final syllable is raised in tone (.. ˙) the resulting word means promise (the noun); if the last two syllables are raised in tone (. ˙ ˙) the resulting word means poison (the noun). Words keep their tones independently of the sense of an utterance in which they occur. One result that Carrington points out is that a tonal language cannot be effectively whispered—the meaning will not always come clear. Tonal languages are known in many places other than Africa, and not all African languages are tonal. In a given linguistic family, some languages may be tonal and others not.

What African talking drums do, as exemplified among the Lokele, is reproduce the tones of words, not the vowel or consonant sounds as such. To reproduce two tones (which suffice for Lokele), one drum with two tones is commonly used. Carrington wisely notes that the term "drum" is derived from other cultures and applied, not with complete success, to the African instruments. A typical two-toned wooden "drum" might be styled more properly, a wooden gong or a slit-gong—an "idiophone," the whole of which vibrates when struck, like a metal gong or a xylophone bar or a tuning fork or a bell. The African wooden slit-gong is typically, though not always, a section of tree trunk, and thus a cylinder, some two to six feet or so in length, hollowed out with a slit an inch or so in width running almost its entire length. The hollowing can be done, laboriously, through the slit, but more commonly the log is opened at the ends, which are then plugged up again afterwards.

The hollowing is done in such a way that the two lips of the slit produce two different tones. Generally the low tone is considered the male "voice" and the high tone the female "voice." But the Lokele conceive of the contrast in terms not of the common Western metaphor "low" and "high" but in terms of "stronger" and "weaker," so that if in a given case the high note of a drum carries farther, it is considered the "male" (p. 25). Some wooden "gong" drums are structured differently from the simple cylinder models, and some are even carved in the shapes of animals, but they all work in essentially the same way, with "lips" of different tones. The word *lisaka* (...), pond, can be signaled by striking the male lip three times; *lisaka* (.. ˙), promise, by striking first the male lip twice and then the female once; *lisaka* (. ˙˙), poison, by striking the male lip twice, the female once.

This kind of tonal differentiation can be and is effected also with African stretched-skin drums, "membranophones," in which a vibrating membrane is stretched over a resonator, like the drums common in Western orchestras. For "talking" two such true drums are used, a "husband" (lower pitch) and a "wife" (higher pitch). In fact, the same drum language can be "spoken" by contrasting two pitches produced by almost anything. It is actually "spoken" by using two differently pitched whistled notes (produced with the lips or with instruments), or by using horns or string instruments, or by two contrasting spoken syllables— the Lokele thus use the syllable "ki" and "li" (Carrington's transcription, p. 98, in French spelling) for the female voice, "ke" and "le" for the male. Compared to other instruments, however, drums have the advantage of carrying farther—perhaps a normal maximum of around four or five miles under favorable conditions (usually along a quiet river, and at night), though Carrington reports (p. 34) from his own experience an exceptional case of a gong, the largest he has ever seen, which carried twenty-five kilometers (about fifteen miles) along a quiet river at night. Longer distances can be covered by relays of drums. Stories one hears of individual drums carrying sixty miles are based, at best, on ignorance.

Obviously, gong or drum "talk" of this sort can be understood at great distances even though heard faintly because all that need be distinguished in it are two different tones or pitches. But the fact that drum language is based only on the tones of words creates problems. *Lisaka* (...) is not the only three-syllable word in Lokele pronounced with three low tones, nor are *lisaka* (.. ˙) or *lisaka* (. ˙ ˙) the only three-syllable words with their sequence of tones. A given sequence of tones does not signal a very determined meaning at all, but remains quite ambiguous. If, however, a set of tones is put into a context, the context can eliminate many or all of the ambiguities, can "disambiguate" a given tone pattern, especially if the supplied context is a stereotyped one.

So the "words" on the drums are set into stereotyped contexts or patterns. To say "moon" the drummer does not simply strike the tones for the Lokele word for moon, *songe* (˙ ˙), for two high tones could mean many things besides moon (p. 39). Rather, he strikes the tones for the stereotyped phrase meaning "moon look toward the earth" (˙ ˙ . ˙ . . . .). The tones of "look toward the earth," also themselves ambiguous, limit and are limited by the tones of the "moon." "Moon look toward the earth" is beat out on the drum every time the drummer wants to say "moon." And so with the rest of the drum lexicon. For each simple word of ordinary speech, the drum language substitutes a much longer expression. These expressions moreover are stereotyped, fixed in the drumming tradition, and must be learned by each novice drummer: a drummer cannot make up his own stereotyped expression at whim. For "cadaver," the Lokele drummer must say "cadaver which lies on its back upon clods of earth." For "war", the stereotyped phrase is "war which calls attention to ambushes." And so on through the drummer's entire drum vocabularly.

It takes much longer to say something on a drum than *viva voce*, on the average eight times as long. The insertion of an ambiguous drum word into a standard context in order to "disambiguate" the word suggests a similar practice, not mentioned by Carrington, *lien-hsi* or "joining," in Chinese, a language having many homonyms. Spoken Chinese has more such problems with ambiguities than written Chinese, since in a set of written homonyms each will often be represented by a different character, though they may sound the same.[6]

The expanded or stereotyped expression on the drums, however, never becomes an abstract code of high and low tones: the drummers think of it as consisting not of tones alone but of words represented by the tones. However, when the drummers are asked to say what the words in their drummed phrases are, it is found that some of the words they say have lost their significance in the spoken language. In the stereotyped phrase for a young girl (pp. 41–42), *boseka botilakende linginda*, "the young girl will not go to the '*linginda*,'" the Lokele drummers are sure that the last word is *linginda* but they are no longer agreed as to what *linginda* means—perhaps a kind of fishing net (tabu to young girls, thought to bring users of this net bad luck by their presence), or perhaps a council of the elders of the clan (obviously not frequented by young girls). It is obvious that drummed Lokele is a

6. See C. P. Fitzgerald, *The Birth of Communist China* (Baltimore, Md.: Penguin Books, 1964), p. 154: "In colloquial [Chinese] speech one does not say 'chin' for gold, because many other words sounded 'chin' exist; 'huang chin'—yellow gold—is the colloquial term, which identifies the 'chin' in this phrase. But in writing [classical Chinese] it was not necessary to use two words [because Chinese written characters for the various words pronounced 'chin' differ from one another]; only the word of primary meaning was employed and thus a page of the classical style read aloud became a wholly unintelligible string of phonemes."

very special form of Lokele, which even native Lokele speakers can learn only with some effort.

IV

This brief summary of relevant portions of Carrington's account will perhaps suffice to identify some of the connections between the noetic economy of the drums and that of oral cultures as such when these are contrasted with writing and print cultures. The point here is not simply that verbalization in primary oral cultures and drum language operate in the same sensory field, that of sound. Obviously, they do. The point is, rather, that the structures given to expression and to knowledge itself by the verbalization patterns of oral cultures are strikingly characteristic of drum language as such. The drums are oral or oral-aural not merely in their sensory field of operation but even more basically in their idiom. Talking drums belong to the lifeworld of primary oral cultures, though not all primary oral cultures have used them.

What are the salient features—or, to resort to oral rather than visual or visual-tactile metaphors, the assertive strains, the principal accents—of an oral culture that are advertised or amplified in the use of talking drums? They can be enumerated as follows, under headings which overlap somewhat but which nevertheless appear serviceable in the present state of our knowledge: (1) stereotyped or formulaic expression, (2) standardization of themes, (3) epithetic identification for "disambiguation" of classes or of individuals, (4) generation of "heavy" or ceremonial characters, (5) formulary, ceremonial appropriation of history, (6) cultivation of praise and vituperation, (7) copiousness. These features of oral cultures generally, as contrasted with cultures using writing and print, and particularly the alphabet, have been worked out largely by scholars interested primarily in the transit from orality to literacy in Western classical culture and its consequents. However, grounds for generalization to primary oral cultures as such have appeared in the work of Albert B. Lord and Eric A. Havelock and have been discussed further in my own work, *The Presence of the Word*. The features, as just enumerated, can be taken up in order here with reference to drum language.

Stereotyped or formulaic expression. Carrington has made clear that the use of stereotyped expressions or formulas lies at the heart of drum language. It should be noted that a similar point has been made also by Lord and Havelock and others[7] concerning oral epic performances and indeed concerning careful expression generally throughout oral cultures. The Homeric poems as well as more recent oral or residually oral epics consist largely, if not entirely, of fixed expressions—the "clichés" which oral cultures live on and which literate cultures teach their members to scorn. Havelock has pointed out, moreover, that the use of formulaic phrases in an oral culture is not restricted to poets,[8] but is also necessary for many prosaic purposes. Stereotyped expressions enable primary oral cultures to preserve their knowledge and to recall it when needed. Formulas are necessary for history: the formulary genealogy, set up for the repetition on demand, preserves knowledge of ancestors which would otherwise vanish. Formulas are also necessary for administrative purposes: to get a lengthy message from Sardis to Athens a public official in early, oral Greek society had to cast the message in mnemonic formulas of some sort or it would not be preserved in the messenger's mind for delivery (or in the sender's mind for recall).

One can go further: oral cultures not only express themselves in formulas but also think in formulas. We know what we can

7. Albert B. Lord, *The Singer of Tales*, Harvard Studies in Comparative Literature, 24 (Cambridge, Mass.: Harvard University Press, 1960), pp. 30–67, and *passim;* Eric A. Havelock, *Preface to Plato* (Cambridge, Mass.: Belknap Press of Harvard University Press, 1963), pp. 134–142; Robert P. Creed, "A New Approach to the Rhythm of *Beowulf*," *PMLA*, 81 (1966), 23–33; Michael N. Nagler, *Spontaneity and Tradition: A Study in the Oral Art of Homer* (Berkeley: University of California Press, 1974); John Miles Foley, "Formula and Theme in Old English Poetry," in B. A. Stolz and R. S. Shannon, eds., *Oral Literature and the Formula* (Ann Arbor, Mich.: Center for Coordination of Ancient and Modern Studies, 1976), pp. 207–238—see also the other papers in this volume and the comprehensive annotated bibliography in James P. Holoka, "Homeric Originality: A Survey," *Classical World*, 66 (1973), 257–293.

8. Havelock, *Preface to Plato*, p. 140.

recall. If one thinks of something once and never again, one does not say that one knows it. Without writing, if one does not think formulary, mnemonically structured thoughts, how can one really know them, that is, be able to retrieve them, if the thoughts are of even moderate complexity? In a culture without writing one cannot first work out in verbal form an elaborate pattern of thought and then memorize it afterwards: once said, it is gone, is no longer there to be memorized. Thoughts must be elaborated mnemonically in the first instance to be recoverable. Oral cultures thus think by means of memorable thoughts, thoughts processed for retrieval in various ways, or, in other words, fixed, formulaic, stereotyped. The formulaic expressions so common in oral cultures—proverbs, epithets, balances of various sorts, and other heavy patterning—are not added to thought or expression but are the substance of thought, and by the same token of expression as well. Oral cultures think *in* formulas, and communicate *in* them. When drums do the same, persons in a primary oral culture do not find the mode of expression at all so different from the normal as do literate folk.

In a sense, of course, every word is a mnemonic device, a formula, something more or less fixed and retrievable, bringing back to mind an element in consciousness otherwise elusive. Writing and print thus involve themselves in memory simply by the use of words, and they even occasionally make use of set phrases. But oral cultures need set phrases in quantity, for nothing can be "looked up." Primary oral cultures use formulas as units somewhat as writing cultures use words as units. This is one reason why such oral cultures are less "analytic": their thought has to be kept in larger chunks to survive and to flourish.

The same forces in an oral culture that tend to make speech formulaic also tend to make speech redundant. Redundancy is repetition. In a noetic economy dependent on large-scale repetition for its life, efforts to avoid repetition are not only difficult but also often inadvisable. Better too much repetition than too little. Too little repetition is fatal: knowledge not repeated enough vanishes. Too much repetition at worst is only annoying, and in a noetic economy obligated to value repetition, it takes a great deal of repetition indeed to annoy anyone. Not only purely oral cultures but also residually oral cultures, such as the European Middle Ages and Renaissance, are much addicted to "amplification" of a subject—verbal inflation which strikes more chirographic and typographic personality structures as at best flatulent.

For these reasons, and for other reasons to be treated later here in discussing copiousness, verbalization, and particularly highly formal or eventful verbalization, in oral cultures tends to be elaborately verbose. Set expressions themselves tend to be inflated or to be used at times when modern information theory would consider them useless. Why keep saying "wily Odysseus" over and over again when "Odysseus" is a perfectly clear reference?

But perhaps nowhere else in primary oral cultures is set expression so inveterately elaborate as it is on the drums. To translate from the French one of Carrington's examples (p. 46), the spoken expression, "Don't be afraid" becomes in drum language "Bring your heart back down out of your mouth, your heart out of your mouth, get it back from up there." Or again, "Come back" is rendered on the drum "Make your feet come back the way they went, make your legs come back the way they went, plant your feet and your legs below, in the village which belongs to us."

Of course, the reason for this somewhat fantastic lengthening is that to the ordinary oral delight in amplification there is added a special need to "disambiguate" because of the binary nature of the drum signal. The need can be expressed in a formula familiar to telephone engineers and cited by Carrington (p. 47) from an article by R. V. L. Hartley, in the *Bell System Technical Journal:* $H = N \log_2 S$, where H is the amount of information to be conveyed in a given message, N is the number of signs in the same message, and S the total possible *different* signs in the sign system. The lesser the number of possible different signs, the longer the message has to be. Spoken Lokele is said (p. 47) to have 266 possible different signs (each a combination of one of nineteen consonants, one of seven vowels, and one of two tones); drummed Lokele has only two possible different signs, the two tones, so that the number of signs in a given message increases enormously on the drums. Or, to use another example, a binary system of notation results in the use of many more digits to express a given number than a decimal system does. Amplification of phrases, endemic to oral cultures, is thus exaggerated in drum talk almost to the point of caricature.

Use of stereotyped phrases, and of the specialized themes next to be treated here, make oral cultures highly conservative. Drum language, Carrington points out (p. 44) is still more conservative than the spoken word in cultures which know both.

Standardization of themes. Oral noetics, as manifested in poetry and narration of primary oral cultures, organizes thought largely around a controlled set of themes, more or less central to the human lifeworld: birth, marriage, death, celebration, struggle (ceremonial or ludic, and polemic or martial), initiation rites, dance and other ceremonies, arrivals and departures, descriptions or manipulations of implements (shields, swords, plows, boats, looms), and so on. It is true, of course, that all knowledge is organized in some way around themes in the large sense of subject matters—there is no other way to organize it. But the themes that govern oral discourse tend to be relatively limited and bound to the human lifeworld, if only because, as Havelock has explained,[9] elaboration of scientific categories or of quasi-scientific categories (such as are used, for example, in the modern writing of history) depends on the development of writing. There would be no reason to believe that drum talk would not follow similar thematic patterns, and Carrington's report, especially his Chapter 8 (pp. 81–90), leads one to believe that it indeed does (although he himself does not advert to this subject explicitly).

Drum language in fact appears to reinforce the thematic standardization or simplification normal in oral cultures because of the binary signaling system of the drums. Since expressions have to be made very long in a binary signal in order to be relatively unambiguous, multiplication of categories or areas of discourse will make for more and more involved expression, which would soon become so labyrinthine that new depths of

9. Ibid., pp. 166–190.

ambiguity would appear. Disambiguation by the lengthening of expressions has certain limits. Hence drum talk is encouraged to exploit the standard themes. These will vary to some extent, of course, from culture to culture. What the oil palm is to the West African, the seal is to the Eskimo.

Standardization of themes does not mean that expression is moribund. It does not preclude reference, for example, to new events in individuals' lives. It is quite possible to drum a message that Boyoko is on his way to Kisangani to buy a motorcycle for his brother. But even in such a drum message, the thematic framework asserts itself, assimilating to itself the individuals involved. Boyoko's ordinary name is not a theme, so Boyoko becomes, for drumming purposes (to translate into English Carrington's French translation from Lokele, p. 54), "The-palm-tree-full-of-stinging-ants-where-one-climbs-and-then-has-to-get-rid-of-the-insects." Palm trees and stinging ants, means of sustenance and sources of annoyance in the human lifeworld, thematically absorb and define the individual.

Neither does standardization of themes mean that the drum culture cannot truly appropriate or interiorize new ideas. In fact, appropriation and interiorization are often expertly achieved on the drums. Carrington gives a remarkable instance (p. 93) of appropriation through formulaic expression. Early Christians at Yakusu had problems in finding a suitable word in Lokele to convey the Christian way of conceiving of God. Because the Lokele had thought of God as far off and indifferent to man (as Aristotle had thought of him) except at the time of birth or death or when invoked by sorcerers to curse someone, a common animist word for God was *itoko,* which also meant "smallpox" (imminent death, more or less). When they understood how Christians conceived of God, the drummers, uncoached by European missionaries, worked out on their own a new drum formula to express their new understanding: God as conceived by Christians is *liuwe lisango likasekweleke likolo kondause,* "Living Father who has come down from above." They had got the message and made it their own. But again, standard themes from the human lifeworld are the denominators: life, father, descent (the high, the low).

Epithetic identification for "disambiguation" of classes or of individuals. One of the forms of "disambiguation" is the epithet or standard qualifier. Some of the instances already given consist in such epithets. Other epithets would be these: for "banana" (*likondo*) the drums say (p. 40) "pole-supported banana" (*likondo lobotumbela*), for "forest" (*lokonda*), "dry-wood forest" (*lokonda teketeke*). Similarly, an individual may be designated with the help of an epithetic word or phrase, these often derived from an event in the individual's life. Epithets are a specific manifestation of formulaic tendencies, but common and distinctive enough to warrant separate mention. They are particularly in evidence in establishing the "heavy" characters next discussed here.

Generation of "heavy" or ceremonial characters. Havelock has shown here, in the absence of the elaborate categorizations with which writing makes it possible to rack up knowledge more "abstractly," oral cultures commonly organize their knowledge in thematic narrative, peopled with impressive or "heavy" figures, often type characters (wise Nestor, clever Odysseus, faithful Penelope). Around such heavily accoutered figures (and themes associated with them) the lore of the culture is focused. The use of drum language carries ceremonialization to new heights. Again, because of the ambiguities in a sign system with only two variants (low and high tones), to be identifiable on the drum an individual needs epithetic and other ceremonial accouterments which will set his name in extremely high relief. Thus, assigned a drum name made up of his own given drum name plus those of his father and mother, as is customary, a Lokele known to his acquaintances in ordinary oral communication simply as Boyele (p. 52) finds himself exalted on the drums into "The Always Poisonous Cobra, Son of the Evil Spirit with the Lance, Nephew of the Men of Yagonde." "The Always Poisonous Cobra" was his grandfather's drum name, "Evil Spirit with the Lance," his father's.

Any name, even in ordinary parlance, is to some degree ceremonial: it fixes a person ritually or conventionally in a relationship to his fellows, though in patterns which of course vary from culture to culture. When the name is massive, as it has to be on the drums, and is used in its entirety every time the individual is mentioned, as it usually is on the drums, the ceremonial weight of discourse becomes exceedingly heavy. Primary oral culture commonly encourages very formal discourse, but the drums once again here exaggerate oral emphases. (The quasi-confidential public address customary today on radio and television is seemingly unknown in primary oral cultures or even in the residually oral writing and print cultures: it is a late development within the secondary oral culture produced by the electronic media, which for their existence and operation depend upon writing and print.)

Formulary, ceremonial appropriation of history. The history which a society knows is a selection of matter out of the continuum of the society's existence. "History" does not exist on its own but comes into being when human consciousness focuses on certain points in its temporal existence, isolates certain connections, and thereby frames certain elements into what consciousness can register as "events." What in a given society constitutes history—true, well-founded history, for we are not concerned here with unfounded or false history—will depend on a society's ways of constituting and selecting events from the continuum around it, its ways of appropriating its past.

Whereas highly developed writing and print cultures tend to appropriate the past analytically when they verbalize it, oral cultures tend to appropriate the past ceremonially, which is to say in stylized, formulary fashion. How this is so can be seen in part from their handling of names. In an oral culture, as we have seen, knowledge in its entirety tends to be organized around the action of individuals. Hence names, which distinguish individuals from one another, can serve as especially important foci for noetic organization in oral cultures, and in particular for the organization of history. They can become quite complicated because of the load of history they bear. Drum names can become even more complicated.

In all cultures names come from history in one way or another. They refer the individual to his own history, and in doing so help constitute that history in a formulary fashion that confers on it a certain ceremonial weight. An individual may be named "after" an ancestor or another person older than himself, being assigned a "given" name which is or was that of the other person. In addition, he may at the same time automatically bear his father and grandfather's or mother's name as well, thus acquiring further anchorages in history. In another pattern, names may derive directly from an historical event in the individual's own life or that of another or of a group. Drum names appear to work in both these patterns. The drum name for Boyele, just mentioned, incorporates ancestral drum names and thus fixes Boyele in history at the same time that it records history by fixing it in his own given drum name. The drum name given Carrington in a village he once visited records an historical fact in his life (p. 65): "The White Man Who Travels with the Man with Heavy Eyebrows." On a Camerounian village's drums, European colonial power (p. 66) is named in terms of some of its historical effects: "It reduces the country to slavery; those who survive it makes slaves." Or again, a certain medical assistant was named in drum language in accord with his behavior, "The Proud Man Who Listens to No Advice from Another" (p. 54). Another drum name given to Carrington (p. 55) is both patronymic and event-recording. Knowing that his father, who did not have a drum name of his own, had been a member of a group of folk dancers in England, the drummers designated Carrington as "The European, Son of the European Whom the Villagers Laughed at When he Leaped in the Air." Despite the historical rooting of many if not most names through the many cultures around the globe, few other names carry the load of explicit information often borne by drum names as recorded by Carrington.

The fixing of the past achieved in the nomenclature of human beings is affected also by other weighty, ceremonial formulas in the drum tradition. Villages have their own special drum names, at times, Carrington notes (p. 55), reflecting the history of the region. At other times, villagers change their names in accord with their fortunes: the village whose gong name had been "They had medicine to overcome curses," when defeated in war, changed its name to "The evil spirit has no friend nor kin."[10] Often the formulas register cultural institutions, the product of a longstanding experience, as when manioc or cassava is called "manioc which remains in the ground that lies fallow" (manioc roots can be left in the ground for more than a year before being harvested)—a whole agricultural tradition is caught here (p. 40).

It is tempting to regard the elaboration of drum names solely as a disambiguating process which does no more than add specificity by adding more and more separate units or "bits" of information. In fact, drum names do far more than this. The need to add separate units is an inducement to appropriate history. For drummers are historians, who study the flux around them to select the items worth recording. Carrington reports (p. 61) how, when a stranger arrives, before assigning him a drum name, the drummer will want to wait to see what happens to and around the stranger. "Let us watch a little to see how he dances," one drummer said of a new arrival. But the nature of the discourse into which knowledge—historical or other—is to be inserted helps determine the kind of knowledge generated. Havelock has explained how "the psychology of oral memorization and oral record required the content of what is memorized to be a set of doings" and that "this in turn presupposes actors or agents."[11] Because their names necessarily become so protracted, agents (individual human beings) figuring in drum communication would appear to constitute exaggerated and thus highly informative paradigms of actors or agents in oral culture generally and would thus appear to illustrate spectacularly the role of such agents in determining the cast of knowledge in such cultures.

Cultivation of praise and vituperation. An oral noetic economy, as has been seen, necessarily stores knowledge largely in narrative

10. Carrington, "The Talking Drums of Africa," p. 93.
11. Havelock, *Preface to Plato,* p. 171.

concerned with interacting human or quasi-human figures, involved normally in quite conspicuous struggle with one another. Such a noetic economy is sure to carry a heavy load of praise and vituperation. Indeed, the preoccupation with praise and vituperation, characteristic of primary oral culture generally, remains long after writing in the West, so long as orality is actively fostered by the concerted study of rhetoric (that is, basically, public speaking). Such study continues until the romantic movement finally matures.[12] European Renaissance literature still carried a heavy oral residue and thus was preoccupied with praise and vituperation, often highly ceremonial, to a degree which strikes technological man today as utterly bizarre but which in its persistence suggests the depths at which earlier sets of mind were structured into consciousness.

The drum language shows the characteristic praise-blame polarity of oral cultures generally, but again in intensified or exaggerated form. Drum soubriquets are often simply praise formulas, common in oral cultures, but elaborated by the paraphrasis which drum language enforces. Indeed, Herskovits reports how drum language can actually come to be largely restricted in a given region to praise of kings and chiefs and to their messages.[13] And Carrington explains how small children use whistles they have fashioned "to broadcast praise names outside the house of some important villager, expecting a reward for doing so."[14] Soubriquets can be vituperative as well as laudatory. Thus the Batomba (p. 66) have two typically polarized paraphrastic names for white foreigners: "The white man, honored by all, companion of our chiefs" or, as occasion may demand, the pointed expression, "You do not touch a poisonous caterpillar."

The drums or slit-gongs themselves become a focus of the personalized praise-blame noetic economy, as they themselves are

12. See Walter J. Ong, *Rhetoric, Romance, and Technology* (Ithaca, N.Y.: Cornell University Press, 1971), pp. 12–20, 254–283; Ong, *The Presence of the Word*, pp. 252–255.
13. Melville J. Herskovits, *Dahomey: An Ancient West African Kingdom* (New York: J. J. Augustin, 1938), II, 318–319.
14. Carrington, "The Talking Drums of Africa," p. 94.

given names, which are beaten out at the start or end of a message. The Yamongbanga clan of Bokondo names its gong with a praise name, "The bolongo tree is not beaten with the hand for fear of its thorns." But discouraged—as many African villages are—by the exodus of their young people to the city, the Bakama of Bandio call their two gongs "We eat the last bits of food" and "Ears of mine, do not listen to what other people say" (in mockery).[15]

The agonistic ethos of oral cultures commonly mixes praise and vituperation (oral agonistic) with physical struggle. This conjuncture is evident in the *liango,* a special kind of wrestling contest reported by Carrington and involving drums (pp. 84–86). For the *liango,* representatives of two opposing clans or villages encircle their contestants as the drums beat. One contestant steps forward and defies the other side with a scornful gesture (the equivalent of "fliting" or ceremonial exchange of insults, as in the story of David and Goliath or in the *Iliad* or *Beowulf*). The drum thereupon calls out the praise of the defiant contestant, "The hero, full of pride." The wrestling begins to the enthusiastic accompaniment of the drum, and when one of the contestants is downed, the drum begins to praise the winner. Up and down the river villagers at work can listen to the broadcast praises.

On other occasions drum contest is simply verbal, or at least begins as verbal: insults are exchanged on the drums in typical fliting fashion (p. 96). But this verbal polemic can readily modulate into physical attack and thence to enduring feuds between families and entire clans. In oral cultures, speech is a conspicuously aggressive weapon and on the drum, which carries for miles, a particularly forceful one. There are many other uses of the drum for laudatory or vituperative purposes. Among the Tiv, Paul Bohannan has reported the drummed insults which can lead to physical violence and even death.[16] Perhaps the most compelling or efficacious drumming reported by Carrington (p. 95)

15. *Ibid.*
16. *Justice and Judgment among the Tiv* (London: Oxford University Press for the International African Institute, 1957), pp. 142–144.

was in a village wanting to get rid of a loose-living woman who had dropped in on them: the gong beaters drummed her out of town in the fullest sense of the word, insulting her, for everyone to hear for miles around, with "very frank anatomical precision."

Related to its use for praise and blame is the use of the drum for humorous effects, which will at times get a whole village laughing (pp. 95–96).

Copiousness. Oral performance demands flow: though pauses may be used effectively in public speaking, hesitancy is always a vice. Writing has no such strictures. Quite the contrary, good writing is often the product of halts for reflection, of revisions, of all sorts of false starts and stammerings. The smoothest flowing text is likely to be the product of great hesitancy. The economy of oral verbalization is quite different. An orator must have at his immediate command an abundance of things to say and of ways to say them, *copia* in Latin rhetoric, "flow," "abundance," such as Erasmus sought to provide for his residually oral literary milieu in his textbook *De duplici copia verborum ac rerum.* Because of concern for flow, an orator in the old, formally oratorical tradition (pre-television) commonly strikes a chirographically and typographically conditioned denizen of the technological world as gushingly verbose, flatulent, often boring, and conspicuously in love with his own voice. An oral culture would not so readily regard such a speaker this way.

Oral cultures need repetition, redundancy, verboseness for several reasons. First, as has already been noted in other connections, *verba volant:* spoken words fly away. A reader can pause over a point he wants to reflect on, or go back a few pages to return to it. The inscribed word is still there. The spoken word is gone. So the orator repeats himself, to help his hearers think it over. Second, spoken words do not infallibly carry equally well to everyone in an audience: synonyms, parallelisms, repetitions, neat oppositions, give the individual hearer a second chance if he did not hear well the first time. If he missed the "not only," he can probably reconstruct it from the "but also." Finally, the orator's thoughts do not always come as fast as he would wish, and even the best orator is at times inclined to repeat what he has just said in order to "mark time" while he is undertaking to find what move to make next.

All of these reasons for verbosity obtain in the case of drum talk, and often with great force. First, the peculiar ambiguities of a language restricted phonemically to tones, without any vowels or consonants at all in the ordinary sense of these terms, make drummed words even more evanescent than spoken words and thus, as has been seen, encourage manifold repetition, even to such an extent that the formula may become a compounding of itself. Examples already cited for other purposes illustrate this point: "Make your feet come back the way they went, make your legs come back the way they went . . ." (p. 46), or "Bring your heart back down out of your mouth, your heart out of your mouth . . ." (p. 46).

Second, parallelisms, synonyms, and the like are common in drum language, as many of the examples already cited show. These are not mere ornamental devices but practical strategies.

The way in which such devices, or formulary devices generally, can implement reconstruction of a part of a drum message the hearer has missed was strikingly illustrated in discussion at a round table in Yaounde with Camerounian poets, novelists, and other writers over which I recently presided. There as here, I had been calling attention to the evanescent character of sound: a sound exists only when it is going out of existence, so that for example when I pronounce the last syllable "-tence" of the word "existence," the first two syllables are gone. One of the Camerounians in the round table intervened: "I am not so sure about the sound's disappearance. I recall many years ago when my great-grandfather caught the sound of a drum in our village, he picked up his fly whisk and waved it imperiously as though he were clearing the air. This also quieted us children. And he could tell what the drum had said even before the point at which he had begun to pay attention to it after he had quieted us." In discussion, the Camerounian speaker agreed that what had happened was that his great-grandfather had caught enough of the stereotyped phrase or the repetition or the parallelism to be able to reconstruct the anterior portion he had not heard or not heard clearly.

Despite this apparent capitulation of my interlocutor, however, his objection in its original bearing was valid in a way. Although sound is ineluctably time-bound, existing only when it is going out of existence, in a certain way the formula, in oral speech or on the drum, gives sound some independence of time. It spreads out the perception of sound, not only beyond the present physical instant, but also beyond the lengthier psychological "present," *la durée* of Henri Bergson. The formula, in this peculiar function, appears as a precocious equivalent of writing—a fact which I have never seen (or heard) commented on before.

Third, there is a good deal of marking time in much drum talk, where it is even more obvious than its equivalent in oral performance. Stereotyped phrases allow an oral poet or an old-style orator to organize his not yet formed thought: once a stereotyped phrase or a repetition is started, it can move to its conclusion more or less automatically so that the speaker's attention can be turned to working out what is coming next. The same advantage attaches to the stereotyped phrases and repetitions which are common, as has been seen, in drum talk: these gain time for thinking.

But the drummers go further, it appears, and develop special "words" serving precisely for marking time. Lokele drummers, Carrington explains (p. 69), have a way of "punctuating" messages by striking simultaneously on both the male and female lip of the drum to produce a sound which they vocalize as "kpei, kpei" (the vowels in this transcription again have French values). Carrington goes on to remark that one has the impression that the drummer who beats out "kpei, kpei" several times in succession is doing so really to gain time for lining up his next phrases. In this connection, it is worth recalling that written punctuation itself was originally thought of as working something like "kpei, kpei," that is, as marking pauses or delays as such. Today technological societies commonly represent punctuation as registering the "structure" or quasi-architectural organization which we impute to discourse: a word or phrase in *apposition* is *set off* by commas; adjectives in a *series* not *connected* by a *conjunction* are *separated* by commas; and so on. Such a structuralist understanding of punctuation and of language is of recent provenience. As late as 1640, the posthumously published *English Grammar* by Ben Jonson (1573?–1637) explains punctuation marks not in such fashion, but as marking the pauses useful for "breathing." Jonson was still thinking of writing and print in basically oral terms.[17] The "kpei, kpei" patterns are thus indeed quite like "punctuation" marks as these were conceived in cultures closer to primary orality.

V

From the evidence adduced here, it appears that African drum talk is an important variant of specifically oral communication not merely in the obvious sense that it operates in a world of sound but more particularly in the deeper sense that it manifests and even exaggerates many features which are distinctive of primary orality (orality untouched by writing or print) as compared with written and printed communication. Drum talk makes extraordinarily conspicuous use of typical oral strategies for gathering, storing, retrieving, and communicating knowledge, such as formulaic expression, standardization of themes, epithetic conceptualization, "heavy" or ceremonial human figures, formulary appropriation of history, polarization of existence in terms of praise and blame, and calculated "copiousness" (verbosity).

Since these strategies are constantly resorted to in normal speech in oral cultures and even more in designedly artistic speech in such cultures, it is hardly surprising that the drummers, too, would employ them. But these strategies are not immutable. They admit of diminution, intensification, and alteration. Certain media of communication work against them. Writing gradually reduces and finally more or less eliminates them—this is why

17. Walter J. Ong, "Historical Backgrounds of Elizabethan and Jacobean Punctuation Theory," *PMLA*, 59 (1944), 349–360.

they now stand out as phenomena distinctive of orality as compared to literacy. The drums or slit-gongs appear to move thought and communication in the opposite direction from writing, since, instead of reducing the use of typical oral noetic and expressive strategies, they intensify their use. The drums belong, in a particularly intense way, to the oral world.

This fact has several implications. First, it should warn against too facile assimilation of the drum messages to messages with which the electronic technological world typically deals. For example, the binary signal used by the drums of the Lokele and of other Africans suggests the binary signal of computers, but computers are posttypographic knowledge-storing devices, whereas drums do not store knowledge themselves but rather deal with knowledge stored in the mind of the drummer—which is to say with knowledge conceived in the way demanded by primary orality. Secondly, it appears that African drum language is not simply one among many alternative means of communication, any more than writing or print or radio or television are simply alternative means, each doing no more than what any other mode or medium of communication does, circulating "bits" of information. Each of the various media—oral, chirographic, typographic, electronic—determines differently the constitution of the thought it communicates. Communication in an oral culture, of which drum talk is a part, commonly is less purely concerned with "information," in the sense of knowledge new to the recipient, than communication typically is in writing and print cultures (once these have eliminated their oral residue, which they retain for a long while) or in modern electronic culture. Primary oral communication necessarily deals to a great extent with what the audience already knows: the typical oral narrative, for example, poetic or prose, normally recounts in familiar formulas what the audience has heard before, so that communication here is in fact an invitation to participation, not simply a transfer of knowledge from a place where it was to a place where it was not. Other messages in primary oral culture share, more or less, this involvement with the familiar. Drum language certainly conveys new knowledge or "information," but it likewise imbeds this in an extensive network of the already known. The familiar is not mere superfluity or "noise," as it might be in communication for a technological world: it is part of the message, and the need for it determines the quality of thought: an oral culture necessarily thinks conservatively.

The rooting of drum language in oral modes of thought needs to be taken into account in questions about the future of drum language, questions which are sure to arise—and indeed do arise in Carrington's book itself. Drum talk is already on the wane (pp. 107–110), so much so that it is now being taught in some schools which teach principally reading and writing, in an understandable effort to keep this important part of the African heritage alive in a literate age. Carrington asks (p. 92) whether drum talk is restricted to matters of the past, or at least to matters long traditional, whether it can adapt to change. Drum language can certainly coin new terms for new things, as he shows, such as river steamers or cigarettes. And until electronic communication better penetrates the interior of Africa, the drums will continue to serve very practical, and indeed changing, daily needs for rapid communication over distances. But in the fuller perspectives suggested here, the question of the relationship of drum language to the future involves more than new lexical adjustments, as Carrington himself is well aware.

One cannot be very specific about implications of drum languages for the future. Indeed, some would consider the question of such implications already moot, given the evident progressive decline in skill with the drums. Drums will be of only antiquarian interest in the future, some have contended. Drums will certainly be of antiquarian interest and, what is more important and not the same thing, of historical interest. But there is more than that to the question of their implications for the future. The widespread use of talking drums in Africa suggests an extraordinarily strong current of orality in African cultures, and this suggestion is further reinforced by the way in which the use of slit-gongs and drums for talking merges with their use for other, nonverbalizing

purposes throughout African cultures in civil and religious ceremonies of all sorts, in the dance, in sports, in celebrations, in war,
in work, and many other areas of existence.

Cultures bring their past to their present and their future. It
appears gratuitous to hold, though some do, that because of some
supposedly superhuman technology all cultures everywhere are
destined soon to be entirely the same. Marks left by history are
permanent. The African entry into the technological world is
being made not only from a signally oral base but also in a state
of consciousness different from that which governed the entry of
the West. The movement from orality in the West to the modern
technological world took some six thousand years (calculating the
departure from orality as dating from the beginning of script
around 3500 B.C.), and it was quite unconscious in the sense that
only in the past few decades has the Western world effectively
taken note even of the existence of oral cultures as radically
distinct from writing and print cultures. In Africa the transit
from orality through writing and print to electronic communication is taking place, not over six thousand years, but in two or
three generations, and for many in even less time. Moreover, it is
taking place consciously, and often with exquisite self-conscious-
ness. Being more conscious, the transit in Africa is thereby more
human than it was in the West. Perhaps the present study can
contribute to developing ways of assessing this rapid transit.

5

"I See What You Say":
Sense Analogues for Intellect

Bernard Lonergan's philosophical investigations of man's noetic activities are among the richest investigations of this vast subject that we have. Together with other work of his, they have warranted the calling of an international congress devoted to the discussion of what he has had to say on this and other matters. His best known work on the nature of knowledge and of knowing is the still seminal book *Insight* (1957), but his other contributions on this subject are vast. In a little-known talk on "Consciousness and the Trinity" given in the late spring of 1963 at the North American College in Rome and circulated in typescript to participants at the First International Lonergan Congress, held at St. Leo College in Florida in March, 1970, he makes some points concerning the analogies between understanding and the activities of the various senses which can lead into our concerns about the evolution of consciousness from a largely oral to a more visual base. Father Lonergan specifies some of the deficiencies of considering the activities of the mind by analogy exclusively with sight:

Now, if human knowing is to be conceived exclusively, by an epistemological necessity, as similar to ocular vision, it follows as a first consequence that human understanding must be excluded from human knowledge. For understanding is not like seeing. Understanding grows with time: you understand one point, then another, and a third, a fourth, a fifth, a sixth, and your understanding changes several times until you have things right. Seeing is not like that, so that to say that knowing is like seeing is to disregard understanding as a constitutive element in human knowledge.

A further consequence of conceiving knowing on the analogy of the popular notion of vision, is the exclusion of the conscious subject. Objects are paraded before spectators, and if the spectator wants to know himself, he must get out in the parade and be looked at. There are no subjects anywhere; for being a subject is not being something that is being looked at, it is being the one who is looking.

This brief quotation provides a wealth of starting points for reflections which I wish to offer. First, simply by way of amplification, one might remark that to consider knowing by analogy with visual perception, "to say that knowing is like seeing," is also to rob knowledge of its interiority—a statement closely related to Lonergan's observation that the analogy divorces knowledge from understanding and from subjectivity. Sight or vision is a limited analogue for intelligence for one reason that can be readily discovered: our sight or vision presents us optimally with surfaces. Basically, this is so because vision is geared to diffusely reflected light. Looking at a light source, not only at a source of the magnitude of the sun but even at a match flame, dazzles the eye, leaving us squinting and unsatisfied. As against diffuse reflection (for example, from this sheet of paper) specular reflection from the surface of a mirror is visually deceptive, requiring correction: what registers is not the object being looked at directly (the mirror) but other objects seemingly "in" the mirror giving off diffusely reflected light from their surfaces. Sight is at optimum only with light coming diffusely off the outside of something, off a surface perceived as such. Hence a field of sight suggests always a beyond or a beneath which is not seen. By contrast, sound gives perception of interiors as interiors without their being opened up into surfaces: I can tap an object and learn thereby whether it is solid or hollow. Without resort to other senses such as kinesthesia, vision as such knows no hollows and no echoes.

Because sight is thus keyed to surfaces, when knowledge is likened to sight it becomes pretty exclusively a matter of explanation or explication, a laying out on a surface, perhaps in chartlike form, or an unfolding, to present maximum exteriority. (For various reasons, the colors purveyed by sight function very little, if directly at all, when vision is taken as an analogue or symbol of knowing.)[1] To say that knowing means being able to explain impoverishes knowing. Explanation is invaluable, but any mere explanation or explication is pretty thin stuff compared either with actuality or with understanding.

I have gone into these and related matters to the best of my present ability and in considerable detail in *The Presence of the Word* and shall not repeat myself further here except to note again, in the hope that someone will take me up to corroborate or refute me, that the Kantian problem of the noumenon and the phenomenon appears closely connected—how closely I suspect no one knows—with a propensity to take vision as a perfectly adequate analogue for intellectual knowing. As we have just mentioned, in a field of sight there is always a beyond or a beneath which is not seen. Kant maintains that this is true, too, of intellectual knowing—as it certainly is so far as such knowing is assimilable to sight. But is it entirely assimilable?

Lonergan suggests some ways in which it is not. Besides excluding understanding (a kind of interiority) from knowing, if we conceive of knowing as only a kind of seeing, Lonergan points out, we also exclude the subject (another and related kind of interiority). Lonergan suggests that if knowing is like sight, the subject can know himself only by making himself something to be looked at. Translated in terms of the description of sight we have just given, as concerned with surfaces only, this is to say that the subject can know himself only by making himself an exterior, despite the fact that he is to himself and to other conscious beings as well an interior, a beneath-surface or beyond-surface. In the last analysis, you cannot quite make your self an exterior. Although you can be the object of your own knowledge, you can be so only in a quite special way.

I have called ocular vision an analogue for intellectual know-

1. Walter J. Ong, *Ramus, Method, and the Decay of Dialogue* (Cambridge, Mass.: Harvard University Press, 1958), pp. 108–109.

ing. In the paper that I have just quoted Lonergan speaks of it also as a "symbol" or "myth" for knowing and suggests that when knowing is equated unquestioningly with vision this is because the latter is invested with symbolic or mythological qualities.

Now, ocular vision is a perfect symbol for knowing. . . . That symbol, because it is symbolic, is absolutely convincing. Myths are not mere funny stories; a myth is something you are absolutely certain of. People who hold the earth is flat do not hold that view as a theory or hypothesis or possibility; they hold it as something which simply must be so. Similarly, one can be absolutely convinced that a cognitional act can be a cognitional act only if it resembles ocular vision.

He elaborates in the same place on the consequences of this "myth":

When do you know? When you perform an act that is like an act of seeing. If you perform such an act, it is self-evident, unquestionable, beyond any possible rational doubt, that the object of that act is really and truly known, that it is valid, that it is objective. On the other hand, if a cognitional act is not like seeing, it is equally self-evident, unquestionable and beyond possible doubt, that its object is not really and truly known, that it really is not valid knowledge.

It is easy to identify the habitat of this hypervisualism which Lonergan here descries and to some extent decries. Its habitat is the mentality fostered by the modern world, that is, the Copernican and even more the Newtonian world, where the cosmos is taken to be essentially something seen. In this world the harmony of the spheres, which was not a metaphorical but an operational concept in the old Aristotelian cosmos, is gone. Joseph Addison and others hail the Newtonian universe as "silent,"[2] simply projecting out of their hypervisualism a new pseudoscience, for the physical universe is in fact quite a deafening, exploding assemblage of material, even without the "big bang" theory of cosmic origins. Newton's and Addison's world, purportedly silent because visually construed, is the cosmic correlative of the noetic

2. See Walter J. Ong, *The Presence of the Word* (New Haven: Yale University Press, 1967), pp. 72–73.

world of "clear and distinct" ideas propounded by Descartes and the Encyclopédistes, where you can test whether anything is possible or not by seeing (the term is significant) whether or not you can imagine it (that is, visualize it). This is the world of ocularly construed "evidence," which violently contests in theory (but accepts in practice) the principle *fides ex auditu*. It is a world embarrassed to death by the presence of persons, interiors, the world against which both existentialists and Teilhardists revolt.

Obsessed by problems regarding certainty, this world soon teeters on the brink of what appears to be total doubt. Oscillation into chaos is of course inevitable when sight is taken unreflectively as a pure symbol of intellect. If we assume that everything in cognition hangs on vision, nothing works, for though vision may be the *sensus maxime cognoscitivus* under one aspect, under another and more profound aspect understanding is allied not with vision but with the word and the world of sound, which is the sensory habitat of the word. To become intelligible what we see has to be mediated, in one way or another, through verbal formulation, which as such simply cannot be reduced to a visual presentation, as I have undertaken to show at length throughout *The Presence of the Word*. Hypervisualism tends to neglect this truth and even sets out to reduce sound itself, and for that matter all the other senses, to vision through devices such as charts and wave measurements, mathematical or oscillographic, forgetting that none of these make any noise and that hence, however informative and desirable and useful and indispensable and beautiful and true they may be—and they are all of these—they are not directly sound at all but visual constructs having to do with sound. We generate our certainties not in a solipsistic universe of isolated "observation" but in a total context which includes verbalization and in which we hope others will believe what we say. The scientist is no exception to this rule, only a special instance of its operation.

So long as hypervisualism induces man to pretend that matters are otherwise and, by interpreting a mythical visualist account of knowledge as a total account and a scientific one as well, the question of certainty is going to arise in wildly distorted forms, generating anxieties all the worse because they are malformed.

II

The addiction to visualism which marks our technological culture has a history. In *The Presence of the Word,* and earlier in more specialized and microscopic fashion in *Ramus, Method, and the Decay of Dialogue,* I have treated the by now well-known and well-documented shift from a culture in significant ways favoring auditory syntheses to a culture in significant ways favoring visual syntheses in its way of organizing both physical actuality and knowledge as such. I have also attempted to show how intimately this aural-to-visual shift is tied in with educational procedures and with the transfer of verbalization from its initially oral-aural economy of sound to a more and more silent and spatialized economy of alphabetic writing and of printing from movable alphabetic type, which seems to assemble words out of pre-existent parts, like houses out of bricks. This shift, we now know in great detail, is connected with surprising changes in personality structures as well as in social institutions.

Was it an inevitable shift? Is there something in the structure or nature of the various senses and of the human intellect that fosters the visualism or hypervisualism noted by Lonergan? To gain understanding of the meaning of this visualism, we can examine such questions here. It may be that doing so is metahistory: if it is metahistory, let us make the most of it. Would it be possible for a primarily oral culture to survive indefinitely? And could any other sense have undergone the hypertrophy in relationship to noetic processes which vision has undergone over the past centuries? Were there alternatives to hypervisualism in noetic practice and theory? Could one have expected or proceeded with hypertrophy of hearing, smell, taste, or the manifold senses we group under "touch"?

I do not believe that there were any real alternatives to the way history worked out. This is not to make intellectual history totally deterministic. In intellectual history choices made by individuals do come into significant play at times. If certain mathematicians had in the past decided to speculate on matters other than those they in fact followed, certain branches of mathematics underdeveloped today would no doubt be more developed, and vice versa. But in intellectual history as elsewhere there are limits to what a person can freely choose. First, we can choose only what we somehow know. You cannot deliberately choose to do the unthinkable. Our paleolithic ancestors did not enjoy free choice to invent or not to invent analytic geometry or the theory of natural selection. Not only because of the limitations of their knowledge but also because of the condition of their thought processes, personality structures, and social institutions, such discoveries were not possibilities they could opt for. Second, a given situation forces certain matters on the attention of thinking men and at least favors, if it does not command, the development of thought in certain fields rather than in others. Many discoveries or developments associated with the name of a particular and now famous individual were inevitable at the time, with or without him: if he had not made the discovery, another would fairly soon have made it. The growth of natural history and the technological developments which made travel relatively easy and observation of remote and isolated populations of fauna and flora possible thrust to the fore certain evidence which struck not only Charles Darwin but also simultaneously Alfred Russel Wallace. The two worked out the principles of natural selection independently at the same time. Conditions were ready for this discovery, and someone was bound to have the insight and energy to make it, not necessarily in exactly the same formulations as those of Darwin and Wallace, but in approximately the same. This is not to minimize Darwin or Wallace: after all, they got there first once the race was on.

Finally, of course, intellectual developments are not matters of free choice insofar as they depend on the structure of actuality itself: if you undertake a development which is not consonant with the way things are, it is not likely to come off—as Thomas Hobbes found when he published his purported squaring of the

circle. Individuals are not free to opt for truth or falsehood with
equal hope of success. In all these ways, and in others not discussed here, human freedom is circumscribed so far as intellectual
history is concerned. Human choice is always between limited
options. But within these limits, it is real and has real effects.

With this understanding of inevitability and choice, one can
say that the way visualism developed was indeed inevitable. Of
course, it was not inevitable in the sense that it came about
everywhere simultaneously. Quite the contrary. It proceeded in
part by a series of nonce inventions. The alphabet, printing from
movable alphabetic type, and modern mathematically implemented science, all major steps on the road to modern visualism,
were all invented or, more accurately, developed only once: the
line runs without break, if not entirely straight, from the ancient
Middle East through ancient Eastern Europe into medieval and
modern Western Europe. When one or another of these inventions turns up in places or cultures other than those in which it
first appeared, it is an import or borrowing. The Roman and
Cyrillic and Sanskrit and all other alphabets all derive in one way
or another from the original Semitic alphabet. Alphabetic movable
type originated in Western Europe around A.D. 1450. The
Koreans and Uigur Turks had the alphabet and movable type,
but they did not invent alphabetic movable type: their movable
types were word types, not alphabetic types. And modern science
had no starting point, though it has had many augmentations,
outside sixteenth- and seventeenth-century Western Europe, conditioned by centuries of scholastic physics and other scholastic
philosophy.

Outside this line of visualist nonce inventions other developments, many of them fascinating, were taking place in other
cultures. But none of them worked so directly to produce the
modern scientific and technological world. In this sense man's
movement into visualism was inevitable: the other routes opened
for cultural development did not lead to this world. Only one
route did. Once it was discovered, people from other routes made
their way into it wherever they could. For the visualism to which

it led, despite exaggerations which we do well to resent, accorded in some profound fashion with the way things really are.

III

In the development of the modern scientific and technological world, vision was maximized in the sensory field in a special way: in its connection with vocalization. Primitive man has keen eyes, and in many ways observes more acutely and accurately than does technological man: a primitive hunter sees all sorts of things happening in the woods around him of which his urbanized visitor is completely unaware. But he cannot expatiate on them or describe or analyze them accurately to any appreciable extent. He may react to excruciatingly detailed patterns in the behavior of elk or salmon. He may have a hundred different words for different kinds of snow or camels and no generic word—a quite ordinary lexical situation, incidentally, not just for primitives but for any specialist: "horsey" people have countless specific words but no exclusively generic word for horse (for them a "horse" means normally an adult male horse, contrasting with a mare, filly, and so on), dog fanciers have countless specific words but no exclusively generic word for dog ("dog" means normally an adult male dog). But, however specific his visual and other perceptions and however rich his nomenclature, early man has no science of elk or salmon or camels or snow. Despite his lexical abundance, he has not thought to ask in words the questions a scientist needs to have asked and consequently, despite his acute powers of observation, many specific things a scientist needs to observe he has not observed.

What is distinctive of the visualist development leading to our modern technological culture is that it learns to vocalize visual observation far more accurately and elaborately than primitive man, by vocalizing it manages to intellectualize it, and by intellectualizing it comes to generate further specific visual observation, and so on. The visualism we are talking of is thus a visualism strengthened by intimate association with voice, directly in speech or indirectly through script. This association is capital.

For if vision is the most tempting symbol for knowing, noetic activity itself is rooted directly or indirectly in the world of sound, through vocalization and hearing. In order to make what we see scientifically usable, we have to be able to verbalize it, and that in elaborately controlled ways. For man there is no understanding without some involvement in words.

IV

This contrast between primitive and modern visualism warns us of the complexities within the sensorium itself, particularly when it connects with noetic or mental processes. Perhaps these complexities explain why study of the sensory bases of individual concepts is almost totally neglected by lexicographers, linguists, anthropologists, psychologists, literary critics, philosophers, and theologians, although all of these are constantly turning up material which invites this study and on rare occasions generates a small amount of it. Scholars and scientists occasionally spy out the model underlying one or another kind of thinking in order to disqualify or note inadequacies in the model,[3] but seldom sight the underlying problems or offer alternatives. An exception would be Milič Čapek, who in *The Philosophic Impact of Contemporary Physics*[4] proposes that instead of operating only with visual models, physicists would do well also to think of the universe as a harmony—which of course is not to use a "model" at all insofar as a model is thought of as something visually and tactilely apprehended.

3. See, for example, Alphonse Chapanis, "Men, Machines, and Models," *American Psychologist*, 16 (1961), 113–131, where it is noted that "models invite overgeneralization," "the relationship between variables may be incorrect" in a model, "the constants assumed in the model may be incorrect," "models are too often not validated," and "model building diverts useful energy into nonproductive activity" (pp. 126–131); also Sigmund Koch, "Psychological Sciences versus the Science-Humanism Antinomy: Intimations of a Significant Science of Man," *American Psychologist*, 16 (1961), 629–639, where it is noted that psychology has imagined "its ends and means on the model of physics" (p. 630).
4. New York: Van Nostrand, 1961, pp. 170–171.

Of the fields just mentioned, literary criticism is one which might be expected to attend to all the senses in every possible way. Certainly literary expression involves itself in all the senses. Yet one of the most surprising features of literary criticism, past and present, is its virtually total neglect of the diversity of the sensory bases of the terms of which literary works or passages consist, and this despite the addiction of present literary criticism to studies of "imagery."[5] Besides the visual imagination and its imagery, there are also auditory, olfactory, gustatory and tactile imaginations and imageries: acts of these senses, too, can be and are called into consciousness in the known absence of an external object. Some of the impoverishment incident to unreflective visualism is evident here, for the terms and concepts "image" and "imagination" which are the best standard critical equipment, themselves refer primarily to the visual field, so that interior representations of the other senses themselves tend to be studied as variants of vision, if they are studied at all. Besides "imagination" and its cognates we have virtually no other terms except those in the series "phantasm," "fantasy," "fancy," which preserve in only slightly attenuated form the same visualist base, only Greek-rooted instead of Latin-rooted, and which, since Coleridge, have been set in paired opposition to "imagination." You will read a lot of criticism before you find any advertence at all to the fact that terms such as "stand," "run," "upside-down," as well as "dynamism," "order," or "apprehension" involve basically the tactile (or tactile-kinesthetic) imagination, or that in many or most contexts a term such as "tumble" or "gush" or "hammer" (verb) or "vibrate" is auditory or kinesthetic and tactile at least as much as visual, or that sound evokes kinesthetic as well as auditory response. Instead, you encounter only an insatiable hunt for striking visual presentation, the "speaking pic-

5. For an account of the failure to attend to kinesthesia, see William C. Forrest, *Literary Kinesthesia* (Diss. Saint Louis University, 1960; Ann Arbor, Mich.: University Microfilms, 1961). Some semantic studies do attend in detail to sensory bases of terms, e.g., Stephen Ullmann, *The Principles of Semantics* (Oxford: Blackwell, 1957).

ture"—often attended by the standard misreading of Horace's "ut pictura poesis."[6]

This neglect in literary criticism is matched in the other fields mentioned above, including the philosophical study of noetics, where the sensory base of conceptualization would appear to be of most fundamental importance. The present paper attempts no more than a sally into this latter unattended area, moving out from borders on which I tentatively set foot some years ago.[7]

We can begin by a tally of some of the English terms in common use for conceptualizing noetic matters.

No language can be representative of all others, but English is fortunately rich in borrowings, especially from the classical languages in which so much Western thought is rooted, and thus is particularly representative of a range of conceptualization much wider than its own. Some of the terms listed here have for any native English-speaker a sensory base which is readily discernible, in some cases immediately and in others after brief reflection on cognates and etymologies. Such terms I list without comment. In other, less obvious, cases the reasons for listings under a particular sense are suggested.

6. The lines read:

> Ut pictura poesis: erit quae, si propius stes,
> te capiat magis, et quaedam, si longius abstes;
> haec amat obscurum, volet haec sub luce videri,
> iudicis argutum quae non formidat acumen;
> haec placuit semel, haec deciens repetita placebit.

—"De arte poetica," ll. 361–365, in *Q. Horatii Flacci Opera,* ed. Fridericus Klingner, 3d ed. (Leipzig: Teubner, 1969), p. 307. This can be rendered, "A poem is like a picture: a certain one will please you at close range, another at a greater distance; this one loves shadow, this one prefers to be seen in light with no fear of the critic's close scrutiny; this one pleases once, this at each of ten viewings." Horace's point here has nothing to do with whether or not a poem presents striking visual *detail,* although, like most critics, he rather imperceptively likens the whole business of apprehending a poem, rhythmically, subconsciously, intellectually, sensorially in all the perceptual fields, to seeing something—the usual assimilation of all knowing to an act of seeing.

7. See, for example, Walter J. Ong, *Rhetoric, Romance, and Technology* (Ithaca, N.Y.: Cornell University Press, 1971), Ch. 9, "Pysche and the Geometers: Associationist Critical Theory."

Some visually based terms used
in thinking of intellect and its work

(t) = especially noteworthy admixture of tactile.

insight (t)

intuition (t)

theory

idea

evidence, evident, etc. (t)

species, specific, etc. (t)

speculation

suspicion (t)

intellectual vision

glimmering of

cast light on

illuminate, illuminating

elucidate (t)

clear, clarity

descry

make out

observe, observation

represent, representation

demonstrate

show

apodictic

exposition

explicate, explication, etc.

explain, explanation, etc.

analyze, analysis (t)

discern

distinguish, distinct, etc. (t)

define, definition, etc. (t—*draw* a
line around, make a border)

form (cf. matter) (t)

outline (t)

chart

plan

table

tabula rasa

list

area of knowledge (t)

field of knowledge

level of knowledge (t)

content (of the mind, of thought, of
a statement, etc.) (t)

object—of knowledge, etc. (t)

subject—of discourse, etc. (t)

connect (t)

copula (t)

Some tactilely based terms

(k) = noteworthy kinesthetic component.
(Note that touch is not one sense but a manifold of senses.)

deduce, deduction (k)

induce, induction (k)

infer, inference (k)

consequence

follow

draw a conclusion (k)

decide

apprehend, apprehension (k)

comprehend, comprehension

perceive, perception, etc.

proposition (k)

composition (k)

arrange (k)

order (k)

system

method

establish (k)

genus, generic (having to do with
origins, from which something
is drawn or taken)

conceive, conception, etc.

express (k)

confute, confutation

refute, refutation

convince

confirm (k)

matter (moldable, carvable)

hesitate (*root* stick, cling)

doubt (*root* waver, vibrate)

prove (*root* forward, through, ahead of)

agent intellect (*intellectus* agens)

patient, intellect (*intellectus* patiens)

Some aurally based terms

category (an accusation, charge in the public assembly)

predicate (something cried out)

judgment, verdict, sentence, decree, criticism—and other results of reasoning

logic (remote visual-tactile base early in Greek etymology)

dialectic (remote visualist base early in Greek etymology)

response (remote visualist base early in Greek etymology)

question (visualist and kinesthetic and olfactory connections: "questing" by sight or by manual exploration or by scenting)

This list is far from complete, but it is fairly representative. It can elicit a number of remarks. First, it suggests that we would be incapacitated for dealing with knowledge and intellection without massive visualist conceptualization, that is, without conceiving of intelligence through models applying initially to vision. The visualist formulations in this list are apparently not just casual metaphors which one can avoid or sidestep. They are inevitable, at least in many cases. In explaining any one of these metaphors, you commonly substitute another. To explain what you mean by "explain" (*ex-planare*—lay out flat, open up) you substitute "explicate" (*ex-plicare*—unfold) or "analyze" (*analyein*—unloose, undo) or "make evident" (*e-videre*—see out) or "make plain" or "clarify," and so on. Your meaning does not come clear by moving away from or transcending the sight-intellect equation, but only by asserting it over and over again. To "explain" something is to undertake intellectual operations with it like those possible in an extended field apprehended visually (with some admixture of tactility). And so with many other visualist noetic concepts, if not all of them. The entire philosophy of noetics, including the Platonic idea, Cartesian clarity and distinctiveness, Lockean sensational noetics, the Kantian phenomenon, Hegelian phenomenology, Sartrean opacity, and much else, is inextricably involved with thinking of intellection by analogy with vision.

A second remark about the list of terms might be that the dominant visualism it evinces is often complemented by tactility. Tactility asserts itself in two ways. First, alongside the visualist repertoire is another, perhaps not quite so large, but sizable repertoire of tactile terms: deduce (lead out), induce (lead in or up), and so on. Secondly, many visualist terms themselves include a tactile element; for example, insight, intuition—for the concepts of "in" and "out" are tactilely based, deriving from our sense, kinesthetic and otherwise tactile, of our own body.[8] The association of visual and tactile, so we shall see, is due to the fact that sight and touch are at opposite extremes in the economy of the sensorium and thus make up for each other's grossest deficiencies.

A third remark about the list of terms is that aurally based terms are rare, but some of them are supremely or centrally operative: category, predicate, judgment, logic, question. The combination of a visual or visual-tactile term with an aurally based term is probably necessary for any definition or adequate description of the plenary act of the intellect, the judgment.[9] Somewhere in such a definition or description the noetic act will be referred to sensory perception, and in order to honor the inclusiveness of (intellectual) understanding, reference will have to be made to more than one sense, for any one is simply too specialized and hence too impoverished to represent intellection. Sight gives precision, but lacks intimacy: it operates only at a distance—eyeball-to-eyeball vision is impossible. Touch is intimate, but lacks clear definition. And so on. Moreover, the ten-

8. Ong, *The Presence of the Word*, pp. 117–122.
9. Ong, *Ramus, Method, and the Decay of Dialogue*, pp. 106–109.

dency of vision and touch to associate even in the sensory field in order to correct one another will not suffice to provide a usable analogue for understanding. For extremes meet, and these two meet in that each resides, in its own peculiar way, in extension, in space. Sound better represents another world, of dynamism, action, and being-in-time (sound necessarily signals the present use of power as no other sensible phenomenon necessarily does although it also exists only when it is going out of existence). Hence it complements both vision and touch more complexly and richly than either of these complements the other. Understanding in man involves process. And sound is the process sense par excellence.

I have been taking for granted here that the economy of the sensorium is familiar to all: by the sensorium I mean simply the various sense taken conjointly. But it will help here to note that man's senses can be arranged in a scale as follows.

Touch————taste————smell————hearing————sight

Movement in this direction → is:

toward greater distance from object physically;

toward greater abstraction;

toward greater formalization ("form" is a highly visualist concept, mixed with some tactility which diminishes at consummation: you "form" something with the hands, but you perceive the finished or consummated form typically with the eye; the Greek equivalents, *eidos* or *idea,* are patently visual, from the same root as the term "vision");

toward objectivity, nonsubjectivity;

toward idealism, divorced from actual existence.

Movement in the opposite direction ← is:

toward propinquity of sense organ to source of stimulus;

toward concreteness;

toward matter, potency, indistinctness (sight and hearing are not easily confused with one another; smell and taste are, taste and touch are; touch so lacks distinctness that no one knows how many senses it really is—Geldard tentatively proposes 27);

toward subjectivity (I normally feel myself feeling even while I
    feel an objective actuality which is not me)
toward actual extrasubjective (as well as subjective) existence
    ("real as this stone I clutch").

With some help from this scale, in reference to the economy of
the senses and what we have thus far had to say about it, we can
move to some concluding questions. What brings about the drift
to visual analogues which we have discerned ("discerned"—
there we go again!) in our conceptualization of intellect or understanding? Can it be that sight really is some kind of supersense
leading toward intellect more directly than other senses do? If
it is, what does this say about the nature of intellection? What are
we saying when we label sight the most cognoscitive sense (*sensus
maxime cognoscitivus*)? And if it is so paramount, why is a blind
child not threatened by the atrophy of intellect which, until
recent sophisticated methods were devised for introducing the
deaf indirectly into the world of sound, made deaf mutes regularly and distressingly subnormal in power of thought? To learn
to think and understand, it is far more necessary to be able to
hear and talk than to be able to see. This is a counterindication
apparently denying primacy to sight in favor of hearing. What
strange forces are at work here?

I have addressed myself in *The Presence of the Word* to the
role of the spoken word, of hearing, and of sound in intellection,
and shall focus here on the visual. ("Focus"—there it is again!)

The drive to consider intellectual knowing, which at its term
is understanding, by analogy with vision responds to the need
to "formalize" intellectual knowledge, to give it definition, distinctness, edge, precision, clarity, qualities like those paramount
in vision. Why the need to formalize? Answering positively, we
can say that to achieve formalization is from one point of view (!)
to work our intellectual knowledge up to the way things are, for
the actuality we encounter is in fact quite diversified actuality,
but it comes to us tumbled together in confusion, where one thing
may lose itself in another. Definition preserves against threat-

ening undifferentiated chaos. Answering negatively, formalization is needed because our knowledge is both fragmenting and distancing. First, intellectual knowledge, like vision, is fragmenting: we need apartness. We come to tell *what* one thing is by cutting it off from other things—and "whatness" is of the essence of our knowing. We know by putting together what we have taken apart: this is the essential movement in predication, in the judgment, which is two-membered, made up of subject and predicate, though its truth is one.

Now sight, as Merleau-Ponty[10] has beautifully (and again!) elucidated, is a fragmenting or dissecting sense. It thus serves as an analogue for our understanding because it cuts apart. It dismembers, and thus registers the dissolution inherent in all direct objects of our knowledge. More frankly, it kills. For man's knowing is even in a way murderous insofar as it is analogous to vision. The letter (visually apprehended verbalized meaning) kills, the spirit (breath, on which the sound of the word rides) gives life. Secondly, our intellectual knowledge is "distancing": typically, though knowledge is union with what we know, to achieve fullest union, that is, understanding, we first distance what we want to know, manufacturing abstractions between it and us. We understand a living animal that we can touch via an intermediary science of biology. Now, of all the senses sight is the most distancing sense: it requires always that eye and object be removed to a considerable extent from one another, and it can operate very well even at distances measurable only in light years.

What has just been said about formalization can be put in another and perhaps more basic way in terms of the generic and specific. Intellectual knowledge can be considered by analogy with the various senses in the scale of the senses presented above, as has been hinted: it is in various ways like touch, taste, smell, hearing, or sight. The movement from the analogy of touch to

10. Maurice Merleau-Ponty, "L'Oeil et l'esprit," *Les temps modernes,* 18, Nos. 184–185 (1961), Numéro spécial: Maurice Merleau-Ponty, pp. 193–227.

the analogy of sight is a movement from the generic to the specific. First of all, the term "genus" has a strong tactile base (*gens*, origin, source, what something is "drawn" from, "derives" from, "comes out of," etc.), while the term "species" has a clearly visual setting (*specio*, to look at, behold; English cognates such as spectacle, speculate, inspect, etc.—species is the Latin equivalent of the Greek *idea*, (*w*)*idea*, which has the same root as the Latin *videre*, to see). Secondly, the condition of these terms represents the underlying contrastive state of affairs to which they refer: whatever is generic is in fact more like what is tactilely apprehended and what is specific more like that which is visually apprehended, for the generic is more corporeal, allied to material indeterminacy, and the specific more removed from corporeality. The definition of man as a rational animal shows the basic state of affairs: "animal" is more apprehensible tactilely than is "rational." In a recent study, I suggested substituting for the term "world view," which is somewhat biased culturally toward visualism and hence not entirely applicable to primitive cultures, the term "world sense."[11] Although I did not advert to the fact at the time, I now note that "sense" is strikingly more general and more tactile than is "view." To "sense" something is, in a very basic way, to "feel" it. Other evidence (!) aligning the generic and the tactile is found in our typical repertory of terms to describe thinking which is not specific or not "clear," but too general: the terms typically involve tactility—the thought is fuzzy, vague, (*vagus,* wandering—kinesthetic), rambling, and so on. Negatively, the same thought is deficient in visualist desiderata: unclear, imprecise, ill-defined (some of these involve mixtures of tactility, as noted above).

For some knowledge, however, definition, distinctness, edge, precision, clarity is irrelevant or even devastating. Knowledge of another person is not typically perfected by such qualities. Explanation, which such qualities do perfect, is at best only an adjunct

11. "World as View and Word as Event," *American Anthropologist,* 81 (1969), 634–647.

of, never a basis for, interpersonal knowledge and understanding. When a married couple or even a group of friends try to base their understanding of one another on explanation, on a knowledge which has definition, distinctness, precision, the bond is headed for disaster. The drive to symbolize intellection and understanding by vision, that is, to consider intellection and understanding by analogy with vision thus corresponds to the drive to objectify knowledge, to make it into something which is clearly thing-like, nonsubjective, yielding meaning not in depth but off of surface, meaning which can be spread out, ex-plained.

Sight presents surfaces (it is keyed to *reflected* light; light coming directly from its source, such as fire, an electric lamp, the sun, rather dazzles and blinds us) ; smell suggests presences or absences (its association with memory is a commonplace) and is connected with the attractiveness (expecially sexual) or repulsiveness of bodies which one is near or which one is seeking ("I smelled him out") : smell is a come-or-go signal. Hence "It stinks" expresses maximum rejection or repulsion: do not even go near—the farther away the better—do not even think about it. Taste above all discriminates, distinguishing what is agreeable or disagreeable for intussusception by one's own organism (food) or psyche (aesthetic taste). . . .

Sound, on the other hand, reveals the interior without the necessity of physical invasion. Thus we tap a wall to discover where it is hollow inside, or we ring a silver-colored coin to discover whether it is perhaps lead inside. To discover such things by sight, we should have to open what we examine, making the inside the outside, destroying its interiority as such. Sound reveals interiors because its nature is determined by interior relationships. The sound of a violin is determined by the interior structure of its strings, of its bridge, and of the wood in its sound-board, by the shape of the interior cavity in the body of the violin, and other interior conditions. Filled with concrete or water, the violin would sound different.[12]

Because of this contrast between sight and sound, knowledge of things (Buber's world of "it") is more immediately assimilable to knowledge by sight; knowledge of persons (Buber's world of

12. Ong, *The Presence of the Word,* pp. 117–118.

"I-Thou") more immediately assimilable to knowledge by hearing. But in neither case is the assimilation entirely adequate. Knowledge of things and knowledge of persons are not entirely unlike or distinct from one another. We are always involved in both "thou" and "it" though at different times more in one than in the other.

V

Discussion of the ways in which the senses serve as analogues for intellect is always introverted: it must itself rely on the analogies it is discussing. Even a casual examination of what has just been said here about understanding will show that many concepts employed assume the likeness between intellectual processes and vision which they undertake to elucidate, and indeed that other concepts here assume, less obtrusively perhaps, likenesses between intellectual processes and the other senses. Such assumptions are unavoidable, for the old logion *nil in intellectu quod non prius aliquo modo in sensibus* applies here with a vengeance: even in its reflection on its own identity, the intellect must make its way to itself through the identity of each of the senses. The intellect is not even in itself except by being in some way in one or another or all of the senses.

This means in short that we can never entirely dispense with sight (or any other sense knowledge—but here we are concerned principally with sight) as an analogue for intellectual knowing, either by avoiding all reference to sight or by defining sight analogues in terms which transcend sight. The analogy remains both indispensable and defective. We can deal with its defectiveness chiefly by reflection, which is here negatively corrective. Since the intellect can reflect, it can transcend its own limits insofar as it knows them to be limits and thus knows the unlimited or at least the beyond-these-limits as a possibility.

We have noted already how the senses themselves tend to supplement one another. Touch, the first used and the most immediate (non-distancing) and basic of the senses, associates itself exteriorly or imaginatively with probably most other sense perceptions and particularly with perception by sight, because the immediacy of touch is needed to make up for the abstracting and fragmenting operations which vision in particular entails. The tactile component is obvious in a very great number of the visualist terms in the list here above, and upon close attention can be detected in many other, if not all, of these terms. Thus the sight analogues for intellect often come to us partly corrected by touch analogues if we give them close attention. For example, "insight" and "intuition" are not only visual but also, because of the prefix "in-," strongly tactile. As just noted above, our concepts of "interior" and "exterior" are kinesthetically based, derived from our sense of being somehow inside our skins or bodies with all that is not ourselves outside. "In" and "out," like "up" and "down" or "left" and "right" cannot be defined simply in terms of visual or mathematical data. The "in-" of "insight" and "intuition" introduces experience of kinesthesia. The same can be said of positioning prepositions and prepositional affixes generally—and perhaps even of all prepositions, since seemingly all prepositions have some vaguely positioning function.[13] Thus the term "understanding" is very strongly kinesthetic: directly or indirectly, "under" suggests muscular perceptions and so does the verb "stand" (hold oneself erect). Both "under" and "stand" can be conceived of in a visual field, too, but not without some reference to touch: underneathness and erectness (verticality) necessarily involve the sense of gravity, which is kinesthetic. Without reference to a gravitational field "under" is no different from "over." Because "understanding" is etymologically so strongly kinesthetic, it readily includes in its meanings feeling, empathy, and sympathy—these last two terms involve suffering, with its inevitable reference to tactility. The Latin *intellectus* and its English cognates "intellect," etc., are also tactile (*inter,* be-

13. See Paula Menyuk, *Sentences Children Use,* Research Monograph No. 52 (Cambridge, Mass.: The M.I.T. Press, 1969), pp. 35–36, 44, etc., where it is reported how children beginning to speak often use an undifferentiated "uh" (in English) for all their prepositions ("in," "at," "under," etc.).

tween; *legere,* to gather, collect—derivatively, to read) but not so "heavily" or gravitationally tactile, and hence do not so strongly suggest sympathy or empathy.

VI

This is the sensorial setting for Lonergan's remarks concerning understanding in the passage with which we began. The concept of "understanding" does indeed imply an analogy of intellectual knowing to sensory knowing, but in significant ways to kinesthetic knowing rather more than to sight. In terms of sensory analogues as well as in terms of what it represents in intellectual activity, it is incompatible with mere vision.

To move from Lonergan's myth of vision to cosmic mythology, we can say that vision has a paramountcy among the senses corresponding to that of the male sky god in a pantheon. For father sky and mother earth as modes of knowing or coming to terms with the universe around us can be related in terms of the economy of the senses we have earlier described. Mother (earth) and father (sky) are related to one another as tactile to visual. Mother and earth are close to us, ground our sense of touch (which develops in contact with mother), and deeply involved in subjectivity; father and sky are more remote, more object-like, apprehended more by sight than by touch (which, when attesting to existence of objects attests to our own subjectivity at the same time—I feel myself feeling something *other* than me).

Hearing mediates between the two. It is both yang and yin. Since intellection also is somehow both, hearing serves as a prime analogue for knowing. "I hear what you say" indicates a fuller experience than does "I see what you say," though not a clearer experience. But it will not do to take hearing alone as the only symbol or myth for noetic processes any more than it will do to take sight. For understanding resides also in the silence out of which man's word emerges and into which it disappears. Unlike "the word of the Lord," which endures forever, man's word perishes and only inaudible silence endures, at best inhabited by echoes. But sight does not fully correct the deficiencies of hearing either.[14] The object of sight is not so evanescent as the word and hence is somewhat like silence, but, since, unlike silence, it is not set off against the word, instead of being truly—that is, permanently and forever—enduring, it is at best merely quiescent.

"The truth shall set you free." It may be somehow liberating to know the depths of our bondage.

14. A fascinating account of ways in which adjectives first applying to one sense shift to apply to another sense ("quiet" applies first to sound, then to color) is given by Joseph M. Williams in "Synaesthetic Adjectives: A Possible Law of Semantic Change," *Language,* 52 (1976), 461–478. Williams finds evidence that there are regular sequences in such changes: touch-words transfer to taste, color, or sound; taste-words to smell and sound; color words shift only to sound; sound-words shift only to color; etc. Starting with English, Williams discovers similar patterns in Indo-European cognates and in Japanese and suggests that the patterns may well be found to apply to any language.

III

CLOSURE AND PRINT

6

Typographic Rhapsody: Ravisius Textor, Zwinger, and Shakespeare

Commonplaces and Their Significance

Writing in *Chapters in Western Civilization,* Professor Paul Oskar Kristeller notes that "the frequency of quotations and of commonplaces repeated in the moral literature in the Renaissance gives to all but its very best products an air of triviality that is often very boring to the modern critical reader."[1] The Renaissance exploitation of commonplace material is of course not restricted to moral treatises. Such material shows everywhere through the Renaissance, from speculative theology and medical treatises to lyric and dramatic poetry, where, however, its use is often less cumbersome than among the moralists. And at its best, in the "pointed" style which derives in part from Seneca, such material becomes brilliant, "illustrating" the subject with flashes of insight and wit.

A great many studies treat in one way or another what we may here style the commonplace tradition. Looking for the roots of the literary heritage of the West, in his *European Literature and the Latin Middle Ages* Ernst Robert Curtius devotes a great deal of attention to the various "topics" (*topoi* or *loci,* places, commonplaces) which have provided both themes and ways of managing themes to writers from classical antiquity on. Thus he treats the "topics of consolatory oratory," "historical topics,"

1. Paul Oskar Kristeller, "The Moral Thought of Renaissance Humanism," in *Chapters in Western Civilization,* ed. the Contemporary Civilization Staff of Columbia College, Columbia University, 3d ed. (New York: Columbia University Press, 1961), I, 305.

"topics of the exordium," and other "topics" explicitly labelled as such.[2] Many of his chapter headings indicate that individual chapters are devoted to the discussion of further individual topics. Thus, "The Goddess Natura," "Heroes and Rulers," "The Ideal Landscape," "Poetry and Philosophy," "The Book as Symbol," and so on. A brief but tightly packed study by August Beck, *Die 'Studia Humanitatis' und ihre Methode,* explains a great deal directly on the use of commonplaces, especially as prescribed in works on education, from Rudolph Agricola and Erasmus on to the time of Montaigne.[3] Studies of sixteenth- and seventeenth-century writers, particularly by American scholars, who constitute the largest group by far of experts on the rhetorical tradition, often treat the commonplaces in various ways. One of the most thorough-going of such treatments is T. W. Baldwin's monumental landmark, *William Shakspere's Small Latine and Lesse Greeke,* which works patiently through large numbers of commonplace collections in use in Shakespeare's milieu by schoolboys as well as by adults.[4] Sister Joan Marie Lechner has provided an invaluable survey of Renaissance views and practice in her *Renaissance Concepts of the Commonplaces.*[5]

Out of these studies there emerges a major question: Why was the commonplace tradition once so important, since it now seems so affected and boring and aesthetically counterproductive? None of the studies just mentioned, nor others like them, really broach this question. The question can be answered only by situating the commonplace tradition in the broader perspectives of noetic history, examining how the tradition relates to the evolution of means of accumulation, storage, and retrieval of knowledge, and thus eventually how it relates to the history of the human psyche and of culture. This is what the present study

2. Ernst Robert Curtius, *European Literature and the Latin Middle Ages,* trans. Willard Trask, Bollingen Series, 36 (New York: Pantheon Books, 1953), pp. 79–105.

3. Bibliothèque d'Humanisme et Renaissance, 21 (1959), 273–290.

4. Two vols. (Urbana, Ill.: University of Illinois Press, 1944).

5. New York: Pageant Press, 1962; reprinted: Westport, Conn.: Greenwood Press, 1974.

undertakes to do, working with a certain few significant Renaissance writers. Until the commonplaces are related to the evolving noetic economy, they remain antiquarian curiosities, quaint phenomena, whose obtrusiveness in the past is no more explicable than their eclipse in the present.

"Commonplace" of course has several, more or less related, senses, some of them quite technical.[6] But in all its senses the term has to do in one way or another with the exploitation of what is already known, and indeed often of what is exceedingly well known. The "places" provided access to a culture's noetic store. In classical rhetorical doctrine, places (*topoi* in Greek, in Latin *loci*) refer to the "seats" or, as we today would commonly conceptualize them, to the "headings" to which one betook oneself to draw out of the stock of knowledge the things one could say concerning a given subject. These headings implemented analysis of one's subject: for a person, one might, by a kind of analytic process, consider his family, descent, sex, age, education, and the like; or, more generally, for all sorts of things, one could look to definition, opposites, causes, effects, related matters, and so on. This meaning of *topos* or *locus* or "place" is approximated still in our present term "topic" (from *topikos,* the Greek adjectival form corresponding to the noun *topos*). In his *Rhetoric* (I.ii.21–1358a) Aristotle notes two classes of "places": (*a*) "common" places, headings providing materials for any and all subjects, and (*b*) "special" places, headings offering matter for certain individual subjects, such as law or physics. But this distinction was too fastidious to survive the hurly-burly of rhetorical doctrine and practice, where "places" (*loci*) and "commonplaces" (*loci communes*) were often used interchangeably.[7]

A "commonplace" might also have another meaning, somewhat deviously related to this first: a "commonplace" could be

6. See Ong, *The Presence of the Word* (New Haven: Yale University Press, 1967), pp. 56–66, 79–87, etc.; Lechner, *Renaissance Concepts of the Commonplaces.* In *European Literature and the Latin Middle Ages,* Curtius is concerned largely, sometimes explicitly and sometimes implicitly, with the central commonplace tradition of the West.

7. See Ong, *The Presence of the Word,* p. 82.

a standard brief disquisition or purple patch on any of hundreds or thousands of given subjects—loyalty, treachery, brotherhood, theft, decadence (Cicero's *O tempora! O mores!* passage is a commonplace on this subject), and so on; these prefabricated disquisitions were excerpted from one's reading or listening or worked up by oneself (generally out of material taken or adapted from others). Quintilian explains this meaning of *locus communis* in his *Institutiones oratoriae* 5. 5. 12—cf. *ibid*. 1. 11. 12.—after treating other usages of *locus* earlier in the same work (5. 10. 20).

Even in antiquity, as Quintilian testifies, commonplaces in the sense of standard brief disquisitions or purple patches were often committed to writing, and by the Middle Ages and the Renaissance came to be regularly stored in commonplace books or "copie" books or copybooks (books assuring *copia,* or the free flow of discourse essential for oratory). The medieval *florilegia* or collections of *exempla* and other useful bits for use in subsequent discourse belong to this tradition. To it can also be assimilated collections such as Erasmus' *De duplici copia verborum ac rerum,* where the entries are often less than disquisitions, being in many instances quite short expressions, mere phrases or turns of diction, such as the Latin equivalents of "white as snow," "soft as the ear lobe," for these phrases, too, are presented as stock ways of treating a particular subject, however briefly, got together for subsequent use.[8]

It is helpful sometimes to refer to commonplaces in this latter sense of garnered standard disquisitions or purple patches on a set subject as "cumulative" commonplaces, and to places or com-

8. Many of Erasmus' works are collections of what in one way or another is basically commonplace material: thus his *Adagia,* his *Apophthegmata,* his *Colloquia,* the *De duplici copia verborum ac rerum,* the *Epigrammata* and the *Parabola sive Similia.* Moreover, his editions of collections of brief lives by Epiphanius, Sophronius, St. Jerome, and Plutarch are primary sources of commonplace exempla, as are also his editions of Lucian of Samosata's *Dialogi* and other works. As was the case with most humanists, Erasmus regarded reading generally as furnishing commonplace grist for the reader's own rhetorical mill. A great deal of his influence as an educator was due to the fact that he was the most influential collector of commonplace material the Western world has ever seen.

monplaces in the earlier sense of headings as "analytic" places or commonplaces. By the term "commonplace tradition" I shall refer here to the practice, more or less reflective, of exploiting both analytic and cumulative places or commonplaces. "Commonplace collections" here refers to assemblages in writing or print of cumulative commonplaces, these latter being understood to include both lengthy passages and briefer expressions, down to mere *modus dicendi,* as in Erasmus' *De copia,* stocked in formulaic fashion out of the extant store of knowledge for further exploitation as occasion might demand.

As Eric Havelock has shown, the noetic economy of an oral culture demands that knowledge be processed in more or less formulary style and that it be constantly recycled orally—otherwise it simply vanishes for good unless it be discovered anew.[9] The whole commonplace tradition, an organized trafficking in what in one way or another is already known, is obviously part and parcel of the ancient oral world, the primitive human noetic universe, to which the Renaissance rhetorical doctrine of imitation also obviously relates. Elsewhere I have undertaken to show that the persistence of such material in more or less conspicuous form provides one rule-of-thumb indication of how oral or residually oral a given culture may be—which is also to say how oral or residually oral the culture's typical personality structures and its state of consciousness itself may be.[10]

Ioannes Ravisius Textor: Exemplary Collector

As an instance of some of the workings of the commonplace tradition in the Renaissance and a point of departure for reflection on the tradition, I should like to adduce here two collections of commonplace materials got up by a much neglected sixteenth-century French Neo-Latin writer, Jean Tixier, Seigneur de Ravisi, who latinized his name as Ioannes Ravisius Textor. Al-

9. Eric A. Havelock, *Preface to Plato* (Cambridge, Mass.: Belknap Press of Harvard University Press, 1963), pp. 36–60.
10. Walter J. Ong, *Rhetoric, Romance, and Technology* (Ithaca, N.Y.: Cornell University Press, 1971), pp. 23–47.

though Ravisius Textor was familiar to sixteenth- and early seventeenth-century schoolboys across western Europe—including, it would appear certain, William Shakespeare[11]—he remains a neglected figure today and indeed promises to be neglected even more effectively in the future, for he published in Latin and the knowledge of Latin is becoming less and less common even among scholars—a fact which we should by now frankly admit is severely warping many studies of the Renaissance.

Ioannes Ravisius Textor was born very likely around 1470, but perhaps as late as 1480, probably at Saint-Saulge in the Nivernais. He studied at the University of Paris under his compatriot Jean Beluacus in the Collège de Navarre, with which Textor's entire life was thereafter identified. There it was that he became professor of rhetoric, helping to make this college the best of all the Paris colleges for the study of humanities. In 1520 he was elected Rector of the University and in 1524 he died in Paris. Although a Nivernais by birth and a Parisian by adoption, Ravisius Textor, like many humanists, was international in his reputation and influence: editions of his works appear not only in Paris, Rouen, and Lyons, but also in Basel, Venice, Antwerp, Douai, and London.[12] Few studies of Ioannes Ravisius Textor have ever appeared, and there is no definitive study at all, so far as I can ascertain.[13] Textor's published works—all Latin, as we

11. See T. W. Baldwin, *William Shakspere's Small Latine and Lesse Greeke*, 11, 391, 414–416; cf. the many other references to Textor locatable through Baldwin's indexes.

12. Including one London edition not listed in the Pollard and Redgrave *Short-Title Catalogue*, namely *Epistolae Ioannis Ravisii Textoris non vulgaris eruditionis: nunc recens in gratiam studiosae iuventutis multo quam antehac unquam emendatiores in lucem editae* (London: ex Typographia Societatis Stationariorum, 1628). I have not seen a copy of this edition, but a copy was listed for sale in Maggs Brothers (London), *Catalogue No. 901* (January 1966).

13. Another study of Ravisius Textor, and a valuable one, has appeared in the same volume in which the present study was first published: I. D. McFarlane, "Reflections on Ravisius Textor's *Specimen epithetorum*," pp. 81–90 in R. R. Bolgar, ed., *Classical Influences on European Culture A.D. 1500–1700* (Cambridge and New York: Cambridge University Press, 1976). There is a brief treatment of Ravisius Textor in Maurice Mignon, *Études de littérature nivernaise: Tixier de Ravisy, Augustin Berthier, Adam Billaut, Cotignon de la Charnaye, Jules Renard* (Gap: Editions Ophrys,

have just noted—include mostly productions of a routine humanist sort: dialogues (written to be staged, as they indeed often
were), epigrams, letters, and editions of Ulrich von Hutten's
Aula and *Dialogus* and of other authors' works, including a collection of short pieces on distinguished women by various writers.
The two works of Textor's to be glanced at here are his *Officina*
(a title which can be rendered into English as *Workshop*) and

---

1946), esp. pp. 9–10. An earlier work by J. Vodoz, *Le Théâtre latin de
Ravisius Textor 1470–1524* (Winterthur: Imprimerie Geschwister Ziegler,
1898), treats Textor's *Dialogi,* which were written to be staged as *moralités,
soties, et farces,* but, as would be normal or even inevitable at the time this
work was done, of course says nothing about the influence of epithet-collecting
or commonplaces on Textor's work. Vodoz cites (p. 137) the *Roman de la
rose* as a frequent source for Textor's ideas, but the complexity of Textor's
sources is so little adverted to that one is unsure as to how directly operative
this medieval romance as such actually was. A still earlier doctoral dissertation by L. Massebieau, *De Ravisii Textoris comoediis seu De Comoediis collegiorum in Gallia praesertim ineunto sexto decimo saeculo disquisitionem
Facultati Litterarum Parisiensi proponebat L. Massebieau* (Paris: J. Bonheure, 1878), goes into the staging of Textor's comedies (that is, his *Dialogi*).
Massebieau notes (pp. 47–48) some antecedents of Hamlet's gravedigger scene
in Villon, Carolus Aurelianensis, Ravisius, and Reuchlin, but without reference
to Ravisius's *Officina* or *Epitheta.* He is aware of Textor's reliance on the
commonplace tradition, as his remarks about what Textor takes "ex communi fonte" here shows (p. 56): "Quaecumque autem Ravisius aut excogitavit aut ex communi fonte hauserit aut quidem imitatus sit, at omnia
libero impetu, vividisque verbis expressit, raro paganis nominibus respersa
nec umquam circuitionum elegantiis oppressa." The late Professor Don
Cameron Allen, in his *Francis Meres's Treatise 'Poetrie': A Critical Edition,*
University of Illinois Studies in Language and Literature, 16, nos. 3–4
(Urbana, Ill.: University of Illinois Press, 1933), pp. 32–37 and *passim,*
notes that in the 'Poetrie' section of his English-language work *Palladis
Tamia* Francis Meres borrows much of his material directly from Ravisius
Textor. In reviewing ways by which Meres might have known Textor—
and these are vast, for many editions were in circulation—Allen makes no
mention of Thomas Johnson's work *Cornucopiae, or Divers Secrets: wherein
is contained the rare secrets in man, beasts . . . plantes, stones, and such
like . . . and not before committed to be printed in English, newlie drawen
out of divers Latine authors . . .* (London: for W. Bailey, 1595). Both the
title and the content of this work—it lists places which abound in various
things and places which lack various things, just as Textor's *Cornucopia* does
(as explained here below)—suggest direct derivation from Textor. But the
interweaving of commonplace collections makes such derivation a little less
than certain unless someone checks out the matter, as I have not myself
done. Hyder Rollins, in his "Deloney's Sources for Euphuistic Learning,"
PMLA, 51 (1936), 398–406, notes that Thomas Deloney's erudite anecdotes
come from, among other sources, Johnson's *Cornucopiae.* And so the *loci*
yield their hold to generation after generation.

his *Epitheta* (*Epithets*). These continue the copybook (*copia-book*) tradition of Erasmus, whom Textor much admired, as his prefatory letter to his 1519 edition of Hutten's *Aula* makes clear,[14] and as his brother Iacobus (Jacques Tixier de Ravisi) also indicates in his own prefatory letter to his 1524 edition of Ioannes's *Epitheta*.[15] The *Officina* and the *Epitheta*, like several of Erasmus' works, arrange in collections for subsequent use[16] bits and pieces out of Latin texts.

Essentially the *Officina* is simply a dictionary of classified excerpts or mini-excerpts from extant writing—"examples," such as Erasmus' copybook program calls for. The excerpts present students with things to say and Latin words to say them with. No Greek as such appears anywhere in the work. Everything originally in Greek is put into Latin. The sources are mostly the ancients, such as Virgil or Ovid, but also extend to Textor's own contemporaries or near-contemporaries, such as Pontanus or Erasmus, with medieval writers of course scrupulously excluded. The content of the examples in at least ninety percent of the cases is concerned with antiquity even when the citation is from one of Textor's contemporaries, but on rare occasions citations from the later writers will have to do with a contemporary or near-contemporary matter, such as an event in the life of King Ferdinand of Spain.

The *Officina* first appeared in Paris in 1520 and apparently

14. *Ulrich de Hutten Equitis Germani Aula. Dialogus.* Textor emaculavit (Paris: Antonius Aussurdus, 1519), fol. *2.

15. *Ioannis Ravisii Textoris Nivernensis Epitheta . . . ab authore suo recognita et in novam formam redacta* [ed. Iacobus Ravisius Textor] (Paris: Reginaldus Chauldière, 1524), fol. 2.

16. Collections of commonplace materials were used not only by orators, poets, "philosophers" (including natural scientists), physicians, divines, and others getting up "original" works under their own names, but even more assiduously by other collectors in their own commonplace collections, published as well as unpublished. As the late Professor Don Cameron Allen points out, in his 1933 edition of the "Poetrie" section of Francis Meres's *Palladis Tamia* or *Wit's Treasury* (1598), a commonplace collection of similes in English which gives us so much of our biographical material on some of the colourful literary hacks of sixteenth-century London, all of Meres's historical examples (for his similes) come from Ravisius Textor's *Officina,* as most of his similes themselves come from Erasmus' *Parabola sive Similia.*

was not reprinted until 1532.[17] But after this date editions of the work in its entirety and in epitomes multiplied. More will be said of the editions later. One particular section of the *Officina* appeared frequently as a separate work under its own section title, *Cornucopia*. I have record of some thirty editions of the *Officina* in whole or in part, the last in 1626, with most editions appearing before 1600. Some editions, revised by Conrad Lycosthenes (Wolffhardt), appear under the title *Theatrum poeticum atque historicum: sive Officina.*

Certainly the *Officina* of Ravisius Textor is in many ways one of the most intriguing collections of commonplace material that was ever assembled. If the work were in French or English or German or any other modern vernacular rather than in Latin, it would certainly be a constant point of reference for literary commentators or curio seekers, or for connoisseurs of the unconsciously comic. In its studied pursuit of conspicuously useless detail it rivals even Burton's *Anatomy of Melancholy* or Sterne's *Tristram Shandy,* and in its nose for the bizarre it can compete with Rabelais. Textor is somewhat apologetic about the zany confusion of his work and in a set of elegiacs to the reader at the beginning sets out to disarm criticism by protesting that the *Officina* is not for "learned poets" but "for uneducated boys" (*rudibus pueris*) who are for the first time "sweating in the dust and still imbibing words in the course of elementary instruction."[18] It is hard, however, to imagine the collection as being put directly into the hands of little boys, for, other reasons aside, the earlier editions of the *Officina* are large folios which would be very expensive even for masters. Probably masters used the work for self-improvement and as a teacher's manual.

17. *Io. Ravisii Textoris Officina partim historicis partim poeticis refertis disciplina* . . . ([Paris:] Reginaldus Chauldière, 1520)—copies in British Museum and Cambridge University Library. *Ioan Ravisii Textoris Officina . . . auctior additis ab ipso authore ante quam e vita excederit rebus prope innumeris . . . cui etiam accessit index copiosissimus . . .* ([Paris:] Reginaldus Chauldière, 1532)—copies in the British Museum and the Bibliothèque Nationale, Paris.

18. *Officina* (1532), fol. [Ai^v].

As a dictionary of quotations the *Officina* differs from today's dictionaries most spectacularly in the nature of its headings. There are some 350 subject headings in the first edition of the book, with often large numbers of entries under each heading. The reader opening the first edition is plunged into a blood-bath perhaps suggesting that Textor was projecting into his subject matter some of the aggressions against oneself which the gruelling work of a lexicographer can well generate (witness the case of Samuel Johnson, who in his *Dictionary* wryly defines a lexicographer—that is, himself and those like him—as a "harmless drudge"). Here are the first two dozen or so entries under which Textor ranges his selections of materials from writers in classical antiquity, translated from Textor's Latin and presented in exactly the sequence in which he gives them, beginning right after his preface. The reader (in Textor's plan, a little boy! *puer*) encounters first a list of suicides (all the cases from classical antiquity that Textor can find), then parricides, drowned persons, those who have given their names to bodies of water by being drowned in them, persons killed or dismembered by horses, persons killed by the fall of horses, those killed by serpents, those killed by boars, those killed by lions, those killed by dogs, killed by other beasts, individuals struck by lightning, dead from hanging and crucifixion, dead from thirst and hunger, consumed by fire, persons cast off precipices, dead from falling staircases, people swallowed up by the earth, individuals done away with by poison, victims of sudden death (such a heading shows that Textor's standards for close timing were pretty high), dead from joy and laughter, dead from too much food and drink.

Under each of these headings Textor gives a list of the individual cases he has read of. His research was not casual. He exhibits one hundred and eighty-five suicides, eleven killed by dogs, and so on. Each instance is accompanied by an explanation which provides a varying amount of circumstantial detail for the case in question, together with references and quotations in many cases, though not in all.

In the particular sequence of headings just given, like items tend to cluster together, but elsewhere sampling of the classics is more random. One finds, for instance, a fairly sustained section on learned persons, and in rather intelligible succession such items as stonecutters (*sculptores*), engravers, statuary sculptors, marble cutters, painters, and pigments. But on the other hand one also encounters sequences such as the following (and I am giving these in the order in which they occur); trainers of monsters and wild beasts, the four elements, sycophants, buffoons, parasites, fat and thin men, famous and memorable gardens, public criers, sleepy people (*somnolentes*), fullers, the columns of Hercules. Every so often Textor avails himself of catch-all headings, such as "those famous for various things." He has further sections on geometricians, astrologers, various types of measures, lousy distemper (*morbus pedicularis*), men who smelt bad (a *topos* which I have found recurrent in collections of this sort), dwarfs, pigmies, the four harpies, various types of haircuts, brute animals to which statues were erected, arguments drawn from the impossible, various kinds of excrement, descriptions of a long time, descriptions of night, and a long strung-out list of various kinds of worms.

The part of the *Officina* labelled *Cornucopia*[19] is a little curio in its own right, constituting a major section of the book that outranks in size the sections under other headings. The title *Cornucopia,* or horn of plenty, is employed because this section is devoted exclusively to a catalogue of things which can be found in great abundance in specified places. Thus the reader here learns what countries abound in bees or cheese or cinnamon or whales, ants, iron, marble, and so on. The *Cornucopia* concludes with its own contrary, listing various things not found in various places. There is no gold in the Nile, alone of all rivers (a sweeping bit of information, but backed by classical references), there are no deer in Africa, no bears either, no swine in Arabia, "especially in the country of the Scaenites." (This transcendentalizing of an absolute denial seemingly defies logical clarification; there are

19. *Officina* (1532), fols. LIX[v]–XCIIII[r].

none at all, especially in this place!) There are no eagles in Rhodes, no woodpeckers in the fields around Tarentum, there is no thyme in Arcadia, there are no mice in the island of Paris, no mountains in Portugal, no moles in Coronea, and finally, in England there is no oil or wine, only beer.

Ioannes Ravisius Textor's *Epitheta* is a somewhat different but equally fascinating work. It is a collection of standard qualifiers and substitutes for nouns which a writer of Latin poetry imitating the classics might use—and of course which writers of French and Italian and English and German and other poetry also might use and did use, following the Latin. Like the *Officina*, the *Epitheta* draws basically on ancient sources. The two medieval writers whom Professor McFarlane notes that it includes, Martianus Capella (fl. 410–439) and Boethius (480?–?524) would seem to be medieval only by ascription, since the former was a younger contemporary (and fellow countryman) of St. Augustine of Hippo and the latter born only some fifty years after Augustine's death.[20]

The first edition of the *Epitheta,* called *Specimen epithetorum* (*An Exhibit of Epithets*) was put out in 1518 during the lifetime of its author.[21] The second edition, although its title notes that it represents a revision done by its original author, came out posthumously in 1524, as mentioned earlier, under the supervision of the author's brother, Iacobus Ravisius Textor, who with quaint heartlessness observes in his introduction, "My brother was brought to an end before his revision was."[22]

In accord with Erasmus' example, as Iacobus Ravisius Textor tells us in his somewhat defensive introduction to the posthumous second edition, Ioannes collected his *Epitheta* for boys an academic cut higher than those for whom he says the *Officina* was designed, that is, for those in the highest class in rhetoric engaged in doing exercises in themes for declamations or for dialogues, or

---

20. McFarlane, "Reflections," in Bolgar, ed., *Classical Influences,* p. 84.

21. *Specimen epithetorum Ioannis Ravisius Textoris Nivernensis, omnibus artis poeticae studiosis maxime utilium* (Paris: Henricus Stephanus pro Scholis Decretorum, 1518). For the 1524 edition, see n. 15 above.

22. *Epitheta* (1524), fol. *2ᵛ.

other prose or verse.[23] The thinking behind the collection is obviously of a piece with the classical idea of rhetorical ornamentation. The *Officina* proffers more or less bare, hard ideas, "naked" thoughts, whereas the *Epitheta* provides an assortment of options for giving the presumably bare or "naked" thought of the rhetorically untrained weaver of words a richer, more attractive—which is to say more commonplace!—texture.

The collection of epithets which Ioannes Ravisius Textor assembled is sizable. It runs to 311 leaves (that is, 622 pages) of folio size in the 1518 edition. Textor's industry appears to have flagged as he worked through the alphabet. *A* to *L* (10 letters, no *J* or *K*) take up fols. 1–206, *M–Z* (11 letters, but only two entries under *X*) take up only fols. 207–303, despite all the *S*s. (In comparison, large Latin dictionaries commonly divide almost evenly between *A–L* and *M–Z*.)

Running through these individual entries is far from a boring occupation today. The coins which Textor proffers have been worn smooth by use, but they still ring true in countless associations. In the *A*'s the searcher for epithets can find 113 of them referrable to Apollo, and 163 for *amor* (love). The complementary *bellum* or war merits a 36-page entry, and death (*mors*) has 95 epithets. Achilles warrants 48 epithets, such as—translated into English—tireless, untamed, trusted, furious. Africa is glowing, fertile, full of fords, bristling, teeming with wild beasts. The associations which countless poems and prose writings had established with Arabia are well recorded here. The inhabitants of the land, the Arabs, are rich in odours, palm-bearing, incense-collecting, tender, Oriental, wealthy, ardent, opulent, and so on. One thinks of Othello's dying declamation full of Arabia, wealth, odours, gums, and tender feelings. Coleridge's River Alph is here too, *Alphēus* in Latin. It is not sacred but it is definitely alien, clear, and swift. One could find here the accouterments and often

---

23. Iacobus Ravisius Textor, prefatory letter to Ludovicus Lassereus, in *Epitheta* (1524), fol. *2ᵛ: "supremae classis rhetorices, quos convenit assiduis declamationum dialogorumque thematibus omnique tum solutae tum numerosae orationis genere exerceri."

the substance of thousands of poems of Western Europe through the Renaissance and indefinitely later.

Renaissance Interactions with the Commonplace Tradition

The management of commonplace material has a long and complex history, which can be sketched here and then brought into focus around Textor's and related works. The source of the tradition, as we have noted above, is ultimately the primitive oral culture of all mankind. Memorable sayings from this culture—and in an oral culture, expression, and thought as well, not mnemonically patterned for recall to all intents and purposes does not exist—from simple turns of expression, epithets, and anecdotes to highly sophisticated aphorisms, gnomes, apophthegms, moralistic fables, and brilliant paradoxes, are woven from the ancient oral store into early writing, which in its most artistic forms continues the oral practice of reiterating and embellishing the already known. In this morass of commonly shared mnemonically structured knowledge there is no footing for anyone seeking an answer to the question, "Who first said . . . ?" Everybody is quoting everybody else, and has been for tens of thousands of years before the written records began, on purpose and with a feeling of achievement.

In classical antiquity, which remained always close to the primitive oral world, the use of commonplace material was always conspicuous and eventually, with the help of writing, had become the object of elaborate reflection, some of it more speculative, as in Aristotle's *Topika,* and some of it more practical, as in Cicero or Quintilian or Dionysius of Halicarnassus or Hermogenes. Despite the currency of writing, however, compilation of commonplace material, though not unknown in antiquity—conspicuous examples of compilation would be the Sapiential books in the Old Testament—was not highly developed before the Middle Ages. Ancient Greek and Roman authors wrote collections of biographies, such as those by Plutarch, and vaguely "encyclopedic" works treating individual words and subject matters (as in Pliny's *Natural History*). They did relatively little in the way of collecting excerpts.[24] By contrast, the *Speculum* of Vincent of Beauvais (ca. 1190–1264), a famous medieval "encyclopedia," consists chiefly of excerpts from other writers. Following beginnings in the patristic period, the Middle Ages specialised in *florilegia,* collections of gnomic quotations, *exempla* (illustrative stories, historical or fictional), sermon excerpts, and other kinds of bits and pieces, culled from sources as distant as the Far East (the *Panchatantra,* a collection of beast fables ultimately from India, was taken over deviously by the Middle Ages in Europe as the *Directorium vitae humanae*). The number of *florilegia* is so vast that no even moderately complete study of the genre, of even monograph size, has ever been published, nor has even an inventory of known or extant *florilegia.*[25] Titles would certainly run into the hundreds. Despite their scribal provenience, however, the contents of the inscribed medieval *florilegia* were often presented as "sayings" or orally conveyed narrative and were intended to be recycled through the oral world, just as the education in the universities, despite the fact that in many ways it was far more text-centred than education in classical antiquity,[26] was calculated nevertheless to provide basically an oral formation for the student.[27]

During the Renaissance, the commonplace heritage of antiquity and the Middle Ages became in many ways more important than ever before. First, by comparison with classical antiquity, the Renaissance needed to become even more self-conscious about commonplace material because Latin, normally the only lan-

24. A good summary treatment, with references, can be found in the article "Encyclopaedia," *Encyclopaedia Britannica* (Chicago: Encyclopaedia Britannica, 1973), VIII, 364–365.

25. Art. "Florilegia," *New Catholic Encyclopedia* (New York: McGraw-Hill, 1967), V, 979–980.

26. Ong, *The Presence of the Word,* pp. 58–61.

27. See István Hajnal, *L'Enseignement de l'écriture aux universités médiévales* (Budapest: Academia Scientiarum Hungarica Budapestini, 1954), p. 64.

guage one studied and used in school (except for a generally quite small amount of Greek),[28] was a foreign language to all its users, and had been so for roughly a millennium. Unlike schoolboys in ancient Greece or Rome studying their vernacular Greek or Latin, and unlike schoolchildren today who address themselves to their own vernaculars in the classroom, Renaissance schoolboys normally came to the Latin which was the *pièce de résistance* of their academic menu with no store at all of common expressions or sayings from ordinary Latin conversation. These had to be artificially cultivated in academic circles.

Secondly, although the Middle Ages, for much the same reasons as the Renaissance, had had to exploit artificially a store of common Latin expressions or sayings, the Renaissance felt the need somewhat more keenly because of its keener and more self-conscious ambition to echo the Latin of classical antiquity. One had to be relatively sure that one's idiom, which included various *modus dicendi,* turns of expressions, Latin proverbs and comparisons and sayings, was more or less of a piece with that of classical antiquity. We need not exaggerate the Renaissance drive to Ciceronianism, which was usually relatively restrained in various ways, but we must acknowledge the existence and the real force of a desire to imitate ancient Latin quite closely. Good Latin writers, such as Erasmus, wrote not purely Ciceronian language but they did not write in medieval style either, though they were influenced by the latter. They wrote their own classically toned Latin.

Thirdly, in settling on the corpus of classical work as its more or less strict norm, the Renaissance fixed its attention on material visually stored and retrievable. Its lexical and linguistic base was not an orally possessed language as such, but a body of texts—a controlled and closed field, at least in principle more or less ex-

28. Robert R. Bolgar, *The Classical Heritage and Its Beneficiaries* (Cambridge: The University Press, 1958), p. 359, reports that, although in later editions of the Jesuit *Ratio Studiorum* Greek was to be begun simultaneously with Latin, in fact it was given only about one-sixth of the time given to Latin at the Jesuit college at Messina. Such proportioning of time appears typical of the better Renaissance schools—in the less good schools Greek got even shorter shrift. See Bolgar, ibid. pp. 332–333, etc.

plicitly bounded. The adoption of this base was crucial in the history of commonplace materials, for it was to mark the beginning of the end of the commonplace tradition. Commonplaces had their deepest roots in the noetic needs of an oral world. The Renaissance preoccupation with texts, inherited from the Middle Ages but intensified by print, tended to shift the focus of verbalization from the world of sound to the surface of the page, from the aural to the visual. This is not to say there were not competing tendencies in the Renaissance, such as the accentuation of the oral fostered by the cult of the classical orator, but the effect of print was ultimately to prove overwhelming.

Various arrangements for visual retrieval of material in texts had been physically possible since writing was invented. Indeed, this was what writing was all about: words, though irreducibly sounds, could now be recovered by the eye (for reconstitution as sounds). But writing is far less effective than print in fixing verbalized material in space for widespread storage and ready visual access.

Once a fixed order is established in print, it can be multiplied with little effort almost without limit. This makes it more worthwhile to do the arduous work of elaborating serviceable arrangements and—what is all important—of devising complex, visually serviceable indexes. A hundred dictated handwritten copies of a work would normally require a hundred indexes, for the material would appear on different pages in different copies, whereas five thousand or more printed copies of an edition of a given work would all be served by one and the same index. Within a few generations after the invention of print, the index became a conspicuous feature of printed commonplace collections, much advertised on title pages.[29]

Besides facilitating retrieval through indexing, the printed page also facilitated retrieval simply because it normally proved easier to read than most manuscripts. This was, of course, less true at the beginning of print. Earlier printed books kept close to the format and style of the manuscript with which they were com-

29. I have given a few instances in *The Presence of the Word*, pp. 85–6.

peting: the pages were indubitably handsome, but not necessarily adapted to speed reading. However, as it gradually dawned on consciousness that printing was not just imitation handwriting, solid pages of close-set type gave way to pages with well spaced words, the paragraph in the modern sense of this term—a unit of thought visually advertised by an indentation—was invented and became functional, and in countless other ways the feeling gradually developed that words could be arranged on a surface in ways facilitating visual retrieval (albeit for processing in one way or another through the auditory world—for words remain at root always sounds).

Development of the feeling for visual retrieval can be seen everywhere, but most spectacularly in the title pages of Renaissance books. Everyone familiar with Renaissance editions will recall how an early title page will often split even its principal words with hyphens, printing successive parts of the same word on successive lines in different sizes or different fonts of type. An example—one of hundreds—would be the title page of the first edition (Paris: Andreas Wechel, 1572) of Peter Ramus' final revision of his *Dialectica*.[30] The full title of this edition is: *P. Rami Regii Professoris Dialecticae libri duo* (*The Two Books of the Dialectic of Peter Ramus, Regius Professor*). On the 1572 title page, the words are dismembered. The first line presents, in upper-case type about 24-point in size, the fragmented "P. RAMI RE-"; the next line drops to smaller upper-case type, about 18-point in size, in which it presents the last two syllables of one word and the first three of another: "GII PROFESSO-"; the third line, in 14-point upper-case type, provides the fourth syllable of one word and the whole of another, "RIS DIALECTICAE," and the following line, in 10-point upper-case type, concludes the title with the two words "LIBRI DUO." This last line is the first of the four to present the reader with words not chopped into pieces.

The overall visual appearance of this title page is far from

30. I cite this title page because it can be found reproduced in facsimile in Walter J. Ong, *Ramus and Talon Inventory* (Cambridge, Mass.: Harvard University Press, 1958), opposite p. 192.

unpleasant. Quite the contrary, as an inverted pyramid arrangement of black marks on a white surface, the page, which includes the printer's mark and imprint, is aesthetically very pleasing and decorative. It would be attractive framed. It is, however, by present-day standards, not easy to read. As soon as it is read aloud, it is understandable, but it does not come into the visual field in such a way as to facilitate apprehension in lexical units with the ease which later typography would demand. There is no sense of what printers and advertisers today would call "display." The reason is that the words are not thought of primarily as being picked off the page as units by the eye, but rather as being made into units within the auditory imagination—or more likely, within the voice box, since many of Ramus' contemporaries were, it seems, still reading aloud or in a mumble when they read to themselves—with only casual relation to the visual. Presentation was improving somewhat. Words came soon to be set with very evident spaces between them, as they were often not in early print, but the verbal visual unit as such was still relatively weak.

   In the gradual movement from the state of affairs typified by this 1572 title page toward a more functionally visual economy of verbalized knowledge, collections of "places" prove to be a recognizable focus of development. Vision is a fractioning sense, as Merleau-Ponty[31] and others have remarked. So in its own way was the commonplace tradition, which, even in its original oral roots, had tended to fragment discourse into the bits assembled by oral narrators and orators—"rhapsodizers" or "song-stitchers," in the original Greek meaning of this term, who sewed together the commonplace bits out of which thought and discourse were made. It was not on the face of it unlikely that the fragmenting possibilities of the visual field would be exploited somehow when commonplaces were subject to the visual regimen of print. Some of the more complex ways in which this exploitation was carried out will be discussed here shortly, but it will be well to note initially the central interaction of the old oral commonplace tradi-

31. Maurice Merleau-Ponty, "L'Oeil et l'esprit," *Temps Modernes,* 18, nos. 184–185 (1961), 193–227.

tion and the newly improved visual medium. This took place in the development in the index, just mentioned. Our present term "index" itself is an abridged form of the earlier *index locorum* (index of places) or *index locorum communium* (index of commonplaces) which one meets with in early printed books.[32] The elements into which an index breaks down a book are, basically, "places" in the text and simultaneously topics or "places" (*topoi, loci*) in the mind—in the physical world and in the conscious world both—thought of as pieces out of which a whole is constituted. The rhetorical and dialectical term "place" (*topos, locus*), conceptualized as some kind of vague region in consciousness or in a "field" of knowledge,[33] here acquires a truly local habitation, becoming a gross physical reality, truly a place on a surface. With typography far more operative in noetic management, the locale was identical now upon thousands of surfaces, where a "unit" of verbalization and thought could be pinned down. The concept "place" had become thoroughly functional.

At this point an older primary oral world is dying out in a certain sense within consciousness and a new visual-verbal world is gaining credibility. The effects on the accumulation, storage, and retrieval of knowledge will be vast, as will the effects on the kind of knowledge to which the mind shapes itself. In the noetic economy, purportedly inert "facts" rather than intrinsically evanescent sayings will have the ascendancy as never before.

Evolution of Visual Retrieval:
Textor, Theodor Zwinger and Others

If we look at Textor's *Officina* and *Epitheta* in terms of knowledge storage and retrieval—there are of course other ways of looking at them—their editorial history shows them to be in a

32. See Walter J. Ong, *Ramus, Method, and the Decay of Dialogue* (Cambridge, Mass.: Harvard University Press, 1958), pp. 313–314.

33. Not without some vague reference to a text at a very early period, it must be said, for *topos* and *locus* could in antiquity also mean a place in a written text, though this meaning was less obtrusive than the rhetorical and dialectical meaning connected with invention (*inventio*) or "finding" arguments, as earlier noted here.

way between the two worlds we have just mentioned, that of the old oral economy of all early human cultures (to which composition by formula was indigenous) and the new visual world of the inscribed word, which had come into germinal being with the invention of writing and which in Textor's day was finally maturing through the newly developing alphabetic print of the West.[34]

In the ancient world of letters, which had remained more dominantly oral than its medieval or Renaissance counterparts, the commonplace tradition had kept the noetic store alive and accessible largely through actual oral performance. One mastered commonplaces largely by hearing them. Although it is true, as has been noted earlier, that Quintilian and others report and advocate some use of writing to implement oratory, antiquity did not compile written lists of things that had been said with the fervor later obsessing medieval Europeans, who, as we have just noted, set out to establish massive textual—which is to say visual—bases, such as *florilegia,* within their own attenuated latter-day orality. The Renaissance, for all its programmatic rejection of the Middle Ages, was actually generated and kept alive largely by the medieval addiction to texts as such. What we have seen in Textor is a sweeping design for textual (visual) management of the noetic store: precipitate out of all classical texts all

34. Modern cultures emerging from orality into print and into electronic culture—at a rate hundreds of times faster than Europe's and with full consciousness, impossible in early Europe, of the evolution being undergone—are manifesting the same passion as that of the European Renaissance for collecting in print the proverbs and other formulaic sayings on which the earlier oral cultures always relied. Thus, for example, at Onitsha, Nigerian printers have been flooding the popular market with printed collections of proverbial materials. See Emmanuel Obiechina, *An African Popular Literature: A Study of Onitsha Market Pamphlets* (Cambridge: The University Press, 1973); Bernth Lindfors, "Perverted Proverbs in Nigerian Chapbooks," *Proverbium,* 15 (1970), 62 (482)–71 (487). Like their Renaissance counterparts, producers and users of these popular collections in Nigeria appear unaware that print makes cultivation of proverbs outmoded or even counterproductive, though Nigerian scholars are often exquisitely aware of this fact, as their Renaissance counterparts were not. The novels of Chinua Achebe, and of other African writers, counterpoint proverbial materials against growing technological developments, with great literary success.

the suicides, haircuts, sleepy people, astrologers, worms, or whatever, so that all of each class can be grouped together in space.
The growing appetite for beginning the study of any field of
knowledge with "history" in the sense of patiently recorded
"examples" from the given field providing grounds for "induction," such as was advocated, for instance, by Francis Bacon, is
certainly here receiving some encouragement which has seldom if
ever been attended to. "Induction" is being encouraged here,
subtly but really, by typographically supported developments
within the commonplace tradition. The units are not individual
observations or experiments, but bits of texts.

These developments show that the age's concern with particularities is not due simply to interest in physical science, that is,
to interest in "induction" from individual experienced instances
such as will lead to a universal scientific principle or "rule."
Speculation about scientific induction there was in plenty in the
Renaissance, as, for that matter, there had been in earlier ages.
But concern for particulars in the extramental world of the
Renaissance patently intermingles here with a concern for textual
particulars, which, though outside the mind, on paper or parch-
ment, in fact had to do with the mental world, since texts represented thought and its formulation and expression. In the case of
Theodor Zwinger, to be discussed below, we see the two concerns
merged or confused.

The new world of humanism and print in which Textor
operated did not, however, immediately maximize all the fuller
possibilities which print offered for particularized knowledge storage and retrieval. The new medium was too new, and many of
the new procedures which it would ultimately make operative
were slow to be realized. Successive editions of Textor's *Officina*
and *Epitheta* only gradually implement the possibilities of rapid
visual retrieval inherent in print from the beginning. But this
makes them all the more interesting, for, despite the inertia in all
cultural institutions, they do move eventually and inexorably
toward more effective implementation.

We have already noted the often chaotic sequence of materials in the original text itself of the *Officina*. Comparable chaos rules the finding apparatus provided in the volume for pulling items out of the text. In the first edition of the *Officina* (1520), the headings are arranged at the beginning of the book in an index or table of chapters, not alphabetically but simply in their order of occurrence in the work. Visual retrieval is a matter of concern here, but not of urgent concern: the effort to expedite such retrieval is, by later standards, half-hearted. The 1532 Paris edition and subsequent editions, however, take visual access more seriously: they provide an introductory alphabetical index. The later editions of the *Officina* prepared by Lycosthenes further implement visual access by organizing the body of the collection itself into clearly defined sections.[35]

Similarly, in the original edition of the *Epitheta,* entries themselves are presented in alphabetical order, but in a way which again shows that visual retrieval of material was still not attended to with full seriousness by later standards. Alphabetization is by first letter only: all the "a"s are together, but "al-" might occur before "ag-" or "ab-." This could indicate, and perhaps does to some degree indicate, haste in getting the material together. But that is not all. It is quite clear that alphabetic ordering as such is quite low in Textor's priorities, for he himself deliberately puts the entry on "Apollo" first of all and explains that he does so because, although alphabetically "Apollo" strictly belongs a little further down among the "a"s, it is most fitting that a collection of epithets for writing poetry should start with epithets that apply to the patron of poetry, Apollo.[36] Hierarchy and the realities of the human lifeworld take ready precedence over mechanical alphabetic arrangement, which is to say over arrangement for fully implemented visual access.

Instances of casual visual organization of materials in this period can be multiplied indefinitely, as can instances of progres-

35. Don Cameron Allen's statement in his edition of Francis Meres's treatise *Poetrie,* p. 23, that Textor's *Officina* is divided into seven major sections shows that he was using one of Lycosthenes' editions: the sections do not exist in Textor's original work.

36. *Specimen epithetorum* (1518), fol. 1,

sively better organization for visual retrieval. We shall content ourselves with some few more samples here. A work of the scholar and translator Raffaele Maffei (Raphael Maffeius Vollaterranus, 1455–1522), who is credited by Zwinger with being one of Ravisius Textor's chief sources,[37] presents us with a clear case of alphabetization by sound rather than by letter. In his *Commentariorum urbanorum libri octo et triginta* (Rome: Ioannes Besicken Alemanus, 1506),[38] a great mass of commonplace material, encyclopedic in scope and again, judged by later editorial standards, only partly digested, is introduced by various indices in which the letter *H*, not pronounced in Italian and no doubt considered by many Italians to be pronounceable only by barbarians, is printed but disregarded. Thus, for example, on fol. *3[r] we find this alphabetization: "Alyza, Halyzones, Haliartus, Alifa. . . ." The procedure makes sense, of course, but it also shows a disposition to store the words on the page in terms of what they sound like rather than what they look like. Later Italian reference works, though they traffic minimally in the letter *H*, nevertheless commonly acknowledge its existence if not as a sound at least as a visually apprehensible item on the same footing with other letters, and alphabetize it accordingly. It will be noted also in this series of words, that the letters *I* and *Y*, being pronounced alike, are also treated as the same letter: "Halicarnassus, Halyz, Alyza, Halyzones, Haliartus, Alifa."

The casual alphabetization of Textor and the phonetic alphabetization of Maffeius would not be without precedent in manuscript tradition, and thus it is not surprising to find either kind in print. The point about their appearance in print is their brief tenure: this sort of thing is doomed by the new medium, which enforces strictly visual regularity as handwriting had not done. Today no editor would tolerate the casual approach to alphabetization taken in Textor's and other early printed works.

---

37. *Theatrum humanae vitae* (Basel: per Sebastianum Henricpetri, 1604), fol. [ ] : ( ) : (4].

38. The British Museum copy—shelf mark 1487. w.3—which I have used here, has no title page, but it does have a colophon.

We can turn to a final sample which shows both the intense drive to assemble vast masses of commonplace excerpts and an attempt to organize them in another way for visual retrieval. The Basel physician and polymath Theodor Zwinger the Elder (1533–1588) undertook what was in many ways certainly the most comprehensively ambitious compilation of commonplace excerpts up to his time. His *Theatrum humanae vitae* is perhaps the world's largest single collection of commonplace excerpts. It went through five progressively enlarged editions between 1565 and 1604,[39] running to over 5,000 double-column folio pages of small type by the posthumous 1604 edition. In this collection Zwinger marshals tens of thousands of single excerpts from extant writings to try to produce what today would be called ground-work for 'scientific' history—he calls it the work of "historian-rhapsodists" (*rhapsodi historici*),[40] who ferret out and "stitch together" (*rhapsōidein* in Greek) the units of history, as the epic poets or other narrators "rhapsodized" or "stitched together" the themes and formulas out of the commonplace tradition in their

39. *Theatrum vitae humanae* (Basel: per Ioan. Oporinum, Ambrosium et Aurelium Frobenios fratres, 1565); *Theatrum vitae humanae* (Basel: ex officina Frobeniana, 1571); *Theatrum humanae vitae* (Basel, 1576—I have never seen a copy of this edition, and the only notice of it I have is its listing in *Antiquariats Katalog Nr. 159* [1963] of the bookdealer Joseph van Matt, Stans, Switzerland, who had sold the volume by the time I had contacted him but who assured me by letter dated 3 February 1964, that the 1576 imprint is indeed correct); *Theatrum humanae vitae* (Basel: per Eusebium Episcopium, 1586–87); *Theatrum humanae vitae* (Basel: per Sebastianum Henricpetri, 1604). The *Biographie universelle,* under Zwinger, lists a 1596 edition, of which I have found no other trace. This work of Zwinger's was widely distributed: in libraries at Cambridge University alone I have found twenty-four complete copies of one or another edition. King's *Intercollegiate Catalogue* at the Bodleian Library lists fourteen copies in libraries at Oxford.

40. Theodor Zwinger, *Theatrum vitae humanae* [in later editions, *Theatrum humanae vitae*] (Basel, 1571), p. 11. Zwinger may have picked up the term from Sabellicus, one of his many sources. See *Enneades Marci Antonii Sabellici ab urbe condita ad inclinationem Romani Imperii* (Venice, 1498), where Sabellicus uses the term *rhapsodia historiarum,* "a rhapsody of histories," in headings (e.g. fol. aaii) as well as in his *Prefatio* and his concluding "M. Antonius Sabellicus Democrito." But I find no evidence here of any theory of his about *rhapsodia.* Sabellicus refers to various sources and has a general feeling that history is "woven" out of *exempla* ("fartum et tectum inde opus," "a Venetiae civitatis conspectu totam . . . texui historiam"—fol. [GGviiiᵛ]).

oral performances. In Zwinger a new feel for the management of the textual store of knowledge in terms of constituent particulars is simultaneously in contact with the commonplace tradition (itemize and classify for re-use in discourse) and with some kind of more or less Baconian notion of scientific induction (itemize and classify to discover "rules" or "laws").

Zwinger's ponderous work is a product of the Basel milieu, not only financially, but also psychologically and genealogically. Zwinger's mother was the sister of the Basel printer Iohannes Oporinus and Zwinger had close personal connections with other printers: he lodged in Lyons for three years with the printer Bering, was financed on a trip to Italy by the Basel printer Peter Perna, and married Boniface Amerbach's sister-in-law.[41] The *Theatrum humanae vitae* (or, in the first two editions, 1565 and 1571, *Theatrum vitae humanae*) builds largely on the compiling work undertaken earlier by Zwinger's father-in-law, Conrad Lycosthenes (Wolffhardt), a continuator of Erasmus' compilations who has been noted here earlier as editor of some late printings of Ravisius Textor's *Officina*.

In the last edition (1586–87) of the *Theatrum humanae vitae* to appear before his own death, Zwinger lists 510 authors as sources. His son Jakob slightly enlarged the posthumous 1604 edition, which is dedicated to the Triune God—who else? Probably no mere creaturely dedicatee could have survived the now over 5,000 dense pages. Jakob added new *exempla*, especially recent ones, and—an important point noted earlier and to be returned to later—improved the indices. These list 601 authors.[42]

The *Theatrum*, in all editions, undertakes to treat universal history in terms of the good and evil of mankind,[43] and consists

41. For a biographical account of Zwinger, besides the ordinary bio-bibliographical reference works, see Johannes Karcher, *Theodor Zwinger und seine Zeitgenossen: Episode aus dem Ringer der Basler Ärzte um die Grundlehren der Medizin in Zeitalter des Barocks,* Studien zur Geschichte der Wissenschaften in Basel, 3 (Basel: Verlag von Helbling und Lichtenhahn, 1956).

42. The 1604 edition, with some slight variations, is largely a page-for-page resetting of the 1586–87 edition.

43. *Theatrum vitae humanae* (1571), p. 10, "Proscenia."

entirely of short excerpts from published sources. By history in terms of the good and evil of mankind Zwinger appears in fact to mean a large proportion of everything that has ever happened, since there is little in the world which cannot be related directly or deviously to man, for his good or evil. Zwinger's range is quite as indiscriminate as Textor's. The various sections of the work treat good and bad things of the soul, of the body, good and bad chance occurrences, instruments of philosophy (grammar, rhetoric, poetic, logic), practical philosophical habits (including legislation, history, and worth or dignity), temperance and intemperance, money, refinement (as opposed to flattery and fastidiousness), religious and secular justice, mechanical skills (in artists, workmen, craftsmen), the solitary, academic, religious, political, and economic life of man, not to mention other headings.

In all subjects Zwinger casts his net wide. For example, his chapter "De prudentia inventrice bellica sive de strategematis,"[44] a title which we can render "On Inventive Prudence in Warfare, or Strategems," he includes material under the following classifications: conscription of strong men; elimination of the cowardly; conscription willy-nilly; conscription by wager; segregation of the suspect and perfidious and rebellious; military haircuts and beards; deception of the enemy by simulated victory, retreat, peace, friendliness, or by use of smoke, snow, or statues, of fire, gestures, clubs, and noises of all sorts, or by use of the human voice, either through shouting or through the utterance of enigmas; the amassing and conservation of resources; treachery and desertion; the use and misuse of fortifications; the crossings of seas, lakes, rivers; avoidance of wild animals and snakes; kindness toward one's own forces; avarice and desire for booty; the hope of happiness, glory, victory, freedom; etc. His *exempla* include items such as an account of a betting system to recruit oarsmen for galleys[45] and an anecdote (vol. VII, lib. iii) from Frontinus telling how Hannibal induced his reluctant elephants to cross the Rhône by having one of his men slash an elephant under

44. *Theatrum humanae vitae* (1586–87), vol. VII, lib. iii.
45. *Theatrum humanae vitae* (1586–87), p. 1768 (vol. VII, lib. iii).

the ear and then run to the river and swim across with the en-
raged elephant and all his elephant friends in pursuit.[46] A little
later (vol. VII, lib. v) Zwinger is off in another direction with
a series of anecdotes on the fervor of the Anabaptists.[47] He
apologizes in his introduction for not doing a more comprehensive job, noting that collectors of "special places" (in Aristotle's
sense, as contrasted with "common" places), such as those having
to do with oratory or grammar or poetry or sepulchres or mar-
riages or banquets, can do more thorough work than those who,
like himself, are "rhapsodists" of universal history and thus
attempt to excerpt and string together everything that was ever
said on anything.[48]

In breaking down into excerpts and reorganizing the extant
noetic store, Zwinger's aims and his epistemology are beyond a
doubt not only typographically but also topographically conditioned. His title *Theatrum . . .* , matched in scores of other
late sixteenth- and seventeenth-century "theater" titles,[49] advertises his visualist noetics. He explains that the twenty volumes of
the *Theatrum* are in fact twenty scenes.[50] Zwinger thinks of the
printed page as a map on which knowledge itself is laid out. Over
and over again he compares his work to that of geographers and
cartographers. Like geographers, he describes only the larger
places (*loci*) into which he wants to "distribute" his materials,
relegating the "little places" (*locula*) to special supplements.[51]
The spatial implications in the classical notion of the *loci* as
mental "places" where arguments can be located are realized
with a vengeance here, as is true throughout the Ramist tradition[52] in which, to a significant degree, Zwinger operates. The

46. Theodorus Zwingerus, *Theatrum humanae vitae* (1586–87), p. 1811.
47. Ibid., p. 1946.
48. Theodorus Zwingerus, *Theatrum humanae vitae* (Basel: Sebastianus
Henricpetri, 1604), fol. [ ) : ( ) : (5ᵛ].
49. I have accumulated, incidentally, a collection of several dozen such
titles: theaters of botany, of chemistry, of celestial wisdom, of universal
nature, of peace, of consumption (diseases), of God's judgments, of hydro-
technic machines, of politics, of poetry, etc.
50. *Theatrum humanae vitae* (1571), p. 32.
51. "In suos locos distribuenda"—*Theatrum humanae vitae* (1604), fol.
[ ) : ( ) : (5ᵛ].
52. See Ong, *Ramus, Method, and the Decay of Dialogue,* pp. 310–313.

original "places" in the mind, a highly metaphorical conception, have here been transmuted into physical places on the printed page. Zwinger's ranging of *exempla* under titles (*tituli*) is likened to the plotting of travels such as those of Alexander the Great and of Ulysses, and to the geometrical work of Archimedes.[53] In a like vein Peter Ramus had undertaken to organize knowledge in accordance with "Solon's Law," a building code for ancient Athens specifying how far apart houses and walls and other structures had to be—the different bodies of knowledge were to be kept separate from one another in a similar way.[54]

Zwinger's concern for a topography of the mind goes hand in hand with an interest in physical topography. His works include a *Methodus apodemica,* in which he undertakes an outline of how to travel and to describe what one encounters. The work is remarkable for, among other things, a Ramist approach to art and art history: in a typically Ramist dichotomized diagram Zwinger analyzes Verrocchio's equestrian statue of Bartolomeo Colleoni in Venice, plotting the statue in terms of its four causes (material, formal, efficient, and final) so thoroughly as to include a full historical treatment even of the vandalism to which the statue had been subjected.[55] The Basel physician was an omnibus dissectionist in the tradition which gives rise to, among other things, Burton's *Anatomy of Melancholy* and the scores of other "anatomy" titles of the age.[56]

53. Zwinger, ibid.

54. Ong, *Ramus, Method, and the Decay of Dialogue,* pp. 280–281.

55. Theodor Zwinger (Zwingerus), *Methodus apodemica in eorum gratiam qui fructu in quocumque tandem vitae genere peregrinari cupiunt, a Theod. Zwinger Basiliense typis delineata et cum aliis tum quatuor praesertim Athenarum vivis exemplis illustrata, cum indice* (Basel: Eusebii Episcopii opera atque impensis, 1577), p. 398 (lib. iv, cap. ii—the chapter consists entirely of the dichotomized outline, with no other text). The four "Athens" which Zwinger treats are Basel (the Swiss Athens), Paris (the French Athens), Padua (the Italian Athens), and Athens (the Greek Athens). The book is not unlike a modern travel guide in the miscellaneous information it conveys, although a modern traveller would be put off by Zwinger's procrustean organization (the causes, accidents, and species of travel) and by finding himself presented not with "travel suggestions" but with "rules" (*regulae*) for travellers.

56. The number of "anatomy" titles from the mid-1500s through the 1600s has never been calculated, so far as I know. I have accumulated some thirty or so, quite incidentally, mostly of English works—anatomies of the

Zwinger is an outspoken admirer and follower of Ramus, whom he had known when the latter was visiting in Basel in 1569 and who praises Zwinger's *Theatrum* in his *Basilea*[57]—one of the rare Ramist doctors of medicine, for physicians were commonly the most adamant of Ramus' numerous opponents. Zwinger undertakes the organization of his (ultimately) more than five thousand pages of material through Ramist dichotomized outline charts, which introduce each section of the *Theatrum humanae vitae* to show how the heads within the section and the quotations under each head all articulate. Charts on successive pages are linked to one another by asterisks or daggers or other typographical symbols, one of which will be affixed to one of the final brackets of a given page and then will recur at the head of the bracket display on a subsequent page to indicate where the subsequent outline is to be hooked onto the preceding to continue the dichtomized divisions.

Visually neat, the result is so complicated as to be psychologically quite unmanageable. The reader is paralysed by overorganized structural detail. And, in fact, although his *Theatrum humanae vitae* consists entirely of a fabric of citations in the full-blown commonplace tradition, Zwinger has lost all sense of the oral roots of the tradition. His excerpts are hardly conceived of as serving "invention," as providing matter to be fed back into the stream of discourse, the way Textor's had been. Rather, Zwinger's aim is to tidy up knowledge by collecting in snippets everything everyone has said with a view to arranging all the snippets in proper, visually retrievable, order, so that, in a historical "rhap-

mind, of valor, of abuses, of a lover's flatteries, of fortune, of sin, of the world, etc. There are many more anatomy titles of course in Latin and the other vernaculars. Passing references to the anatomy literature are to be found in L. A. Beaurline, "Ben Jonson and the Illusion of Completeness," *PMLA*, 84 (1969), 51–59, and in Karl Josef Höltgen, "Synoptischen Tabellen in der medizinischen Literatur und die Logik Agricolas und Ramus," *Sudhoffs Archiv für Geschichte der Medizin und der Naturwissenschaften* (Wiesbaden: Franz Steiner Verlag), Band 79, Heft 4 (1965), 371–390—this latter study treats Zwinger at some length and explicitly connects the "anatomy" with Ramist dichotomized tables.

57. *Petri Rami Basilea ad senatum populumque Basiliensem* [Lausanne: Ioannes Probus] 1571), pp. 18–19.

sody," as explained here above, one can at long last find out why things are the way they are. Good Ramist that he was, Zwinger felt that somehow the thousands of quotations ranged "logically" in his text represented in some vague way the "structure" of the human lifeworld, the microcosm, and thus in some fashion, no doubt, the macrocosm as well.

The idea of diagrammatic organization has overwhelmed Zwinger without his quite knowing what has happened to him. The same idea would overwhelm many of his Swiss compatriots, for the typographic collecting drive and also the Ramist dichotomized outline appear to have enjoyed a vogue in Basel and elsewhere in Switzerland which they never quite achieved in other parts of the West. Zwinger's mentality may appear today curiously bemused in its addiction to noetic cartography, but the same drive toward consummate tidiness which produced this cartography would continue to manifest itself through the next two centuries in the Cartesian addiction to clarity and distinctness, and, even more conspicuously in the folding chart of knowledge, the *système figuré,* which at the opening of Diderot's and d'Alembert's *Encyclopédie* (1751–1772) epitomizes Enlightenment noetics.

In fact, the use of Ramist dichotomized outline diagrams, by Zwinger and so many others, for all its somewhat zany ineffectuality, was not entirely wrong-headed even though it had more limitations than Ramists might allow. For the Ramist outline would eventually have its day. In its binary organization, as anyone who knows computer programming sees immediately, the Ramist dichotomized outline is in fact nothing other than a computer flow chart. One can, however, hardly have a successful computer operation until one has a computer. This neither Ramus nor Zwinger had, but there can be little doubt that both would have welcomed one.

Ravisius Textor and his congeners, such as Zwinger, I hope it is clear, had no way of viewing what they were doing in the perspectives suggested here—which, it might be noted again, are by no means the only perspectives for viewing the commonplace enterprise of the Renaissance. These perspectives appear useful largely because they help show how, with the emergence of typography, the human imagination, conditioned for thousands of years in the orally grounded commonplace methods of processing the noetic stores of a culture, was evolving new ways of organizing this store outside consciousness, in the silent tidiness of exactly duplicable, printed texts. Yet, even after print, storage processes proper to the original oral culture or manuscript culture, with the latter's very heavy oral residue, persisted through many generations: that is to say, the drive to consider what had been said as demanding perpetual reiteration continued strong. Academia still felt the last thrust of the drive in *gradus ad Parnassum* or metrical Latin phrase books which persisted through the nineteenth century, providing schoolboys with set excerpts and expressions for the construction of Latin verse. Today in technological cultures, however, commonplace collections, or their equivalents, are quite peripheral to serious discourse, being restricted largely to dictionaries of jokes and of quotations compiled basically for desperate after-dinner speakers rather than for the serious playwrights, teachers, scholars, and scientists for whom Renaissance collections (and earlier collections) were typically prepared. In the Renaissance, the commonplace material to which Kristeller rightly draws attention was still part of the grist demanded for even the first-rate intellect.

An oral culture can make no lists of commonplaces, for lists demand writing, but, as has been suggested in the first section of this study, following Havelock, such a culture has as its commonplace collections the formal oral performances such as orations or narrative poetry or prose or other poetry, for these performances are most beautifully woven ("rhapsodized") textures of formulaic materials. The *Iliad*, it will be remembered, not only weaves together fixedly thematic and formulaic materials ("the rosy-fingered dawn," "the wine-dark sea," and so on) but actually includes a nearly four-hundred-line roster of the Greek leaders and their followers. This roster is presented in formulaic fashion itself, but it is a kind of oral equivalent of a list, an oral version of

Ravisius Textor's and Zwinger's printed compilations. An oral culture's poems are the equivalent of commonplace collections (though they are other things besides).

It is of considerable interest that the Renaissance itself still preserved a strong sense that this is what poems and/or other "inventions" were, *inter alia*—assemblages of commonplace materials to which other poets could resort for the matter of their own poems. The Elizabethan anthology is typically presented to its reader not simply as an anthology would be presented today, that is, as a collection of works to enjoy. It is also presented as a collection of materials to be used. *Anthologia* is the Greek word for which the Latin *florilegium* is a calque: both mean etymologically "flower collection," for which the English equivalent is "posies," a term which figures in not a few Elizabethan collections of poems. The conceptual apparatus of "flowers" and "collecting" is tied in with the massive tradition of rhetorical invention (which includes poetic invention) running back into classical antiquity and thence to the oral sources of literature. "Flowers" imply the busy rhetorical "bee" who goes through the garden (or, at times, the forest) of invention to visit the "places" (*loci, topoi*) from which "arguments" are to be extracted. From the garden he gathers nectar to make honey (orations or poems). These themselves can be constituted as bouquets of flowers, in which "arguments" are artfully arranged now rather than naturally grown, and which are still interesting to industrious bees. One goes to an anthology thus conceived not merely to enjoy oneself but also to make out of what one can extract from the "inventions" there other "inventions" or poems of one's own. This is the ideology in play in the titles of anthologies such as John Bodenham's *Belvedere, or the Garden of the Muses* (1600) or John Proctor's *A Gorgeous Gallery of Gallant Inventions* (1578) or Clement Robinson's *A Handfull of Pleasant Delights* (1584).

In this tradition, with a certain effort, not entirely unwarranted, the commonplace book itself can be viewed as a kind of literary genre. If narratives taking shape within oral cultures, such as the *Iliad* or the *Odyssey* or *Beowulf* (or, in the present, the countless similarly formulaic tales and other verbal performances being transcribed in oral cultures everywhere today, particularly in the Third World), are collections of commonplaces in the sense of formulaic materials stitched together in a narrative frame, or if the classical oration is largely a collection of commonplaces framed for persuasion, the commonplace book is a collection of similar materials ranged in a more abstract frame. To this extent, Textor's two collections examined here and Zwinger's more ponderous assemblage and the hundreds of other collections like these three, are in a way more of a piece with the original oral epic than later epics are, such as Milton's *Paradise Lost* or even Virgil's *Aeneid*.[58] The collections of stock materials and the old epics belong to the same noetic world—the world of commonplace thinking. Milton has his share of stock epithets, but he was literate enough to want to minimize them if not to avoid them totally; for fully literate cultures, by contrast with oral cultures, teach their members that verbalization should avoid clichés. (In *The Faerie Queene,* however, it might be noted, for reasons which heretofore have never been fully explained, Spenser uses epithets with many of the techniques and with almost all the abandon of an oral poet, though this is a conspicuously literate poem.)

In these perspectives Textor and even Zwinger appear, if not as poets, which they certainly are not, at least in some sense as typographical equivalents of Homer—weavers, if not of tales, then at least of the elements of tales. For Homer, and oral poets generally, are more than poets are in technological cultures: they are also encyclopedists, the repositories for the culture's noetic store which they retrieve and organize by "weaving." It is interesting that Textor in Latin actually means "weaver," a meaning which its French form Tixier (Tissier—cf. *tisser,* to weave;

---

58. For the way in which Virgil studiously adapted orally based Homeric similes to the demands of written composition, see Gregory Carlson, *Die Verwandlung der homerischen Gleichnisse in Vergils Äneis* (Heidelberg: Ruprecht-Karl-Universität zu Heidelberg, 1972).

tisserand, weaver) at least suggests. An individual's identity is deeply wrapped up in his name, and who knows the deeper forces of consciousness or of culture which may have helped steer this sixteenth-century humanist into his sometimes bizarre achievements?[59]

Effects on Renaissance Literature:
A Sonnet of Shakespeare's

Robert R. Bolgar has made the point that much Renaissance teaching of rhetoric, and particularly the doctrine of imitation, implies that a literary work consists of an assemblage of individually conceived parts.[60] Although too much can be made of implications, this same piecemeal view of literary composition is obviously also implied by the doctrine of the commonplaces here discussed, and in a special way by the studied exploitation of epithets. For epithets—standard or expected qualifiers or substitutes for given nouns, encoding a certain amount of lore (the *sturdy* oak, the *clinging* vine, the *vain* braggart, etc.)—by and large, are the simplest or at least the smallest bits, the least divisible particles in a rhapsodizer's repertoire. A commonplace disquisition on, say, loyalty might run to a thousand words. An epithet is generally one word, a least common denominator, an atom, in commonplace composition. This is doubtless why Ravisius Textor's collection and others like it were useful for relative neophytes in the art of rhetoric. These collections provided the elemental particles of discourse.

If only because of this paradigmatic status of the epithet in the commonplace tradition, the effects of epithet collections on literature is a subject which warrants far more attention than it has received. Renaissance literature often intoxicates itself on epithets. In Book III, Chapter 38, of *Gargantua and Pantagruel,* Pantagruel and Panurge become dithyrambic over Triboulet's

---

59. One thinks immediately also of Ramus, whose name in both this Latin form and in its original French form, La Ramée, means "branch" and who specialized in branched dichotomized outlines or "ramifications" of knowledge, as has been noted here above.

60. Bolgar, *The Classical Heritage and Its Beneficiaries,* pp. 271–273.

unparalleled qualifications as a fool, heaping up some 207 different epithets (some of them quite bizarre, rather than standard,
qualifiers, but forced ironically to serve as epithets anyhow) to
specify exactly what kind of a fool Triboulet is. This is only one
of many such chains of epithets in Rabelais' work. It would be
interesting to check such epithetic dithyrambs in detail against
individual epithet collections and interesting, too, to check John
Lyly's, Thomas Nashe's, or by contrast, Thomas Deloney's prose
against such collections. So, too, with poetry: a recent study
views epithetic poetry as a minor genre under which some of
George Herbert's sonnets can be classified.[61]

In the study of the effects of epithet collections on literature
Ravisius Textor's *Epitheta* must be accorded close attention.
T. W. Baldwin has shown at great length that this work was one
of the most esteemed and most used books for the writing of
Latin and English in Shakespeare's day, and that Shakespeare
himself might well have used it.[62] Ascham's invective against the
book itself attests clearly to Textor's popularity, at the grammar
school level especially.[63]

In a programmatically repetitive milieu such as that of the
commonplace books, one must be careful, of course, in ascribing
any given literary production to a particular commonplace book
as a source. But sometimes startling instances of correspondences
leap to the eye, especially in works or passages which are largely
cascades of epithets. Such an instance is one of Shakespeare's best
known poems, his Sonnet 129, which suggests how deliberately

61. Virginia R. Mollenkott, "George Herbert's Epithet-Sonnets," *Genre,*
5 (1972), 131–137.
62. *William Shakspere's Small Latine and Lesse Greeke,* I, 174; II, 366,
414–16, 455, 508.
63. "Grammar schools have few *epitomes* to hurt them, except *Epitheta
Textoris,* and such beggarly gatherings as Horman, Wittinton, and other
like vulgars for making of Latins"—Roger Ascham, *The Schoolmaster*
(1570), ed. Lawrence V. Ryan (Ithaca, N.Y.: Cornell University Press,
1967), pp. 106–107. It is clear from the context that Ascham is taking
"epitome" to refer to any edition of Textor's *Epitheta* or *Officina,* not simply
to the abridged editions of the *Epitheta* got up by later editors under the
title *Epitome epithetorum.* Indeed "epitome" for Ascham refers pretty much
to commonplace collections in the wide generic sense in which I have been
using the term "commonplace collections" here.

and directly Textor's *Epitheta* may at times have been used. The sonnet treats of lust and its consummation—but in reverse: first briefly (one and one-half lines) of the consummation of lust ("lust in action") and then retrospectively, in the rest of the poem, of lustful desires ("till action, lust").

> Th'expense of spirit in a waste of shame
> Is lust in action; and till action, lust
> Is perjur'd, murd'rous, bloody, full of blame,
> Savage, extreme, rude, cruel, not to trust;
> Enjoy'd no sooner but despised straight;
> Past reason hunted; and no sooner had,
> Past reason hated, as a swallow'd bait
> On purpose laid to make the taker mad:
> Mad in pursuit, and in possession so;
> Had, having, and in quest to have, extreme;
> A bliss in proof, and prov'd a very woe;
> Before a joy propos'd, behind, a dream.
> All this the world well knows; yet none know well
> To shun the heaven that leads men to this hell.

This poem is almost entirely a piling up of epithets.[64] If we turn in Textor's *Epitheta* to the two key terms with which Shakespeare is concerned, *luxuria* or *luxuries* (both these forms occur in Latin) for "lust in action" and *libido* for lustful desires ("till action, lust"), we find striking equivalents for every epithet in this sonnet, and indeed often two or three Latin terms for one or another English word. Shakespeare's keynote for his sonnet, lust's wastefulness, is sounded loud and clear by the very first epithet supplied by Textor under *luxuria* (*luxuries*), the epithet *prodiga* (spendthrift, extravagant, wasteful), represented in Shakespeare's first line by "expense" and by "waste."

---

64. Other connections of the poem have been pointed out which do not invalidate or contravene the connection with the commonplace tradition examined here and which, indeed, often corroborate or further specify this connection. See, for example, Douglas L. Peterson, "A Probable Source for Shakespeare's Sonnett CXXIX," *Shakespeare Quarterly*, 5 (1954), 381–384, which notes relationships between the sonnet and rhetorical schemes such as those discussed in Thomas Wilson's *Arte of Rhetorique*. The schemes Peterson treats are admirably suited to the exploitation of epithets, and are themselves from commonplace books.

Some of the correspondence between Textor's Latin and Shakespeare's English can be noted here, with Textor's Latin terms beneath the word (italicized) in Shakespeare's text which they suggest.

Th'*expense* of spirit in a *waste* of *shame*
    prodiga   prodiga   prava, nefanda, infamis,
                                     turpis, impudens
Is *lust* in action, and *till action, lust*
   (LUXURIES)   (LIBIDO)
Is *perjur'd, murd'rous, bloody, full of blame*
    fallax   scelerata   flagitiosa probrosa, vitiosa, nefaria
Savage,   *extreme,*   *rude,*   *cruel, not to trust*
immoderata, intemperata refrenanda saeva fallax
indomita
Enjoyed no sooner but *despised straight*
blanda   odiosa
Past reason hunted, and no sooner had
inconsulta, intemperans, avida
Past reason hated, as a *swallowed bait*
foeda   occulta, personata, astuta
On purpose laid to make the taker *mad*
                           rabida, insana, furens,
                           vecors
Mad in pursuit,   and *in possession so*
praeceps, effrenata,   saeviens, dira
impetuosa
Had, having, and in quest to have, *extreme*
                        infrenata
A bliss in proof, and prov'd a *very woe*
blanda, fervens   aerumnosa, intolerabilis,
                       noxia
Before a joy proposed; behind, a dream
illecebrosa   perdita, vana
All this the world well knows, yet none knows well
To shun the *heaven*   that leads men to this *hell.*
    carnis amica   perniciosa,
                          damnosa

This exploitation of epithets, encouraged by Textor and the commonplace tradition generally, can strike an age committed to romantic originality and "creativity" as devastatingly artificial, unrelated to the human world. But to Shakespeare the use of epithets seemed quite the opposite, eminently human and urbane. "All this the world well knows." How? By experience? Yes, certainly. But by direct experience? Hardly. The store of experience with which Shakespeare's sonnet resonates would certainly take a great deal of time to accumulate. Moreover, as Roger Ascham (1515 or 1516–1568) had just reminded readers of *The Schoolmaster* (1570—published posthumously by Ascham's widow), experience is the worst teacher: too many die from it before they learn, or even after they have learned, for the lessons experience teaches can prove fatal.

Learning teacheth more in one year than experience in twenty, and learning teacheth safely, when experience maketh more miserable than wise. He hazardeth sore that waxeth wise by experience. An unhappy master he is that is made cunning by many shipwrecks; a miserable merchant, that is neither rich nor wise but after some bankrupts. It is costly wisdom that is brought by experience.[65]

A mature person must have a lot of experience—indeed, more than anyone can have time for directly—but if a person is truly mature, he or she can, and must, supplement direct experience by vicarious and empathetic experience. Even direct experience is normally the richer for the vicarious experience brought to it. Shakespeare was hardly so callow as to believe that all readers of his sonnet would have experienced directly all the degrees of disillusionment that his sonnet deals with, or that they needed to have experienced them directly, or even that it would have been helpful if they had. Experiences of the sort he is concerned with here would not always leave the sensibility intact enough to appreciate this sonnet or any other. Many would normally be destructive experiences, even though not always irreparable.

"All this the world well knows." How then, if not simply from direct experience? From Ravisius Textor, of course, or from his equivalents and thus from the total experience of the vast culture which Textor's excerpts sample. That is to say, from all the

65. Ascham, *The Schoolmaster,* ed. Ryan, p. 50.

literature of classical antiquity—a literature based indeed in one way or another on experience, direct and/or indirect, matured over hundreds of years of classical and postclassical, largely Christian, reflection, and by reflection on reflection. The age's restriction of its references—in principle if not in full actuality— to classical antiquity of course strikes us today as quaint and parochial. There was, after all, much more to mankind's experience than what Mediterranean civilization provided. But at least the civilization built around and in great part out of Mediterranean classical antiquity was large enough in time and in space to provide a sizable body of experience, the most sizable and viable body in fact that anyone in Shakespeare's West had access to. You work with the best you know.

In these perspectives Shakespeare's value becomes once more that of a skilful conservator and reflector of the amassed wisdom of a sizable portion of the human race. Like his contemporaries generally, Shakespeare was not original in the way in which poets since the romantic age have often programed themselves to be original. He did not "create" from nothing. He did not want to, nor did he even consider the possibility. (There is no such possibility.) He wanted to rework the old wisdom in an always fresh and meaningful way. Shakespeare is perhaps our most quotable author in English, or at least the most quoted. It is, or should be, a commonplace that the reason he is quotable is that his text consists so much of quotations—not grossly appropriated, but nuanced, woven into the texture of his work more tightly than is normally possible in any performance, no matter how sophisticated, in the oral tradition, in which the practice of composing out of other compositions is nevertheless grounded, as has been seen. Shakespeare appropriated the oral tradition and exploited it with the condensation and pointedness made possible by writing and even more by print.

And yet the tradition which Shakespeare here exploits in Sonnet 129 and elsewhere in his works—the individual reader can study out for himself where else and how—was moribund at the very time Shakespeare was using it to the maximum. By now it is gone, at least in its Renaissance form. We cannot compose in this way any more. When the heritage of the past is exploited with comparable deliberateness and calculation today, and with comparable effect, it comes out, as in James Joyce's *Ulysses* or *Finnegans Wake,* woven into infinitely more complications than even Shakespeare managed—or wanted to manage—and into different kinds of complications. Shakespeare's world was not what ours is in its relationship to the store of human knowledge—which store itself was different from ours, though not discontinuous with ours. Shakespeare belonged to a world in which typographical culture had not had its full impact, a world in which the accumulation of circumstantial information, vast as it was, could not match that at hand today, and in which information could not be codified so neatly as it can in our superindexed books and supercatalogued libraries and superprogramed electronic computers.

But Shakespeare's world was moving toward ours. With typography and the possibilities it brought of greater codification, the age of intensified information-collecting was beginning to succeed the age more given to utterance-collecting. Soon commonplace collections, which were essentially collections of what persons had said (or, later, written), would be absorbed and superseded by encyclopedias in the modern sense, beginning with the primitive "methodized" works of Johann Heinrich Alsted and terminating in such works as today's *Britannica,* which set before the reader stores of "data" and "information." Encyclopedia users today commonly do not advert to the fact that even today encyclopedia articles, and even dictionary definitions, still represent something that someone "says" (writes) about a subject. There is no way to lay hold of a "fact" without some kind of intervention of voice. But we live in a world which tends to feel that pure "facts," without voice, are there, "contained" in the silent, visible words which are contained in the sentences which are contained in the paragraphs which are contained in the pages which are contained in the volume which is contained in the set which can be located with the help of a trustworthy and convincingly abstract system

(Dewey or Library of Congress) upon a specified shelf contained in the library.

Shakespeare lived on the verge of this supercodification or superlocalization of the noetic world. But in Shakespeare's day, the codifying, localizing process was in great part still turned primarily not toward purportedly nonvocalized "data" but quite overtly toward sayings, which had been the proper preoccupation of the original oral culture of mankind and which remained a major preoccupation of the residually oral culture of the Renaissance. Without decrying our vast expansion of the noetic world and our need to deal with "facts"—perhaps more gingerly and critically than we usually do—we can ask ourselves whether any poetry or literature can forgo delving into the commonplace world of sayings, of communal memory, from which Shakespeare and Ravisius Textor drew, whether it can bypass the wisdom stored in what men and women out of the past have said about actuality and about their experience, matured by subsequent reflection, and sharpened and driven home. It would appear quite feasible to demonstrate that where modern literature is at its peak it retains a living connection of some sort with the commonplace tradition, and when it is poor its poverty is due to its failure to establish this connection—which is to say to its ignorance of itself, of how it comes to be where it is. The older we get, the more mature our literature deserves to be.

7

From Epithet to Logic: Miltonic
Epic and the Closure of Existence

In 1672, two years before his death, John Milton published a logic textbook which he had written, it is quite certain, sometime in the years 1641–1647, and most probably sometime during the years 1645–1647, when he was teaching his two nephews and some other boys. The work is in Latin, as textbooks in all subjects normally had always been in Western Europe from classical times. Milton's concern with logic, evinced by this book, shows itself throughout the corpus of his writings, as many modern studies have made clear.[1] Nowhere perhaps does this concern show itself more than in *Paradise Lost*. It is to certain questions raised by this fact that the present chapter addresses itself.

I

About Milton as logician, one thing can readily be said: he contributed nothing to the internal development of logic, directly or indirectly. *Ioannis Miltoni Artis logicae plenior institutio ad Petri Rami methodum concinnata* (London, 1672), despite its title styling it . . . *Milton's* . . . *Logic* . . . , is essentially no more than an edition of Ramus' *Dialectica* or *Logica* incorporating minor Miltonic idiosyncrasies and a commentary which is largely George Downame's. And Ramus' *Dialectica* itself was

1. Modern studies of Milton's use of logic and of his references to logic in his various works are too numerous to mention here. I have reviewed most of them in the Introduction to the forthcoming English-language edition of Milton's *Logic* (the short English title here used for Milton's Latin work) referred to in n. 4 below. Questions concerning the dating of the *Logic* are also treated in this Introduction.

scientifically uneventful. To the internal development of logic
Ramus had contributed only "random simplification," as Jennifer
Ashworth has neatly put it.[2]

And yet Ramus' logic, and with it Milton's, is highly significant
in the evolution of consciousness, which is to say in the extension
of consciousness into the areas of life formerly preempted by the
unconscious and subconscious. More than most logics, Ramist
logic satisfied an inarticulated desire for closure, for order subject totally to the surveillance of consciousness. Ramist logic was
in effect the perfect closed system: for it contained "method" as
one of its parts, and method prescribed how the logic that contained it was to be organized and consequently how all thought
was to be organized "logically" as a collection of closed fields
separated from one another by "Solon's Law," invoked by Ramus
for noetic organization though devised originally for plotting real
estate in ancient Greece.[3] Milton is at one with Ramus in situating method within logic. He is more explicit than Ramus in
making clear that the "one and only method" of proceeding from
the more general to the more particular applies properly to the
interior organization of knowledge after it has been discovered
and not to discovery as such, and he leaves to orators and poets
rather than to logicians the study of the reversals and other con-
cealments of method (*crypsis methodi*) which are warranted by
audiences not entirely amenable to logic.[4] But method is as integral a part of Milton's as of any other Ramist logic.

In Milton's case, Ramist logic is particularly significant because of its juncture in Milton's own sensibility with the epic
tradition, which itself serves as an important index of the evolu-

2. E. J. Ashworth, "Some Notes on Syllogistic in the Sixteenth and
Seventeenth Centuries," *Notre Dame Journal of Formal Logic*, 11 (1970), 20.

3. Petrus Ramus, *Scholarum rhetoricarum libri XX*, in *Scholae in liberales
artes* (Basel: E. Episcopius et Nicolai fratris haeredes, 1569), cols. 255–256,
also in cols. 237–238, 292, etc.

4. *Artis logicae plenior institutio*, lib. ii, c. xviii, in *The Works of John
Milton*, ed. and trans. Allan H. Gilbert (New York: Columbia University
Press, 1935), IX, 474, 484. A new edition in new English translation by
Walter J. Ong and Charles J. Ermatinger is scheduled for publication soon
by Yale University Press in vol. 8 of *The Complete Prose Works of John
Milton*.

tion of consciousness. The original oral epic derives from and registers an oral noetic economy, in which knowledge was conceived, stored, recalled, and circulated largely through narratives about "heavy" or heroic figures. Heroic figures, as Havelock's work suggests, are typical not simply of epic as such, but of oral cultures as such.[5] To store and retrieve its knowledge, an oral culture must think in heavily patterned forms facilitating recall—antitheses, epithets, assertive rhythms, proverbs, and other formulas of many sorts. Without these, in a purely oral culture thinking is impossible, for, without writing, unless one's articulated thoughts occur in heavy mnemonic patterns they cannot be retained or retrieved. Oral cultures do not add antitheses, proverbs, and other formulas and mnemonic patterning to their thought: their thought consists in such elements from the start. In a completely oral noetic economy, thought which does not consist in memorable patterns is in effect nonthought: you can normally never get it back again. Not merely poetry, but serious discourse of all sorts in such a culture is thus of necessity formulaic—mythology, jurisprudence (consisting in maxims, proverbs, and other sayings and formulas), administrative directives, and the rest.

Heroes are indigenous to this noetic economy. The hero is always a type character, a kind of elaborate personalized formula, such as wise Nestor, wily Odysseus, furious Achilles, a weighted, standardized figure hung with appropriate cultural values or antivalues. In their early, oral stage of learning, children today of course profit from such figures, common in fairy stories, movies, and other productions for children's audiences. Formulary sayings and characters make it possible to conceptualize and manipulate sizable bodies of knowledge, but in ways largely dependent on the unconscious and resistant to conscious analysis. An oral culture can articulate only a rudimentary account of how it itself works.

An organized, abstract articulation of any "body" of knowl-

---

5. Eric A. Havelock, *Preface to Plato* (Cambridge, Mass.: Belknap Press of Harvard University Press, 1963), pp. 94, 106–108, 135, 165–193.

edge—for example, an "art" or "science" of war or speechmaking or hunting or farming—in the linear, consciously reflective form taken for granted in written treatises is quite simply unthinkable in a primary oral culture. (There is that much to say, but not much more, for the old anthropological myth of the prelogical "primitive" mind.) Without writing, the mind cannot work that way. To produce orally a work such as Aristotle's *Rhetoric* or *Physics* one would have to proceed by reciting the entire work extempore from end to end. There is not, and there never was, any way to do such a thing. Primary (preliterate) oral cultures are capable of prodigiously complicated and lengthy verbal performances, but these performances are typically formulaic, not analytic, in cast—which is by no means to say that formal oral narratives, for example, such as epics or formal orations are unsophisticated but only that they are illiterate performances, which is not at all the same thing as unsophisticated performances. Oral epic, as Havelock has shown, is of a piece with the rest of oral noetic activity: the epic poet uses superlatively, in his own fashion and for his own artistic purposes, the kinds of thought processes and concurrent expressions that other formal verbalizers in his culture use for their purposes—administrators, mothers teaching their children, messengers, judges, and witch doctors.

By Milton's time, although the formal logic begun in Aristotle's Greece and matured in medieval Western Europe was no longer actively developing, it had been thoroughly interiorized and was affecting the entire noetic world. Formulaic and heroic codification of knowledge had been more and more superseded by abstract or "logical" analysis for reflective and administrative purposes (though great masses of oral residue remained in cultural practices). Ramists were advertizing their "method" for a logical philosophy of everything, and Machiavelli had earlier expedited the reduction even of practical political administration to "logical" maneuvers. With Milton, who was part of the governmental administration under the Commonwealth, the logic which had superseded the old formulaic and heroic noetics extended itself further: it was imported from reflective (philosophical) and administrative life into the epic itself. Milton's announced aim in *Paradise Lost* is logical or analytic ("To justifie the wayes of God to men") and his characters' speeches, most notably those of God the Father, as has frequently been pointed out, are organized like classroom lectures, are "methodized," that is, to use Ramus' terminology. Pope hit the mark: "In Quibbles, Angel and Archangel join / And God the Father turns a School-Divine."[6] The largely subconscious or unconscious design of the original oral epic has been transmuted by more conscious control.

It was by Milton's time impossible—and it remains today impossible—to organize epic in the old way any more. The discrepancy between Renaissance "epic" writers' announced aims and their actual achievement is testimony to this fact. Edmund Spenser's program for his proposed epic, as declared in his letter to Sir Walter Ralegh prefaced to *The Faerie Queene*, stands in bizarre contrast to his actual performance in the work, and the contrast is paradigmatic for sixteenth- and, even more, for seventeenth-century epic writers. By the eighteenth century, most good writers had given up and attempted only mock epics.

The foregoing points I have developed more at length in a recent study.[7] Here I should like to move on from them to pursue somewhat further the logical reorganization in Milton's *Paradise Lost*, but at a level which was more unconscious, if not indeed totally unconscious, on Milton's part. For logic, like epic and everything else in the noetic world, has both a conscious and an

6. *Imitations of Horace,* Ep. II, 101–102. Because the title might suggest the book's immediate relevance here, it might be noted that *The Logical Epic: A Study of the Argument of Paradise Lost* by Dennis H. Burden (Cambridge, Mass.: Harvard University Press, 1967) does not even mention, so far as I can find, Milton's *Logic* or Ramus or anything about the logical tradition in which Milton was educated and thought, but is concerned rather with the general intellectual consistency of Milton's presentation of Christian teaching in *Paradise Lost.* "Logic" in this sense of general intellectual consistency is of course a part of the diffuse Ramist heritage.

7. Walter J. Ong, "Logic and the Epic Muse: Reflections on Noetic Structures in Milton's Milieu," in *Achievements of the Left Hand: Essays on the Prose of John Milton,* ed. Michael Lieb and John T. Shawcross (Amherst, Mass.: University of Massachusetts Press, 1974), pp. 239–268.

unconscious side, as Gilbert Durand, Michael Polanyi, and others have made evident.[8] In particular, I should like to attend to Milton's practice regarding the epithet or its equivalents, and to the way this practice related to Milton's response to logic as a principle of literary organization.

Connections between epithets and logic have not been exactly a commonplace of scholarly discourse. And yet connections become apparent when we think of both epithets and logic as ways of managing knowledge. We can understand epithet here as either an expected, standardized, formulaic qualifier for a noun (the *sturdy* oak, the *brave* warrior, the *bloody* sword, the *rosy-fingered* dawn) or a standardized, formulary substitute-qualifier for another noun (*whale-road* for the sea, the *wise one* for Nestor, the *clever one* for Odysseus). As has already been suggested, epithets, like other formulas, play an essential role in the pre-chirographic patterning of knowledge which marked the original, oral epic and other oral forms. Homer is full of the "rosy-fingered dawn," the "wine-dark sea," "furious Achilles," "wise Nestor," "clever Odysseus," and so on, and in fact is mostly composed of these and other kinds of formulas.[9] He is a "rhapsodizer" in technical Greek terminology, that is, a "stitcher" or "sewer" who fastens such formulas together to make poetry. Oral narrative and other performance elsewhere across the globe have similar features.[10] In Central and West African drum talk, where the

---

8. Durand has pointed out that formal logic is constrained to play down its unconscious affiliations, to treat statements as though everything in them belonged to the *régime diurne,* or conscious side of thought, and nothing to the *régime nocturne,* or unconscious. This somewhat unnatural insistence produces a strain in the psyche and sets up defenses which can result in the quarrelsomeness that Durand, and others, find exceptionally common among formal logicians in all ages. See Gilbert Durand, *Les Structures anthropologiques de l'imaginaire* (Paris: Presses Universitaires, 1963), pp. 453 ff., also pp. 165, 187, 191–199, 472–473. *Cf.* Michael Polanyi, *Personal Knowledge* (Chicago, Ill.: University of Chicago Press, 1958), pp. 87–131.

9. See Albert B. Lord, *The Singer of Tales,* Harvard Studies in Comparative Literature, 24 (Cambridge, Mass.: Harvard University Press, 1964), especially pp. 141–156.

10. See, for example, Jeff Opland, *"Imbongi Nezibongo:* The Xhosa Tribal Poet and the Contemporary Poetic Tradition," *PMLA,* 90 (1975), 185–208. Lord, *op. cit.,* gives other instances from several cultures.

most assertive features of oral performance are amplified almost beyond belief, one of the features most exaggerated is epithetic identification[11]—a fact which further certifies the centrality of the epithet in the oral noetic economy.

II

The work of Milman Parry and Albert B. Lord already noted, and of those whom they cite as well as those who have followed up on their research, makes clear the contrast between oral epic such as Homer's and written epic such as Virgil's in the management of formulaic expressions. But oral traits did not by any means vanish in narrative immediately with the coming of writing. They tapered off gradually and unevenly. By contrast with writing of later periods, Tudor prose style is still strikingly oral.[12] In the epic tradition, Milton is transitional between Spenser and Pope, the three marking rather clear-cut stages in the evolution from an oral noetic economy to fully interiorized literacy as manifest in the use of the epithet.

In a brilliant study on "Oral Form and Written Craft in Spenser's *Faerie Queene*"[13] John Webster has identified the additive and formulary style of Spenser's great poem as fundamentally that of oral performance and has shown how the easy surface flow of the poem (often contrasting with the frequently tangled plot) is due to its oral techniques. Oral performances must flow freely. (One thinks of the Renaissance preoccupation with *copia*, flow, even gush, picked up from the basically oral world of classical rhetoric.) Professor Webster notes in detail the inability of much earlier criticism, including that of the late C. S. Lewis, to come to grips with the style of *The Faerie Queene* because of the critics' unawareness of what orality consists in and because of their consequent indifference to chirographic and

11. See Chapter 4 above.
12. See Walter J. Ong, *Rhetoric, Romance, and Technology* (Ithaca, N.Y.: Cornell University Press, 1971), Ch. 2, "Oral Residue in Tudor Prose Style."
13. *Studies in English Literature,* 16 (1976), 75–93.

typographic styles as developments growing out of an anterior tradition which was necessarily quite different. Webster of course gives considerable attention to Spenser's use of epithets. Here I should like to give the epithets still further attention, in more specialized focus.

The Faerie Queene is as filled with epithets as one might expect the most oral poems to be. Let us take as a sample the word "tree" (singular and plural forms), which is both a recurrent term and one tolerant of diversified contexts, and see what epithetic equipment the term commands. The Osgood *Concordance*[14] gives us such samples as "aged tree," "living tree," "goodly tree" (recurrent), "stately tree," "withered tree," "forked trees," "naked trees," "faire trees," "loftie trees," "high trees," "highest trees," "heavy trees," "tall trees," "trees up-shooting high," "mossy trees." The qualifiers here are all clearly epithetic, standard adjectives such as one anticipates, given the poetic tradition or perhaps given simply the nature of trees. Many others of Spenser's arboreal adjectives are less immediately and less conspicuously epithetic of themselves but in context appear clearly as epithets: "native tree" (recurrent), "wretched tree," "cursed tree," "hung upon a tree" (recurrent), and so on.

The epithets here are metrically serviceable, and one feels that in their abundance they meet one of the needs that epithets meet in oral verse performance generally: they provide a large assortment of ready-made snippets of lines out of which the poet can without delay stitch together his poem. The oral poet cannot afford to pause, and if one compares *The Faerie Queene* to *Paradise Lost,* one feels in the former a sense of flow or even gush, a need to get on with the line, to keep moving, that suggests the oral performer's heavy dependence on *copia,* a sense of flow hardly, if at all, perceptible in Milton's poem. Equipped

---

14. Charles Grosvenor Osgood, *A Concordance to the Poems of Edmund Spenser* (Washington, D.C.: Carnegie Institute of Washington, 1915), p. 893. References to the exact lines in which these epithets occur are given in this *Concordance* and need not clutter the text here.

with an abundance of epithets, with the *copia* which oral performance absolutely demands—for in oral delivery, while pauses may be effective, hesitation is normally a disaster—the oral poet who feels a tree surfacing in his imagination has an abundance of options for maneuvering the tree gracefully into his metric current: aged tree, living tree, native tree, goodly tree, withered tree, and so on.

All but a few of Spenser's prepositive arboreal epithets, the epithets placed before the noun "tree" or "trees," are like these just cited, disyllabic and accented on the first syllable: the far less common monosyllabic prepositive adjectives such as "faire" or "high" take care of less frequent metrical settings. The epithets for individual species in Spenser's catalog of trees in 1. 1. 8–9 draw from the same classical store and commonly satisfy the same metric condition as do the epithets for the word "tree" itself ("the Warlike Beech," "the Fruitful Olive," "the Cyprusse funerall"), though some few epithets for individual species are more enterprising. But besides these epithetic qualifiers that precede their nouns, Spenser has also a whole battery of postpositive epithetic equipment, normally iambic as the antecedent epithets were normally trochaic. Such postpositives would include: "trees of state," "trees yclad" (clothing for trees remains a standard topos all the way down to Joyce Kilmer, who, critics have enjoyed pointing out, appears to have patronized topical bargain basements), "trees so straight and hy," "trees ymounted high," "trees upshooting high."

To illustrate Spenser's commitment to epithetic formulas there is no need here to instance epithets serving other nouns, since these can be dislodged in superabundance simply by leafing through a concordance. Those wanting further accumulations of Spenserian epithets might begin with concordance entries such as "beauty," "cloud," "courage," "grief"—to note a few under early letters of the alphabet. Much further study is called for and many significant patterns could doubtless be isolated. "Grace," for example, as compared to "trees," has limited epithetic equipment, but the equipment is in constant use; over and over again grace is "heavenly" or "soveraine." Such particular patterns, however, are irrelevant here. Our concern is simply the superabundance of epithetic apparatus.

By analogy with nouns, other parts of speech can of course be managed in epithetic fashion—verbs, for example, can command epithet-like adverbs, and so on. But even limited to adjectives and nouns in *The Faerie Queene,* the epithetic equipment in Spenser's imagination appears staggering. For Spenser himself the wealth of equipment was doubtless reassuring: with such an abundance (*copia*) of epithets roiling in his head, he could day after day face with equanimity and perhaps even with joy the otherwise dismaying prospect of writing still another and another and another and another canto. Spenser's imagination enjoyed free play, within bounds, for the bins churned with possibly useful materials as soon as he turned on the machinery. This is the way an oral poet had had to work.

The epithetic equipment Spenser commands relates to other oral features of the style of *The Faerie Queene,* as Webster has shown. The same equipment also relates to Spenser's characterization. Spenser is writing a poem with not merely type characters but with also somewhat abstract characters, characters verging on and at times matching the totally abstract virtues and vices of the morality play. Abstract characters, virtues and vices, emerge from the oral heritage. In the world of abstract categorization opened by writing, the type characters of the old oral tradition were distilled into pure virtues and vices. "Wise Nestor" was replaced by wisdom or sapience, "furious Achilles" by anger. For a new medium normally does not do away with the phenomena associated with the old but, rather, reinforces them and at the same time utterly transforms them. The formal fixity of Spenser's characters—and I am aware that they are not always entirely fixed—and the formal fixity of his epithets are of a piece. Both are part of the ancient oral noetic. Studies of the persistence of the oral formulaic economy in later epics and other literary traditions are now multiplying,[15] but much remains to be done in deepening understanding of the relation of stylistic developments to the profound changes in the entire noetic world, extraliterary as well as literary, brought about by the movement from orality through writing and print.[16] However, despite the tantalizing lacunae in our present knowledge, it does appear that what has been noted here is utterly typical so far as it goes and that it will suffice to make clear some significant differences between Spenser and Milton as they reflect changes in ways of appropriating and managing knowledge and thus in the development of consciousness.

III

When we turn to Milton the state of epithetic affairs is quite different. John Broadbent has very briefly called attention to Milton's use of epithets in *Paradise Lost* as an inheritance of one of the "minor conventions" of the oral epic and has noted that

15. See, for example, Edmund de Chasca, *Registro de formulas verbales en el Cantar de mio Cid* (Iowa City, Ia.: University of Iowa, 1968), or Opland, in the article just cited, which studies the active interlacing of oral and literary practices among the Xhosa. Anyone familiar with the oral and written productions of other peoples of Subsaharan Africa will be able to suggest further materials for study, for perhaps nowhere in human history has the interaction of orality and literacy been more intense than in this part of the world today. The interaction ranges from the basically spontaneous, unreflective, but after a fashion literary, performance found for example in the Onitsha market pamphlets in Nigeria to the exquisitely selfconscious work of novelists such as Gabriel Okara, Chinua Achebe, and (in French) Camara Laye, and of many African scholars in linguistics. On the aforementioned pamphlets, see Emmanuel Obiechina, *An African Popular Literature: A Study of Onitsha Market Pamphlets* (Cambridge: The University Press, 1973).

16. Many or perhaps most studies of epithets are quite unaware of the significance of formulaic structures as such in the evolution of consciousness. See, for example, Bernard Groom, "The Formation and Use of Compound Epithets in English Poetry from 1579," S.P.E. Tract No. 49, *S.P.E. Tracts,* 3 (London: Oxford University Press, 1961), 293–332. Groom finds that in his formation of compound epithets, Spenser "is less modern than Shakespeare, and a great deal less modern than Milton" (p. 299), but says nothing about epithets, compound or other, as diagnostic of various noetic economies, and consequently finds it difficult to specify what being "modern" comes to.

Milton's "use of this device is subtler than Homer's."[17] But it would seem that Milton's use of epithets, rather than being a minor convention of the oral epic, is simply one manifestation of the major feature of all oral thought and expression, reliance on fixed formulas, and that Milton is "subtler" than Homer because he is literate and cannot be quite so formulary even if he tries.

Let us take a look at the entry "tree," with its plural, "trees," in the new Ingram and Swaim *Concordance*,[18] attending to occurrences only in *Paradise Lost*. The first thing one notices is that Milton uses epithets, in the sense of predictable or expected qualifiers or noun substitutes, rather sparingly, even in situations which would seem to invite epithets. In only about a fifth of the occurrences is the word "tree" attended by any adjective at all. Few of the adjectives which do occur are epithetic in the sense of standard, expected: "high," "highest," "fair," "rich," "stately," and "spreading" each occur only once; "goodliest" occurs twice. Certain other qualifiers can be considered epithetic in context. Some adjectives which would be otherwise unexpected appear quite epithetic for the Biblical Tree of Life in the Garden of Eden setting: "forbidden," "fatal," "interdicted," for example, the last two of which are nonce epithets, although "forbidden" occurs as an epithet twice, once in Book 1 and once in Book 10, and again as a predicative in Book 9. But these are all exceptional: some four-fifths of Milton's trees bear no epithetic accoutrements.

A check of other representative nouns in the Milton *Concordance* reveals the same sparsity of epithets for the most part, in spectacular contrast to Spenser's usage. There are some ex-

17. John Broadbent, *Paradise Lost: Introduction* (London: Cambridge University Press, 1972), pp. 131–132.

18. William Ingram and Kathleen Swaim, *A Concordance to Milton's English Poetry* (Oxford: Clarendon Press, 1972), p. 604. Again, references to the exact lines referred to are readily available in this *Concordance* and thus are omitted here to avoid clutter. On Milton's studied "epic reiteration" generally, see Edward S. Le Comte, *Yet Once More: Verbal and Psychological Pattern in Milton* (New York: Liberal Arts Press, 1959), pp. 19–47.

ceptions. For example, terms which have been part and parcel of epic ideology for centuries appear to be more hospitable to epithets than are other terms. Thus, for example, "conquerour" and "conquerours" tend to be "great" or "proudest," though far less frequently than in Spenser, where all of the seven "conquerors" we find tallied carry epithets: five are "mightie" and the other two are respectively "greatest" and "bedecked." Or again, in his catalog of pagan gods in Book 1, which mimics the catalog of ships and captains in Book 2 of the *Iliad,* Milton imitates Homer's epithetic tags: "Dale of *Sibma* clad with Vines" (1. 410) suggests Homer's "Arne, where the grapes hang thick" (1. 436).[19]

A certain kind of epithet which Milton uses calls perhaps for particular comment. This we may style the epithet of literary allusion: "*Thyestean* Banquet" (10. 688), "*Typhoean* rage" (2. 539), "*Thessalian* Pines" (2. 544), "*Stygian* Council" (2. 506), "*Herculean* Samson" (9. 1060), and the like. Such epithets, in our perspectives here, are indeed epithets and yet in another way anti-epithets. They are epithets because they are predictable, at least in the sense that they are adjectives with classical precedent, the kinds of things that Renaissance epithet books such as the *Epitheta* of Ioannes Ravisius Textor will list as part of the standard literary equipment furnished out of classical antiquity.[20] On the other hand, for effectiveness they demand not a listener but a trained reader with a store of information and a disposition to bookish attention which contrasts with the free-flowing, easy, though skilled, spontaneity governing transactions in the kinds of epithets more frequently emerging in the oral tradition. "Thyestean" calls for a detailed knowledge of the history of the house of Atreus; nothing comparable is required for the epithets in Spenser's expressions such as "stately tree," "forked-tree," or "aged tree."

19. I am indebted to Professor Clarence H. Miller of Saint Louis University for this suggestion about the two catalogs and for other comments generously provided.
20. See Chapter 6 above.

Thus these epithets of literary allusion, rather typically Miltonic, are also anti-epithets in the sense that they are expected only by the exceptionally alert bookish person, unexpected by others. In today's parlance, they are "cool" epithets, epithets of low definition, calling for interpretation by the receiver, whereas "stately tree" or "forked tree" are "hot," conveying their message instantly and insistently, without intensive input from the listener: the difference here parallels, for example, that between "hot" jazz (the French *jazzhot*) and "cool" jazz: the latter demands a more sophisticated audience. Needless to say, "cool" epithets are typical of the literary epic, which by contrast with the oral epic is an elitist art form, dependent upon an elitist noetic economy. Milton is in this sense more bookish than Spenser, and probably in other senses, too. It must be remembered, however, that we are considering here only the epithets in *Paradise Lost*. Milton's lyrics utilize more standard epithets, especially when they are pastoral or verging on pastoral, as, for example, "Lycidas." But this raises a different question. "Lycidas" and the other lyrics are not programmatically "logical."[21]

Doubtless, as in Spenser's case, lengthy and close study would reveal other patterns in Milton's use of epithets in *Paradise Lost*, with greater or lesser frequencies of particular kinds of qualifiers in particular situations. But the instances here cited are entirely representative of many others available in the Milton *Concordance*, and they appear quite adequate for present purposes. They show that, so far as the use of epithets goes, Milton's world is a quite different one from Spenser's. In general, we can say that the qualifiers he uses appear to be subject to more personal control, and to belong to a more bookish noetic economy. Spenser's epithets are not careless—far from it, of course. But they are floated into his poem from a tradition in which he has immersed himself in a way not unlike that of the oral poet.[22] Milton's quali-

21. It might be noted that in a study of "Milton's Epithet *Agonistes*," *Studies in English Literature*, 4 (1964), 137–162, Paul R. Sellin has shown the learned, bookish discrimination evinced by Milton in importing this Greek term as an English epithet into the title of *Samson Agonistes*.

22. See Havelock, *Preface to Plato*, pp. 134–142.

fiers are seemingly the product of more personalized, individual-
ized surveillance, rather directly implemented by reading: in his
use of epithets, Milton controls the tradition, whereas in Spenser's
case the tradition is more in control.

IV

This variation in the use of epithets would be less significant
than it is if the sixteenth and seventeenth centuries had been less
attentive to epithets than they in fact were. The poetics of Spenser's and Milton's age concerned itself about epithets with an
intensity we find hard to believe, so that we often do not know
what Rabelais is spoofing in his frequent epithetic or mock-
epithetic hodge-podges, as when, for example, in *Gargantua and
Pantagruel,* Book 2, Chapter 38, he lists all the different sorts of
fools a person can be. It is a commonplace that the poetics of
the time was preoccupied with itemizing figures of speech of any
and all sorts. But epithets were special favorites: brief, easy to
identify and classify, they adapted immediately to the potentiali-
ties of print for presenting dissected matter in visually structured
order for ready retrieval. Whole books were devoted to culling
from classical antiquity the various expressions which ancient
poets had habitually used and which poets ever after were expected to repeat. Most of the commonplace books of various
sorts, books providing excerpts from classical Latin and Greek
works (the latter generally translated into Latin), furnished
epithets in quantity within the quotations they compiled under
various headings. Erasmus' collections, for example, in great part
fostered epithetic competence, particularly his *De copia verborum
ac rerum.* But there were also entire books consecrated simply to
gathering together epithets, the best known being the *Epitheta*
(in its first edition, Paris, 1518, called *Specimen epithetorum*)
compiled by the University of Paris master of arts Ioannes
Ravisius Textor. Here we find listed by the thousands all the
standard qualifiers which Textor's industry could accumulate
from his readings in the classics, arranged for ready retrieval in

alphabetic order (more or less) under the nouns to which they applied.

The age took its epithets seriously indeed. In doing so, of course, it was somewhat behind the times, as most ages probably are. For the use of heavily epithetic expression belonged to the old oral noetic economy, which had been partly weakened and partly reinforced by writing but which was now being superseded by the new noetic economy associated with print. One no longer had to repeat what one knew to keep it from getting away. Writing had made repetition less mandatory but had not eliminated it, for it was tedious to consult handwritten manuscripts, which were used largely to recycle materials out of and back into the still dominantly oral world.[23] By contrast with writing, print vastly improved visual access to knowledge—for example, by making indexes more practicable (one index for 2,000 identically paginated copies rather than separate indexes for each of 2,000 diversely paginated handwritten copies) and by radically improving legibility and eventually eliminating the slow "myopic" reading which had been the rule until print was finally interiorized in the psyche.[24] In the new visualist noetic economy for words, epithets became noetically dysfunctional, impeding rather than expediting the flow of thought, for thought, no longer condemned to repeating what was known to keep it extant, could now be freed for trafficking in the new.

Knowledge management practices of course change slowly, however irresistibly. The age of Pope would still continue in principle the use of epithets. But a sense of their growing dysfunction in poetry, attendant on their more and more evident dysfunction in scientific and practical thought and expression, was inexorably asserting itself. Epithets were being used wrily, tongue-in-cheek, or savagely, as often in Dryden and Pope, very likely disguising unconscious distaste for the whole epithetic business.

23. See Istvàn Hajnal, *L'Enseignement de l'écriture aux universités médiévales* (Budapest: Academia Scientiarum Hungarica Budapestini, 1954).

24. On the different psychological implications of writing and print, see Walter J. Ong, *The Presence of the Word* (New Haven: Yale University Press, 1967), pp. 17–110.

Epic became mock epic, as has earlier been noted here: the old economy of thought and expression could no longer be made seriously convincing. The age of Wordsworth would more explicitly downgrade epithets.[25] They did not disappear from poetry entirely, of course, but they were ultimately incompatible with what Wordsworth took to be "plain" speech of plain people—which was really not simple speech at all but a stripped-down, highly sophisticated chirographic style, no longer tolerant of the heavy mnemonic patterning found in the original oral cultures of all mankind and in the residual orality of the genuinely unschooled to this day. No serious poet of the Romantic Age wrote poetry from epithet books any more, not in the vernacular at any rate, although the nineteenth century continued to publish the *gradus ad Parnassum*, printed collections of metrically turned phrases from classical Latin poets, implementing the writing of Latin verse from the formulas which the old oral tradition had hallowed. In this ambiguous penumbra of orality in Latin one can identify the classicism to which the Romantic Movement was indeed opposed. The opposition appears as the opposition between orality and fully interiorized print culture. Classical culture is essentially oral culture somewhat bridled by writing (the classical oration was sustained by written works on rhetoric); romantic culture is typographic (there were few if any romantic orators or poets in a purely oral culture).

V

The post-Miltonic world as such is of course beyond the purview of this paper. But I have suggested these larger perspectives to help bring home what the relationship between Milton's use of epithets and his introduction of logic into the epic suggests about the history of logic and of the epic, namely, that to understand either in any decent depth today, we must delve into the evolution of noetic structures, which means ultimately the evolution of consciousness. No longer can we take logic as simply a

25. See Ong, *Rhetoric, Romance, and Technology*, pp. 255–283.

given which either whim or some more or less well-defined con-
viction brought Milton to incorporate into poetry. If Milton's
purportedly "logical" aim, "to justifie the wayes of God to men,"
was deliberately and explicitly espoused, Milton was still not in
complete conscious control of what he was doing or of his reasons for doing it, though he surely wanted to be.

The evidence here adduced seems to show that Milton's restrained use of epithets signaled an increase in conscious organization of knowledge in areas earlier organized more subconsciously.
Epic in its oral original had served not merely aesthetic but also
larger noetic functions: it had been an important way of conceiving, storing, retrieving, and circulating knowledge, a way of
keeping the noetic store from evaporating. Epic resulted from
and helped implement the oral noetic economy, in which knowledge was organized not logically or analytically but mnemonically.
Epithets had been major features of this kind of noetic organization, which proceeded largely by repetitious formula rather than
by more logical analysis. Milton's sparse and controlled use of
epithets marked a move from mnemonic oral noetics to later,
more consciously controlled management of knowledge, implemented by writing and print. Milton's epithets are more consciously powered than Spenser's, less consciously powered than
Pope's. Milton's preferred use of epithets thus belongs to one of
the stages of the increasingly conscious organization of knowledge
that marks human intellectual history. It is of course beyond all
belief that Milton could have been reflectively aware of this fact.
Though he may have had some sort of sense that his way of
managing epithets represented a certain "logical" control, his
adjustment to greater consciousness was in great part unconsciously inspired.

Over the centuries and millennia, as consciousness grows
through the mind's contact with actuality and through reflection,
and particularly as the development of writing, and even more of
print, liberates the mind from the onus of constant repetition of
the noetic store to keep this store from vanishing, consciousness
takes over more and more of the areas in the human lifeworld

where the unconscious had formerly ruled. Milton's strong infusion of logic into the organization of his epic is a moment in this expropriation of parts of the unconscious by consciousness.

Of the two traditions with which Milton is working, that of the epic and that of logic itself, each is marked by a growth of consciousness, and in ways which, as Milton's own case makes clear, are not entirely distinct from one another. In the epic tradition, the Homeric poems had been organized largely through the unconscious—which is not to deny that they were organized with consummate skill or that there was conscious control, and a lot of it. But the inability of an oral culture to develop a reflectively articulated account of what a poet is doing—or, for that matter, of other human action—other than in scattered aphorisms, however profound these may be, suggests how much of the unconscious was inaccessible to any efforts to raise it to consciousness. Hesiod's reflections on the nature of the poetry he practiced, reported and discussed by Havelock,[26] evince genuine "consciousness raising." The Homeric age had been incapable of such reflection. Intermediate between the primary oral culture of Homer and the deeply interiorized literacy of Plato, Hesiod shows consciousness actively invading the purlieus of the unconscious. Homer had invoked the Muse and let it go at that. Hesiod wants to investigate who the Muses are. Virgil goes further: the *Aeneid* is far more consciously programed, sociologically and politically and aesthetically. (Horace's still farther evolved *Ars poetica* was just around the corner.) In his letter to Ralegh, Spenser articulates quite consciously his purposes in composing *The Faerie Queene* and to some extent his organization of the poem, although it is noteworthy, as I have remarked earlier, that these conscious articulations are overridden by unconscious drives, which give the poem contours often quite different from those announced, and perhaps surprising at times even to Spenser. In *Paradise Lost* Milton articulates his conscious purpose much more clearly and achieves it much more completely, despite the

26. *Preface to Plato,* pp. 97–111.

abundant evidence, for example in the critical agitation since Dryden about Satan as hero, which shows that the unconscious was also at work and at times even in charge, at cross-purposes to consciousness. What is left of the epic tradition in the eighteenth century is in many ways still more consciously managed in the mock epics, where it is often trivialized by overconscious control at the expense of unconscious depth, the unconscious often exerting itself most forcefully in the disguised hatred which powers the humor without offering much further sustenance. With vagaries such as these, the epic tradition, however, does register a rise in consciousness, and it is this rise which destroys the tradition. For the epic mode had originated in and belonged to the less consciously, but beautifully, organized noetic economy of primary oral cultures.

The other tradition with which Milton works and which we have considered here, that of logic, likewise has a history in which consciousness emerges more and more distinctly from the unconscious. For the fact is that logic does have a history. The persuasion that it does not, that it must simply be there, comes naturally to most persons in Western cultures, if not to those in other cultures, too, and has come naturally for a long time. So great a mind as Kant's could believe that Aristotle had not only invented logic—as he claimed to have done and in fact did—but had also concluded that there had been nothing new in logic discovered since Aristotle and indeed that there was nothing new to discover. It is true that Immanuel Kant lived when logic had fallen on evil days: the great discoveries of the Middle Ages had been spurned and lost in the Renaissance and, Leibnitz apart, matters would not look up in logic until the mid-nineteenth century with George Boole.[27]

But Kant to the contrary notwithstanding, logic has had a history. There was a time when logic as a formal art did not exist.

---

27. I. M. Bochenski, *A History of Formal Logic,* trans. and ed. Ivo Thomas (Notre Dame, Ind.: University of Notre Dame Press, 1961), pp. 5–9, quotes Kant and others with similar convictions and details the ups and downs in the history of formal logic (pp. 267–270ff., and *passim*) touched on here.

Formal logic grew out of rhetoric and, more remotely, out of verbal combat, for formal logic came into being when the question was raised, Why is it that what you say demolishes what I say? What are the structures in play when yes and no are set in motion against one another? After it was invented by Aristotle, logic had its ups and downs. It took various turns, and much of it atrophied from time to time. In modern times it has taken on a new life such as it has not had since medieval logic, though a new kind of life, one supervised by specialists who, among other things, run computers, rather than a life felt as diffused more or less through all academic disciplines, if in fact not actually honored equally by all.

By Milton's day the rigorous formal logic of the Middle Ages had atrophied or been outlawed, not, as used to be supposed, because it was "decadent" (whatever that could possibly mean) but because it was so powerful an instrument that it had crowded out more necessary disciplines possessing less impeccably formal credentials, disciplines teaching, for example, practical language skills in Latin, social effectiveness in speech, and general knowledgeableness about the human lifeworld and its recurrent problems.[28] But even after devout humanists exorcised the logic-ridden curriculum, logic still haunted the sixteenth- and seventeenth-century mind in the sense that explicitly organized, rational control was the central human ideal. Milton lived in the middle years of the age of theodicy, which logicized even divine Providence. Leibnitz's *Théodicée* (*theos* + *dikē*, God-judgment) was to climax the age in 1710, undoing the Book of Job and showing how God himself operated according to logical laws, which Aristotle had providentially discovered and Ramus had streamlined. For Ramus had been convinced a century and a half earlier that all creation was logical.

In *The Descent from Heaven* Thomas M. Greene discusses the shift in *Paradise Lost* from epic violence to moral concern and

28. See Terrence Heath, "Logical Grammar, Grammatical Logic, and Humanism in Three German Universities," *Studies in the Renaissance,* 18 (1971), 9–64.

suggests that this shift implies a rejection of "part of the basis of epic itself—the balance of objective and subjective action, the balance of executive and deliberative."[29] Milton's shift of ground certainly did reject the violent basis of the original, oral epic itself—and those who have not noticed the shift or have not subscribed to it continue to identify Satan, the most conspicuously violent figure, as the epic hero, which he would have been in an oral original, for in early epic, normally the most conspicuously violent character was of course the hero. Professor Greene finds that "the last of the great poems in conventional epic contained within itself, not accidentally but essentially, the seeds of the genre's destruction." These seeds it certainly did contain, and they had been sown broadcast before Milton came along. They drifted inevitably into his epic, borne by the winds of cultural and psychological change.

The seeds had been produced by the growth of consciousness of which we have treated. The old epic simply could not be held together any more: there was no longer anything in the real management of knowledge in Milton's day that the old ceremonial violence could relate to. The epic would have had to stand apart from the rest of the noetic economy, and this is something no poetry can do if it is to be effective. For the violence had been itself part of the old formulary oral noetic. Contest between heavily laden type figures is a central operation in an oral culture's retention of its articulated knowledge and its sense of identity.[30] The old oral world had had to keep everything as formulaicly fixed as possible, and violent external conflict had been the principal ploy to make a story interesting. The old oral world will be recognized as the one in which little children still want their stories told: typed heroes and gore—though the

29. Thomas M. Greene, *The Descent from Heaven: A Study in Epic Continuity* (New Haven: Yale University Press, 1963), p. 407.

30. Walter J. Ong, *The Presence of the Word*, pp. 192–207; Walter J. Ong, "Agonistic Structures in Academia: Past to Present," *Interchange: A Journal of Educational Studies* (Toronto), 5 (1974), 1–12, and (abridged), *Daedalus*, 1 (Fall 1974), issued as *Proceedings of the American Academy of Arts and Sciences*, 103, No. 4, 229–238.

sophistication of the great epics is wanting in children's tales, as it is in the regressive Westerns and whodunits on television.

Professor Greene knowledgeably catalogs the seeds of destruction within Milton's epic: "the internalization of action . . . the questioning of the hero's independence [his independence of other persons, that is, not of mores, dependence on which is requisite for the hero] . . . the detaching of heroism from the community." All of these work against the communal formalism which governed the old epic for the reason that it governed the noetic economy of all pristine human orality. Logic was one more mode of internalization of action, for logic belongs to the interior human consciousness. Although it can at times have reference to the outside world (provided it is very closely controlled from within), in many of the real events of the outside world logical structure hardly leaps to the eye. Violence, if not more common, is at least more conspicuous as propulsion to action. After the age of logic, narrative will take another turn inward, this time into the novel: typically, at its most serious, a deeply interiorized genre where the narrator's voice is no longer of a piece with society's presuppositions and values, but at odds with them, seeking to convey awareness of the falsity which lies at the surface of society and of some deep, inarticulable, personal truth beneath.

Among the more important, and neglected, indications of the movement of *Paradise Lost* away from the world of communal formalism and toward the newer interiorized world are the features of the poem here discussed: *Paradise Lost* is no longer strongly formulaic in the old conventional way, it is controlled by the noetic economy of the old-style epic hardly at all and its structure is shaped not by communal forces but by a logic which its author has reflectively appropriated and interiorized. Isabel McCaffrey has pointed out how Milton's imagery does not derive from the unconscious in the way that Shakespeare's does, but is more externally managed.[31] This is the other side of the coin. For it is the unconscious, grounded so largely in communally pro-

31. *Paradise Lost as "Myth"* (Cambridge, Mass.: Harvard University Press, 1959).

cessed experience, that logic undertakes to move away from, if always with only limited success. The emergence of logic sets up a new variance between consciousness and the unconscious. Logic establishes new interior distances within the mind. Attempts to describe in depth what happened to the Western European psyche during the sixteenth and seventeenth centuries inevitably find themselves dealing with dissociations—T. S. Eliot's "dissociation of sensibility," for example—which logic registers and defends. To say that logic makes for dissociation is not to downgrade logic entirely. Logic is basically good though not utterly so. For thought to evolve, consciousness must disengage itself from its unconscious roots, since only by doing so can the mind regain possession of these roots more consciously and reflectively. We can hope that the present study has implemented such possession.[32]

32. It would probably be rewarding to pursue further the present line of investigation and to study the use of epithets in the various literary genres with a view to plotting the complex relationships of individual genres to the oral mind-set, more or less residual after the development of writing, and to the chirographic mind-set, increasingly dominant after writing at least until the onset of secondary orality in recent years. The fact that often epithets are less frequent in drama than in literary epic—Shakespeare's plays use a language decidedly less epithetic even than Milton's epic verse, as a glance through a Shakespeare concordance will show—would appear to correlate with the fact that the epic, even when written, remains in some way essentially oral and that the drama, despite its oral presentation, is essentially a written genre, the genre first (from Greek antiquity) completely controlled by writing. Such a study might throw light on a fact all too little adverted to: a dramatic "hero" is not entirely commensurate with an epic hero. It might also suggest ways in which the drama, more perhaps than other genres, abetted the development of chirographic noetic structures and states of consciousness.

8

The Poem as a Closed Field: The Once New Criticism and the Nature of Literature

> A poem should not mean
> But be.
> —Archibald MacLeish, *Ars Poetica*

The new criticism and the poetry which arose with it deserve to be examined in fuller perspectives than those in which they have commonly been viewed. Both are still too often described largely as ad hoc reactions to what went immediately before. The Hulme-Eliot-Pound-Leavis-Richards-Ransom kind of criticism is set against the impressionistic and often autobiographical performances of William Hazlitt, Walter Pater ("the presence that thus rose so strangely beside the waters"), or Oscar Wilde. The doctrine of clear, precise images which entered into the fiber of the New Criticism as well as into the more or less contemporaneous imagist poetry is set against the vagaries of Edwardian and Georgian verse. And eventually the story winds down with the anticulture movement which compromised the New Criticism at mid-century.

We are, however, becoming increasingly aware that the New Criticism calls for more than such short-range description. It was somehow a major cultural development. Some new insight into why and how it was can be gained if the New Criticism is examined in relation to the antecedent rhetorical tradition, which had dominated the theory and practice of expression from antiquity to the romantic age, when the remote beginnings of the New Criticism can be detected in Samuel Taylor Coleridge.

So far as I know, the New Criticism has never been examined in this way, although it has been examined from countless other viewpoints. Even at first blush the rhetorical tradition would appear relevant to the New Criticism not only because the older rhetoric had registered and controlled the dominant attitudes toward poetry for two millennia, but also because the New Criticism from its beginnings has had a lot to say about rhetoric. One of I. A. Richards' earliest books was *The Philosophy of Rhetoric* (1933); and in the United States, where verbal rhetoric is more studied and less practiced than in Great Britain and its dismantled empire, Cleanth Brooks and Robert Penn Warren have influenced millions of teachers and students, directly or indirectly, not only through their *Understanding Poetry,* but also through their companion volume *Modern Rhetoric* and through other textbooks treating poetry and rhetoric under the same covers.

Basically, the relationship between the old rhetoric and the New Criticism is one of opposition. The New Criticism was concerned with rhetoric because by overthrowing the old rhetorical tradition it made imperative an overhauling of the entire noetic economy. The old rhetorical tradition was no small thing. From antiquity the study of rhetoric had encapsulated the most ancient, central, and pervasive tradition of verbalization and of thought known to mankind at least in the West.

Elsewhere I have tried to explain how, until the beginning of the modern technological and romantic age in the later eighteenth century, Western culture in its intellectual and academic manifestations—and, *mutatis mutandis,* very likely all human culture everywhere—can be meaningfully designated rhetorical culture.[1] Basically, rhetorical culture means culture in which, even after the development of writing, the pristine oral-aural modes of knowledge storage and retrieval still dominate noetic activity, including both thought itself and verbal formulation and communication. When writing first appeared, it did not immediately

---

1. Walter J. Ong, *Rhetoric, Romance, and Technology* (Ithaca, N.Y.: Cornell University Press, 1971), pp. 1–22, 255–283.

wipe out or supplant oral-aural modes of thought and verbalization. Rather, it accentuated and codified them. Writing made
scientific analytic thought possible. Directed to the consideration
of communication, such analytic thought produced "rhetoric" as
a formal, reflective *techne* or art.

It is paradoxical and thought provoking that rhetoric was one
of the first fields of knowledge worked up as a formal art with
the aid of writing, for rhetoric means primarily oratory or public
speaking, for which the Greek word is *rhetorike*. The written art
of rhetoric at first focused primarily not on written but on oral
communication, which outproduced and outranked writing not
only at the time when writing first timidly began, but also for
several millennia afterwards. New inventions normally at first
reinforce what they will eventually transform or supplant. The
automobile at first encouraged prolification of the kinds of roads
devised for horses. Superhighways came late. Writing undermines
the oral noetic economy, but only after it first strengthens it by
giving it status in the new "scientific" world which writing made
possible.

From the time the first scripts had been invented around
3500 B.C., the old oral culture had been threatened; but before
the age of letterpress print, beginning around A.D. 1450, writing
had not greatly altered some of the major features of the oral
noetic economy: the organization and exploitation of knowledge through *loci communes* or commonplaces, the use of academic procedures centered upon oral reaction and upon the
agonistic intellectuality which preliterate orality fosters, and an
overall attitude toward expression which, at first overtly and later
less openly but still actually, regarded oratory as the paradigm of
all verbalization. Through the Renaissance and even into the
romantic age, textbooks on "rhetoric" regularly and dutifully
included a section on delivery (*pronuntiatio* or *actio*), which is
to say oral performance, even though most of their users were
being trained in fact chiefly for "literacy," which is to say for
writing. We no longer include a section on delivery in a book on
writing, but we have retained the term "rhetoric" for such a

book, thereby attesting unconsciously the still residual force of pristine oral culture. At root, rhetoric means not writing but speaking.

The rhetoric of the New Criticism represents, however, a rather final break with the older rhetoric in the way it fixes the eye unflinchingly on chirographic and typographic expression. On the one hand, the New Criticism descends from the old academic rhetoric matured in the orality of classical antiquity and rooted in the pristine oral world of mankind, an oral world dominated by male ceremonial contest—fliting, disputation, and formalized debate—and marked by heroic male bonding structures of which the war party was the paradigm. But, on the other hand, the New Critical rhetoric descends also from the vernacular, bourgeois, account-keeping schools designed for training in "reading, writing, and 'rithmetic," with very little of the heroic-oral-combative in them. The vernaculars moved into academia first in the lower grades, from which they worked their way up in the curricula. The New Criticism arose as the universities shifted their central linguistic focus from Latin to English.[2] Before this shift there had never been any developed university criticism of English literature as a whole.

The hallmark of the old rhetoric in the West was the use of Latin, since the sixth century not a mother tongue any more but exclusively a sex-linked, public, male language encoding the agonistic structures of the agora and the academy. Into the twentieth century, the requirement of Latin, in however attenuated a form, marked the schools which trained boys and young men not for business but for academic or public life, for taking positions on issues and fighting them through, for diplomacy and other verbal jousting. The vernacular schools, by contrast, trained boys and, somewhat later, girls for managing the economy, commercial or household, and for other practical, noncombative uses of literacy. The two types of schools influenced one another and often intimately coexisted; in the United States, as late as the

2. Walter J. Ong, *The Barbarian Within* (New York: Macmillan, 1962), pp. 177–205; see also Ong, *Rhetoric, Romance, and Technology*, pp. 113–141.

1920s, the same secondary school often housed two clearly marked courses: the "classical" course (training, roughly, debaters) and the "commercial" course (for account keepers). By and large, women entered the older, "classical" academic world where it was most amenable to influence from the vernacular schools. They seemed to want classical education, but the psychological structures were against it. As women came into academia, Latin went out.

The older rhetorical Latin tradition stood for a committed, agonistic approach to learning and to life. In this tradition, even the study of literature was programed to prepare for taking a position and defending it or for attacking that which another was defending. "For by the reading of his [Homer's] work called *Iliados,* where the assembly of the most noble Greeks against Troy is recited with their affairs, he gathereth courage and strength against his enemies, wisdom and eloquence for consultations, and persuasions to his people and army," Sir Thomas Elyot explains in 1531 in *The Book Named the Governor.* It was still much the same more than three centuries later in *Tom Brown's School Days* (1857). This educational world prepared for contest, for struggle, taking for granted the existence of violence. Significantly, the last bastions of Latin in the British Isles, the public schools, are also the last bastions of the programed use of physical punishment. George Orwell once ventured that without physical punishment it was impossible to teach Latin; on the whole, though not in every particular case, he has been proven right.

In this setting, as was to be expected, poetry as a purely aesthetic activity had little, if any, place. From antiquity through most of the nineteenth century, poetry by and large was conceived of academically as a part or a subsidiary of rhetoric, which was ordered not to creativity but, paradigmatically, to public decision making. Generally speaking, whatever contrary theories may have been more or less in circulation privately, poetry was in fact taught academically not for itself but as an ancillary subject, or semisubject, to develop the linguistic skills and the sensibility re-

quired for an orator or man of public affairs. And academic practice reflected the dominant nonacademic views. Poetry was supposed to teach, to move, and to delight, with a heavy emphasis on
the first two, from Dionysius of Halicarnasses, probably the most
aesthetically oriented ancient rhetorician, through Sir Philip
Sidney and John Milton—who wrote *Paradise Lost* for agonistic
purposes, to "justifie the wayes of God to men"—and on into the
beginning of the romantic movement. In the last analysis, academia felt that speech was essentially for the committed man, an
accomplishment to be used in making and implementing practical
decisions. Deviations from this activist position there were from
antiquity, but most of them were in favor of "philosophy"—that
is, the speculative life, as this was cultivated in the study of logic,
"physics" or natural philosophy, or metaphysics—not in favor of
poetry or any other performance conceived as purely aesthetic.
When humanists such as Lorenzo Valla spoke out in favor of
eloquence, the practical art of winning assent and getting things
done, they identified the enemy not as poetry but as the pursuit
of knowledge for the sake of knowledge, the speculative tradition of the universities.[3]

In these longer historical perspectives, many of the features of
the New Criticism and its concomitant poetry take on much
wider meanings. We can examine one feature here in particular,
the characteristic doctrine concerning the integrity of the literary
work itself. Criticism must begin, the doctrine teaches, by examining a poem or other work of literature on the work's own
grounds, asking of the work itself what it is undertaking to do
and adjudicating its success in terms of its discernible aims. The
literary work exists in its own closed field. This doctrine finds
somewhat different expression and different emphasis in different
critics, but in one or another guise it is present in virtually all
New Criticism and nowhere more significantly than in Cleanth
Brooks's cardinal book, *The Well-Wrought Urn: Studies in the*

---

3. See Jerrold E. Seigel, *Rhetoric and Philosophy in Renaissance Humanism* (Princeton, N.J.: Princeton University Press, 1968), pp. 141–144,
160–169.

Structure of Poetry, which, we are advised on the dedicatory page, was worked out in greater part in a seminar at the University of Michigan in the summer of 1942, during the heyday of the New Criticism. Here, in a variety of ways and through the patient study of diverse texts, the reader is shown over and over again the unity of diversity, the paradoxes, the ironies, the tensions—how the poem's parts are indeed very much parts in that they can tend to fly away from one another, but are nevertheless convincingly held together in the unity of the poem. This holding together, the closed field, *is* the poem, the work of art.

The poem, in other words, is what it is because of its interior economy, not because of the way it ties in at specific points with "life" or with anything else. In this sense a poem does not "mean" or "signify." To say that something has meaning or signification is to refer it outside itself in one way or another. The word *tree* means or signifies a physical object, which is not the word itself. A person's life or actions have meaning when they are referred to something or someone beyond themselves. Meaning or significance thus breaks open any closed field. If, as in typical New Criticism doctrine, the poem is a closed field, to give it "meaning" threatens its whole validity as a poem. "A poem should not mean / But be," Archibald MacLeish proclaims in his *Ars Poetica* (1926). If the poem is related to life, as it of course is, the relationship must be not from without but somehow from within, interior to interior: life relates to the poem and the poem to life in terms of the poem's own inner consistency. This relationship yields meaning, but of a special sort, meaning growing out of the dialectical relationship between art and nature, play and work—terms which define each other.

Even laws of decorum do not refer characters or situations beyond the poem itself. In Appendix 1 of *The Well-Wrought Urn,* "Criticism, History, and Critical Relativism," Professor Brooks speaks strongly for the interrelationship between poetry and life, but he protests that decorum itself is not a matter of relating poetic language point for point to real-life situations— making sure that poetic swains speak and behave like real-life swains—but of relating poetic language to the poem. Within the poem itself, in a sense anything goes. But only in a sense, for the organization of any poem worth the name imposes its own demands, which must be honored. If they are, decorum is achieved and morality guaranteed, for poetry is such that, if it is not of a piece with life, nevertheless it is always consistent with life when it is consistent with itself, with its own unity. "To thine own self be true," and all will be well poetically. There is no way to have a good poem which will be indecorous or morally debilitating. The interior consistency of the poem, if honored, rules out or expels any incipient disaccord. The total poem, if it is good, accords with extrapoetic reality, though its parts individually may not match extrapoetic correlates. How the inner consistency of the poem relates to that of life is a further question we need not broach here. Propounded by its best advocates the doctrine is rigorous and at least as consistent as any competing doctrine.

To a certain extent, it appears that this contention—that each poem must be approached on its own grounds and judged for what it is—is not new. Had not Alexander Pope taken a position like this when he wrote in *An Essay on Criticism,* "A perfect judge will read each work of wit / With the same spirit that its author writ"? Pope does here urge a certain deference to a poem's integrity, but the integrity appears less isolated than what the New Criticism has in mind. Pope seems willing to view the poem as being in contact with external reality through its author. The poem is something someone has said, not a detached existence whose business is simply to "be." Pope does not demand the author's absence once the poetic work is composed with quite the insistence of the New Criticism. He is concerned with fairness to the author at least as much as with fairness to the poem. Hence he does not devote any particular thought to the depersonifying effects of aesthetic distance.

The New Critics do, and their thought is part of us now. In "Tradition and the Individual Talent," T. S. Eliot writes, "Poetry is not the expression of personality but an escape from personality."[4] This echoes John Keats's statement about "negative capability." It is of course quite true and, to us, even obvious. Shakespeare's own personal problems cannot be construed from *Macbeth* or *Hamlet* or *A Midsummer Night's Dream* (although if you know Shakespeare's personal history from other sources you can conceivably relate these plays to it). Some of Eugene O'Neill's personal hang-ups can be construed from *Mourning Becomes Electra* or *Long Day's Journey into Night* and, insofar as they can be, the dramatic effectiveness of these works suffers. They hold together not entirely because of what they are, but partly because of what O'Neill was and the way they touched his life—which means they do not hold together all that well. They sound contrived. Ernest Hemingway's stories tell you much more about Hemingway's lack of maturity than William Faulkner's tell you about Faulkner's problems with alcohol, and Hemingway's inability fully to transcend his own problems in his writing excludes him forever from the rank where Faulkner and Shakespeare and Sophocles stand.

This objectivity or relative dissociation of the work of art from its author has in one way or another been a quality of true art from the start. It was a feature of oral performance before literature began. Individual epic singers had their own styles, but these were not expressions of "personality" in any usual sense. You cannot find Homer's personality in the *Iliad,* although you might find the personality of an entire culture there. But with the New Criticism these matters—disinvolvement with personality, "objectivity" in art, insulation of the poem from direct existential interactions—became burning issues. As never before, it became imperative to treat the poem as a conspicuously closed field, an object disengaged from real persons and indeed from all else. Such an imperative lies back of the "classicism" advocated from T. E. Hulme on, back of T. S. Eliot's "objective correlative," a "set of objects, a situation, a chain of events" which will evoke a "particular emotion," to some extent back of

4. T. S. Eliot, *Selected Essays* (New York: Harcourt Brace, 1950), p. 10.

Wallace Stevens' "supreme fiction," and of course back of imagism in all its avatars.

A strong feeling for the poem as a closed field signals the end of the old rhetorical world by recasting the readers or "audience" in a spectator's rather than an interlocutor's role. So long as a poem was assimilated to rhetoric, it operated within the agonistic framework of real life, of decision and action. The rhetorician addressing his audience is struggling with the audience, interacting with it, though the audience for the moment is mute. And so is the original poet, the oral poet, who remained, unconsciously if not consciously, the paradigmatic poet so long as the old rhetorical tradition survived.

The reader, using his eyes to assimilate a text, is essentially a spectator, outside the action, however interested. His reaction to one page has no effect on what appears on the next. Inviting readers to fill in blank pages, as in Sterne's *Tristram Shandy*, or to shuffle pages around, as in some recent fiction, essentially alters nothing: what the author has written he has written. The live audience is not so necessarily passive: the storyteller's narrative takes on different contours as audience reaction develops differently. Fiction or poetry in this tradition is of a piece with dialogue and with real life in a way the written product is not. (Written narrative or poetry has other ways of being in contact with real life, no less honorable, of course, but different—as, for example, the calculated use of colloquial speech, rare or unknown in artistic oral performance of cultures without writing.) Writing seals off its product from direct dialogue: the writer creates his text in isolation. It is this isolation of his which makes credible and, more than credible, meaningful the doctrine of the poem as a closed field.

The doctrine of the poem as a closed field reveals not only the chirographic roots but also the deep romantic roots of the New Criticism. With romanticism, the old agonistic poetic had been replaced by a new doctrine of creativity. The poet is irenic, or at least neutral, uncommitted, free of dialogic struggle with an audience, since for the "creative" romantic imagination the poem is no longer a riposte but a simple product, an "object" rather than an exchange. This insulation of discourse from dialogue on aesthetic grounds has evident similarities with the isolation or insulation fostered by writing, as just noted, and suggests a subtle alliance between literacy and romanticism complementary to the alliance between rhetoric (oratory) and classicism, as I have attempted elsewhere to show.[5]

The insulation of poetry from dialogue allows poetic in the romantic age (in which we still live) to deflect attention which had been earlier directed to the audience, back to the poet's own self. John Stuart Mill registered the changed emphasis, with no evident awareness of its deeper implications, when, in his "Thoughts on Poetry and Its Varieties," he stated that "eloquence is *heard;* poetry is *overheard.*"[6] Earlier, when "eloquence" would have included poetry as akin to rhetoric, poets wanted desperately to be heard; even when they were not actually competing with one another, they sang to audiences for applause. But not romantic poets, as least in implied principle. They wanted to be alone—which means in effect, of course, that they felt themselves more as writers than as oral speakers.

The romantic feeling for isolation of the poem is strikingly illustrated in the felicitous halftone print on the dust jacket of M. H. Abrams' deeply perceptive recent book on romanticism, *Natural Supernaturalism.*[7] The print reproduces in black and white a painting, *The Bard,* by the romantic John Martin (1789–1854). This painting is certainly one of the most unwittingly informative anachronisms in literary and art history. High on a precipice in a mountain fastness, an ancient bard stands. Harp in hand and wildly gesticulating, he sings at the top of his voice—utterly alone, to no one at all, for the awesome landscape is completely unpeopled. In the castle on a rocky outcropping

5. Ong, *Rhetoric, Romance, and Technology,* pp. 255–283.
6. John Stuart Mill, *Dissertations and Discussions: Political, Philosophical, and Historical* (New York: Henry Holt, 1874–82), I, 97.
7. M. H. Abrams, *Natural Supernaturalism* (New York: Norton, 1971).

opposite, across a deep valley cut by a torrent, no one at all appears. Martin has gone Mill one better: this poetry is not even overheard.

The actuality of all bardic performance, so far as investigation can ascertain, is entirely the opposite of this earnest but grotesque representation. Bards were and are extraordinarily gregarious folk. The real bard encountered by folklorists, anthropologists, or students of oral verbalization will do anything for an audience. He depends on audience reaction, as has been noted, to shape his performance, so that he badly needs an audience, generally speaking, even to get under way. Albert B. Lord shows how bards themselves learned their bardic skills by long hours of listening in such audiences,[8] not by sounding off on mountain crags.

The old poetic tradition associated with rhetoric had socialized the poet in another way, too. It had kept the poet engaged, struggling, not only with an audience but with other poets as well. Rhetorically colored poetic was a poetic of virtuosity, setting poet against poet. The earlier poetic was not always explicitly conscious of its agonistic underpinnings, but the underpinnings were there nevertheless, to be seen if you looked. Contest, ceremonial polemic, was a constitutive element in the noetic organization of the old preromantic rhetorical world and of the poetic this world enfolded. Pope speaks for the dominant poetic of two thousand preromantic years when, in *An Essay on Criticism,* he allies wit with Nature and assigns to the poet the task of producing "what oft was thought, but ne'er so well expressed." This is the pristine rhetorical world speaking, thinking of composition, including poetry, as proceeding by "invention" (*inventio*), retrieval of matter from the accumulated stores of mankind, stores organized by means of the places or commonplaces or topics (*loci* or *topoi*). This topical poetic clearly calls for an agonistic stance for, if the poet deals with the common store of awareness

8. Albert B. Lord, *The Singer of Tales,* Harvard Studies in Comparative Literature, 24 (Cambridge, Mass.: Harvard University Press, 1960), pp. 20–29.

accessible to all, his warrant for saying or singing again what everybody is already familiar with can only be that he can say it better than others. The invocation of the Muse can be paraphrased, "Let me win, outdo all the other singers." In preromantic, rhetorical culture, the poet is essentially a contestant. He must do his work, make his poem, as conspicuous competitor within the dialectic of existence, the struggle—basically not lethal, as Thomas Hobbes and Herbert Spencer thought, but ceremonial—between man and man.

In the oral or residually oral cultures in which rhetorical culture is rooted, the originality which romanticism was to erect into a poetic and artistic principle is normally wasteful and counterproductive, for, in the absence of writing and hence of records, available energies must be channeled into repeating what is already known, lest it slip away forever. The novelty esteemed in such cultures is the novelty of supreme skill with the known, virtuosity in handling the familiar, the ability to excel in a situation where all the factors are in hand, are the same for all, and hence challenge all equally, as in an athletic contest. This is the "exquisiteness" looked for when the Welsh mercilessly graded bards by degrees of proficiency at periodic bardic contests. Hence, in oral or residually oral cultures, contests between poets or other verbal performers are quite normal, from the fliting in the *Iliad* and in *Beowulf* through the poets' contests in the medieval courts of love (real or fictional) to the present-day eisteddfod survivals in Wales and the "dozens" still practiced by our young American blacks.

Poets today still have rivalries (and indeed, on the average poets' egos are very likely more assertive than those of nonpoets), but modern romantic poetic no longer enforces ceremonial virtuosity as the older rhetorical poetic did. Expertise in exploiting a common store of matter is no longer the announced aim of the craft. "Creativity" is, and creativity implies that each poet starts not from a storehouse but *ex nihilo,* making poems which in principle are unique lock, stock, and barrel. "Creativity" is not all of romantic poetic, and it is tempered in fact by doctrines such as Eliot's doctrine of tradition. But the concept has certain basic implications and it is a central feature of romantic poetic—including, incidentally, Eliot's concept of tradition itself.

In a poetic focused on creativity, the sense of struggle weakens at two points. First, involvement with a living audience weakens; in place of rhetorico-poetic concern with teaching, moving, and delighting (*docere, movere, delectare*), poets programed to be "creative" develop concern with image and symbol, which tends to be concern with production in terms of sight, however mediated by words—the "audience" here turns into spectators. Between the spectators and the performers there is no struggle, although there may be communication.

Second, as just suggested, combative involvement of poet with poet weakens. There is no contest, for the common grounds needed for contest have been eliminated or minimized. Instead of bardic contests, the romantic world has poetry "readings," which may be covertly agonistic but are seldom openly programed as combative. Where a sense of poetic contest survives, as it does certainly at points today, the agonistic action is often also muted by being focused on poems in writing (which provide something "objective" to look at, to "examine"), not on recitations or readings.

Such are some of the implications of romantic poetics and of mountaintop bards. Romantic actuality, including modern poetry, of course has not always conformed to such implications. But it frequently or usually has. It is difficult to imagine Wordsworth at an eisteddfod singing *The Prelude* or anything else he wrote. The creative romantic poet does *his* thing, not the communal thing. Wordsworth was his own hero, and had to be.

Seen in these perspectives of the old rhetorical world antecedent to it, the age of the New Criticism clearly is tied in with evolving psychological and social structures more extensively than might otherwise appear. From as far back as we can go into the beginnings of academic history, *agonia* or contest had constituted the mode of instruction in all academic subjects. From rhetoric itself to logic and physics and on through medicine, law, and theology, learning was acquired and tested by oratorical contest, dialectical debate or disputation, defense of theses or attacks upon those which others were defending. These procedures derived from the orality of early culture and from the very nature of oral performance. Oral performance favors not impartial investigation but contest. The typical orator's stance is not, "Let me objectively work through this matter with you, for I do not know the answer as yet," but rather, "Here I take my stand." An orator does in fact typically stand, a combative and precarious posture, inviting overthrow. A writer sits, or squats. He also revises, as an orator can seldom afford to do. The procedures of early oral or rhetorical cultures were typically of a piece with the world of male ceremonial combat, which was held at high value in a literary and academic world powered at its center by the ceremonial male language of Latin, a language resonant with the orality of antiquity and acquired with the help of physical punishment through rituals carried on in the tradition of puberty rites.

The age of the New Criticism provides us with a different setting. Contest as a conspicuous institution for instruction and learning no longer figures in the classroom setting. Deweyan educational reform ruled contest out, although it was on its last legs long before John Dewey intervened. Physical punishment, Latin as an instructional medium and linguistic paradigm, testing by oral defense of theses, academic focus on preparation for the public agora and political arena rather than for commercial or social service, though they remained vestigially here and there, were by World War I moribund. All disappeared from the academic scene about the same time. Their disappearance coincides with the use of the vernacular and the entrance of women into higher education. So far as I know, there was never a formal, scholastic disputation in the old, rigorously formal, ceremonially combative style conducted in English or conducted by women. Women tend to fight when they truly have to, for realities, not for laurels, and to speak the mother tongue, which is truly their own.

If this very sketchy description of one aspect of the state of affairs is valid, it suggests the question, Where have the polemic or agonistic drives gone? It is hard to believe that they have simply disappeared from poetics and from academia generally. The most inclusive answer is that nobody quite knows, although it is certain that the presence of women in the literary and academic world has basically shifted the psychological and noetic structures there toward declared irenicism. What matters here is that by the advent of the New Criticism the verbal world had strikingly downgraded ceremonial combat. The New Criticism generated its own economy of hostilities, but, however fierce, they were largely incidental, not operational.

It adds further to our perspectives to note in conclusion how verbal hostilities have been reconstituted as the age of the New Criticism has shaped itself into a new age. Student demonstrations have revivified verbal polemic, not in the formerly controlled, ceremonially agonistic educational setting, where even scurrilities were ritualized, but in an essentially callow setting of raw confrontation. The rhetoric of liberation movements has fed other hostilities into newly opened verbal channels. Poetry of liberation movements is rhetorical and polemic, in this resembling that of the oral or residually oral culture of the preromantic past. Such resemblance is understandable in many cases because liberation movements are powered largely out of oral cultures—in the case of black liberation, a very highly developed oral culture, complexly related to the literacy around it and to the secondary, literate orality of technological popular art culture.

Moreover, in our day the verbal *agonia* of politics has become real in portions of academia often most shielded from it a few years ago, notably the field of poetry. Poetry, we are told, is and must be an activist political event. Although political stances were being imputed to poetry at the onset of the New Criticism in the 1930s—by Christopher Caudwell, for example—such imputations were pretty well disabled by the aesthetics prevalent in the New Criticism. The reopening of activist approaches to literature recalls the earlier poetic, which was part of or subordinate to the practical concerns of rhetoric, and alerts us to the curious ways in which electronic, secondary orality, though derivative from and permanently dependent on writing and print, reproduces some noetic structures characteristic of early or primary (preliterate) orality.

The new activism will soon be no newer than the New Criticism is, but its emergence has made it clear that the psychological and cultural intellectual forces which produced the age of the New Criticism no longer act in concert as they once did. *Mais, plus ça change, plus c'est la même chose.* If the forces of the New Criticism once acted in concert, we can remind ourselves that "concert" means struggle, contest, *agonia.* The forces in the New Criticism, even in their ascendancy, were never quite at ease with themselves, but were in fact always struggling. Their struggle produced the tremendous outburst of energy and achievement marking the work of Cleanth Brooks and those who have learned from him.

9

Maranatha: *Death and Life in the Text of the Book*

The Bible as Text

The Bible is an altogether special case in the history of textuality.* In its own history as a text it relates uniquely both to oral antecedents and, interiorly, to itself. The unusual problems it presents throw light on textuality as such, and the study of orality and textuality throws light on the Bible and the character of the message it proclaims.

It is commonplace that the Hebrew and Christian scriptures, as compared to other sacred writings, have a special relationship to time. This relationship has commonly been thought of in terms of the attitudes toward time expressed or implied in statements in the Bible. Here relationship to time is defined by what the text says, by its meaningful context. As a result of recent concern with texts as texts, by contrast with oral communication—by text I mean here, quite inclusively, a representation of words in script— a new way of considering the relationship of the Bible to time has begun to take shape. For texts as texts have a special relationship to time. And the Bible is a special kind of text. The present reflections have to do with these matters: texts as texts in their relationship to time, and the Bible in this setting of textuality. Attention to texts as texts is likely to suggest the work of psychoanalytic structuralists such as Jacques Derrida, Jacques Lacan, Michel Leiris, or Roland Barthes, together with Claude Lévi-Strauss,

* This study is an expansion of a paper presented October 29, 1976, in St. Louis, Missouri, at the plenary session of the annual meeting of the American Academy of Religion. It is published here for the first time.

Hans-Georg Gadamer, and others, including now Jeffrey Mehlman, whose recent analysis of four autobiographies carries
forward structuralist contrasts between text and spoken language.[1]
But the present reflections grow out of preoccupations different
from theirs, preoccupations less attentive to theoretical constructs
and more attentive to psychocultural history, and particularly to
the growth of writing and print out of the primary orality of
mankind and to the comparative psychodynamics of oral,
chirographic, and typographic noetic processes.

Much of the productive recent biblical scholarship has resulted
from growing knowledge of oral cultures. Everyone in or near
scriptural studies today is in some way aware that the Bible in
great part comes out of an oral tradition, and in various ways,
although scriptural scholarship as a whole, so far as I can see,
still shows little awareness in depth of the psychodynamics of an
oral culture as these psychodynamics have been worked out by
Albert B. Lord and Eric A. Havelock and some others, so that
the definitive breakthrough in scriptural studies, I believe, is yet
to come.[2]

However, despite the growing awareness of the Bible's oral
matrix and of the massive oral residue it contains, the Bible
remains a text, and most spectacularly when we think of it as a
whole. For the Bible is a whole. Though its canon has been
disputed, the disputes have concerned only a few books or
sections of books.

The Bible is made up of various works, composed in a variety
of ways over a period of some thousand years, but as it has
grown, it has always folded back on itself in memory, the later
parts building a later history out of later states of consciousness
but also building onto and out of and into and through the
earlier parts in a process which we must own is unique. When

1. Jeffrey Mehlman, *A Structural Study of Autobiography: Proust, Leiris,
Sartre, Lévi-Strauss* (Ithaca, N.Y.: Cornell University Press, 1974).

2. Albert B. Lord, *The Singer of Tales,* Harvard Studies in Comparative
Literature, 24 (Cambridge, Mass.: Harvard University Press, 1960); Eric A.
Havelock, *Preface to Plato* (Cambridge, Mass.: Belknap Press of Harvard
University Press, 1963).

Stephen preaches Jesus Christ crucified and risen, as is reported in Acts 7:2–53, his account of Jesus' redemptive work starts with the story of Abraham before Abraham left Mesopotamia for Haran. We have no other book got together as a whole out of a communal memory the way the Bible has been.

This whole is a text. Individual parts of the Bible have oral antecedents, more or less evident and more or less ascertainable. But there is no oral tradition in which the Bible as a whole ever existed or in which its parts simultaneously coexisted (as would be the case, for example, with the *Iliad* and the *Odyssey*). The Bible is what the word *biblos* says it is, a book, the Book.

Text as Monument

Oral cultures, we all know, have a heavy investment in the past, which registers in their highly conservative institutions and in their verbal performances and poetic processes, which are formulaic, relatively invariable, calculated to preserve the hard-won knowledge garnered out of past experience which, since there is no writing to record it, could otherwise slip away. A written work has a somewhat similar relationship to the past: it can fix on the page what an oral culture fixes in continually repeated formulas. The text preserves the past by recording it. But by contrast with oral verbalization, a written or a printed work—textualized work, perhaps we might say, in the absence of any better term or concept to cover generally both writing and print—has a special kind of involvement with the past, namely, its textuality as such. Not just what a text says, but the physical text itself possesses a certain pastness. All texts are preterite. Unlike an utterance, a text is assimilated by the person who receives it not when it is being composed but after its utterance (its "outering") is over with. A text is not a living potential in the human interior as a remembered oral utterance is after the oral utterance has been uttered once and before it has been uttered again. A text is simply there, something over with, a thing out of the past.

A text as such is so much a thing of the past that it carries with it necessarily an aura of accomplished death. In our highly literate culture, where everyone who cannot read and write is considered defective, and culturally is indeed so, literacy is often superstitiously regarded as totally unexceptionable and thus a statement such as this, attributing to literacy a negative quality, associating writing with death, is quite scandalous. Nothing but good should be said about writing and reading as such. Of course, this suggests the Latin saying, *De mortuis nil nisi bonum.*

If, however, we dismantle our defenses and recognize that real words are always sounds, always events, which exist only while they are going out of existence, that real words are not marks on a surface, the truth about texts better appears. In oral or oral-aural communication both speaker and hearer must be alive. Without the speaker's living action, there are no real words. Without a living hearer, the words are ineffective, uneventful, inoperative, a movement toward nothing. This is as true today as it was before script was invented.

The case is quite different with writing. Once I have put a message into writing, it makes no difference so far as the text goes whether I am dead or alive. Once a poet has written out a poem, so far as the poem goes, his own continued existence is irrelevant. Paul Ricoeur has observed that he likes "to say sometimes that to read a book is to consider its author as already dead" and that to meet an author and speak with him about a book of his is to "experience a kind of disturbance."[3] For this disturbance, however, it is not necessary that the author be previously unknown. This fact can be illustrated by a true anecdote. Not long ago I had occasion to telephone my secretary at home. The first thing she said was, "I interrupted reading a book of yours to answer this phone call and you cannot imagine the strange experience it is to hear your living voice. In the book, I was in a different world."

3. Paul Ricoeur, "What Is a Text? Explanation and Interpretation," Appendix, pp. 135–150, in David M. Rasmussen, *Mythic-Symbolic Language and Philosophical Anthropology: A Constructive Interpretation of the Thought of Paul Ricoeur* (The Hague: Martinus Nijhoff, 1971), p. 137.

Turning from the somewhat ghoulish implications of these reflections, we can note that in a certain way writing also perdures into the future and in this sense lives. Writing obviously outlasts speech. It will remain. It will live. But the kind of life writing enjoys remains bizarre, for it is achieved at the price of death. The words that "live" are inert, as no real words can ever be. They are no longer audible, which is to say they are no longer real words, but only marks on the surface which can signal those who know the proper codes how to create certain real words or groups of real words. In this sense, writing "lives" only posthumously and vicariously, only if living people have the skills to give it a share in their lives. When they do this, the words read off are made to enter always into an historical situation other than that in which they were first "set down" (as we well conceive the writing operation).

Analogies between sound recordings and writing of course suggest themselves here, but they must be left aside as complex, not simple, analogies not directly relevant to present concerns though well worth studying in themselves.[4]

4. For retrieval into the aural world, an electronically or mechanically recorded utterance requires not merely a skill, such as the ability to read, but also a machine. It is recoverable, but not simply through action within the human sensorium and psyche, which can reconstitute the visually transformed word in sound but cannot transform the electronic pattern or mechanically incised groove into sound. Thus, although in a way the voice on a sound recording is more immediately accessible than the voice embedded in writing, in a deeper sense it is less immediately accessible: something other that a human being intervenes between record and verbalization. Hence, the recorded spoken voice is in one way curiously less natural than writing, in another way more natural.

Moreover, sound recordings do not involve the psyche, as writing does, in the transaction between the stasis of vision and the dynamic transience of sound. The implication of death in sound recordings is less than in writing. Writing, as will be seen below, is frequently considered to be a "monument," a memorial visually and tactilely perpetuating one who is deceased. It appears less real or less natural to think of sound recordings as "monuments." In one way they are too alive (sound), in another too dead (an overwhelmingly mechanical product).

The relationship of the sound-recorded utterance to the speaker, however, is somewhat like that of the text to the writer in that, once the utterance is recorded, the speaker no longer need be alive for his words to be appre-

In a way, these observations about the inertness of the written word appear banal. But the situation to which they refer is complex, suggesting that covered by the juridical concept of "mortmain." An inalienable holding in real estate under old English common law was conceived of as held in mortmain, which means in "dead hand," in a hand which cannot pass the holding on to anyone else. Those who hold real estate can normally dispose of it as they wish. But not here, for what is mortmain is held in the clutch of death. In Scots law, a corresponding concept is that of "mortification," a putting to death: a gift for religious, charitable, or public use (something we might call an inalienable trust fund in the United States) is called a "mortification." The property constituting the trust has been constituted as "dead" in the sense that its state is fixed once and for all, is no longer subject to change. In this sense, in its changelessness, the fund has been rendered immortal, but the immortality is that of a corpse. A corpse cannot die, for it has already passed through death, the ultimate change. It is faced into the future but not as a living person is. "After the first death, there is no other," writes Dylan Thomas.

In a written work, the author's words are mortmain. They will never die because when he put them down, he fixed them for good. They are a "mortification" because writing them down killed them, as Plato protested in his Seventh Letter and in the *Phaedrus*. By the same token, the author also after a fashion did away with himself, for, as we have seen, once a literary work is written, it makes no difference whether the author is alive or dead, and indeed, ideally speaking, he is as good as dead.

The connection between writing and death is very deep, so deep that it registers almost always in the unconscious or subconscious rather than in consciousness. But it can be brought up into consciousness very readily if we look carefully at what has been

---

hended. Still, in a way, one does not sense that he should be, since his words cannot be made to live by directly human activity but only through a machine.

For other special implications of the traffic between past and present made possible by sound recordings and videotapes, see Chapter 11 below.

written about writing across the centuries. Thousands of references could be cited, and indeed whole books could be written on literary references, open or veiled, to writing and print as death.

Here are a few random instances showing associations, direct or indirect, welcome or protested, of writing and print with death. They are simply selected from the quotations entered under "Book" and "Library" in *The Home Book of Quotations,* edited by Burton Stevenson:[5] "Books are the legacies that a great genius leaves to mankind," Addison, *The Spectator,* No. 166. Books, "the monuments of vanish'd minds," Sir William D'Avenant, *Gondibert.* "Of all the inanimate objects, of all man's creations, books are the nearest to us . . . most of all . . . in their precarious hold on life," Joseph Conrad, *Notes on Life and Letters.* "For half the truths they hold are honoured tombs," George Eliot, *Spanish Gypsy.* "Books are sepulchres of thought / The dead laurels of the dead," Longfellow, *Wind over the Chimney.* "Books are not absolutely dead things," Milton, *Areopagitica*—the protest here ("not absolutely") reveals how truly dead they must be in some sense. "A good book is the precious life-blood of a master spirit, embalmed and treasured up on purpose to a Life beyond Life," Milton, *Areopagitica.* "Alonso of Aragon was wont to say of himself 'That he was a great necromancer, for that he used to ask counsel of the dead' meaning books," Francis Bacon, *Apothegms,* No. 105. "Studious let me sit / And hold high converse with the mighty Dead," James Thomson, *The Seasons: Winter.* "With faded yellow blossoms 'twixt page and page, / To mark great places with due gratitude," Robert Browning, *Pippa Passes.* (The widespread practice of pressing live flowers to death and thus into necrotized immortality between the pages of books deserves investigation—the book as floral necropolis. Flowers are symbols of full but fragile life, and their desiccated corpses are entombed on our bookshelves as in mausoleums.) "Libraries, which are as the shrines where all the relics of the ancient saints, full of true virtue, and that with-

5. Fourth ed., (New York: Dodd, Mead, 1944).

out delusions or imposture, are preserved and imposed," Bacon, *Advancement of Learning*. Libraries "are the tombs of such as cannot die," George Crabbe, *The Library*. "Shelved around us lie / The mummied authors," Bayard Taylor, *The Poet's Journal: Third Evening*. "Thou canst not die. / Here thou art more than safe. / Where every book is thy epitaph," Henry Vaughan, *On Sir Thomas Bodley's Library*.

This presence of death in the text has been suggested not merely in countless secular texts, as sampled here, but abundantly in biblical texts as well. We read, for example, in 2 Corinthians 3:6, "The letter kills but the spirit gives life." The "spirit," *pneuma,* is of course breath, which gives being to sounded words, spoken words, the only real words there were or are or ever will be.

Countless other texts could be cited, from secular and religious sources. The *locus classicus* in the West would be perhaps Horace's final ode constituting the epilogue that concludes his first three books of *Odes*. It triumphantly begins, *"Exegi monumentum aere perennius"* (*Odes* 3. 30. 1): "I have erected a monument more lasting than bronze." Horace had made something, a collection of odes, a work consisting of words. However, he wants to dwell on its permanence; hence he must think of it as something other than words, for words are evanescent, *verba volant*. He could have thought of his collection, the product of his labor, as a limitless number of things, as a tool, or as a machine, or a vehicle, or a dwelling, or a shelter, or a graceful tower, or a pillar of ever-blazing fire, or perhaps as a nontree, as Joyce Kilmer once did. But—and this perhaps is the difference between Horace and Joyce Kilmer—Horace thinks of it precisely as monument, a manmade structure connected with death, which the literary creation, like the monument, is paradoxically to counter. Horace drives the point home in the sixth line, *"Non omnis moriar"*—"I shall not entirely die." But the monument which continues its and his existence after his death is itself dead, a nonliving surrogate for a dead person. Note that there is no way to say in real—that is, in spoken—words what Horace composed in writing. The oral statement "I have erected a monument," referring in parallel fashion to itself, would not be true, for the oral statement would not be a monument, since it always vanishes as soon as it is said. Horace's statement is true of itself only if it is made in writing. The statement must be constituted mortmain.

Literary works are commonly called brainchildren, or some such thing. Why did Horace not call his work here a brainchild? Because children die and Horace wanted to create something which cannot die. A poem is often thought of as a flower: the terms *florilegium* and *anthologia* mean in Latin and Greek respectively a collection of flowers, and thereby a collection of poems or other literary works. Thus there were ample antecedents for calling poems flowers. Why did Horace not call his poems a flower or a collection of flowers? Because flowers die, and do so conspicuously. Flowers, as just noted, are in fact symbols of full but fragile life, of death-in-life. Its obviously coming death is what makes the living rose the haunting symbol that it is.

As monument, Horace's collection of poems inevitably imposes and advertises death. A monument says not, "Death is coming," but "Death has come. I exist within death. I shall not change." In this sense, every written work is the author's own epitaph. Keats's meditation on the immobile coursing figures on his Grecian urn was a meditation on his own poetry and all poetry.

Because writing carries within it always an element of death, the tragic literary work—or simply the serious written work in general, the work which deals with life and death honestly—often turns out to be in some way about itself, as will be seen was the case in *Oedipus Rex* (with what conscious or unconscious authorial intent who knows?) and in *Finnegans Wake* (with both unconscious and very conscious authorial intent). That is to say, a work about death often modulates readily, if eerily, into a work about literature. For death inhabits texts.

Such is the virtue of texts, however, that their ability to absorb death makes death somehow less threatening. For, as already noted, the text assures a kind of life after death, which can readily be disguised as life without death.

Looking more closely at the psychodynamics at work in writing, we may note that, however unobtrusively, death presides at both ends of a writing operation. The basic reason is that the person being addressed as present is in fact absent and because, obversely, the author is not present to the reader although his words will be. The writer of the letter may even be dead by the time his words arrive at the locale to which they are sent. Or the reader presumed to be at the receiving end of the scribal operation may already be dead and buried when the letter is being penned to him by an unaware correspondent. (Curiously enough, during the very days when I was first working out these ideas, I drafted a letter to a correspondent who, as it tragically turned out, had already been dead two days at the time when I was composing my letter to him.)

Like writing, print is related to death, although the relationship is not exactly the same. It is even more definitive. Print comes in after death—that is, writing—has been accomplished. It works on the "body" of the written text which it treats with respect and reverence, as a dead body should be treated. The writer has produced a "body" because he has "executed" his work. (The word-play possible here is by no means coincidental: "execute," from Latin *ex-* and *sequi,* at root means follow through to the end.) Printers, like editors, feel deeply that they must deal with an unalterable, fixed text, and not with the spoken word. The text is sealed off from life and change. What was the author's final intention, his closing choice, the end product? "Final," "closing," "end": these are editors' preoccupations.

I recall the story of the linotype compositor who was approached by the proprietor of the shop where he worked and asked, "Set me up a slug with these words on it," and then was given some words orally. The linotype operator rose to his feet and glared at the shop owner. "If I have to do that, I quit. I set type. I do not take dictation." The source of this story I do not recall, though I know that I did not make it up myself, but even if it is apocryphal, it still represents the state of mind of most linotype compositors I have known. They deal with fixities, with text, not with living words. If you proffer a substitute for a text, you are in trouble. Death is not to be trifled with.

As has already been intimated several times here, writing of course has associations with other things besides the immobility of death. It can be thought of as an ongoing activity, like speech in a way—this is the image of the *calamus scribae velociter scribentis* of Psalm 45:2, the pen of the rapidly writing scribe. But writing leaves a fixed residue, as speech does not—the kind of thing attended to, in perspectives different from ours here, in Edmund Husserl's and Jacques Derrida's concept of the "trace."[6] Writing also has more positive associations with redemption and life, which will be gone into in more detail later. But these associations are paradoxical, realizable only in terms of death.

As contrasted with speech, writing is associated with death because it is never "natural" the way speech is. Unlike speech, writing is not unreflectively acquired by every normal person who grows up to maturity. Writing requires special reflective training, and terrifying restraints.[7] Moreover, the concepts and vocabulary connected with writing often associate the activity itself with activities which are, or can be, lethal, such as cutting and dismembering. The word can be "incised" or cut into a surface (such as marble); the "stylus" means originally a stake, a spearlike instrument; "scribe" connects with the Proto-Indo-European root *skeri,* to cut, separate, the same root that gives us not only "inscribe" (cut into, like "incise") but also "crime," "critic," "crisis," and "hypocrite." The association of writing with death is not total, but it is manifold and inescapable.

The Retrospectivity of Literature

The relationship of the text to death is allied to the relationship of literature to past time. In a recent germinal paper, "On

6. See Jacques Derrida, *De la grammatologie* (Paris: Editions de Minuit, 1967); *L'Ecriture et la différence* (Paris: Editions du Seuil, 1967); "La Différance," in *Théorie d'ensemble,* ed. Phillipe Sollers *et al.* (Paris: Editions du Seuil, 1968).

7. See Walter J. Ong, *The Presence of the Word* (New Haven: Yale University Press, 1967), pp. 134–138.

Literature and the Bible," building on diversified sources in scriptural scholarship, notably on Gerhard von Rad, as well as on modern literary theory, James Nohrnberg has noted that works of literature generally are marked by what he calls "a deep posteriority."[8] The reader's appreciation is necessarily posterior to the "setting down" of the work; it is retrospective. From the reader's standpoint, all literature is preterite. As an instance of what he is referring to by the "deep posteriority" of literature, Nohrnberg cites the "mute and admiring retrospectivity that overtakes us at the end of a long novel," when "all our surmise is a surmise upon things past." He goes ahead to argue, I believe convincingly, that the reader of the Bible is not caught up in such "deep posteriority" and that consequently it is deceptive to regard the Bible as simply and truly "literature." A story ends *"ever after,* just as it began *once upon a time."* A story pattern "crosses into time and out of it at aligned points." But "the Bible does not want to end ever after, however clear it is that the canon itself is closed." To use an instance which Nohrnberg does not use, one might make his point by saying that at the end of the Gospel according to Matthew, for example, the reader simply does not sense a "deep posteriority" or enter into "a surmise upon things past" in the way in which he or she might after reading *The Return of the Native* or *Who's Afraid of Virginia Woolf?* Nor does he or she at the end of the Book of Revelation, the last, and truly climactic, book of the Bible.

We can return later to the matter of the Bible as nonliterature or antiliterature. Let us first reflect further upon the "deep posteriority" and the "surmise upon things past" which Nohrnberg finds in literature as such.

Nohrnberg instances the novel as possessing the "deep posteriority" to which he refers. One can carry his observations further, and in directions he does not undertake to explore. A novel is about a fictionalized past, but some kind of retrospectivity pos-

8. James Nohrnberg, "On Literature and the Bible," *Centrum* (published twice a year by the Minnesota Center for Advanced Studies in Language, Style, and Literary Theory), 2, No. 2 (1974), 27, also 5.

sesses us even when we read a poem whose thematic focus is in the future, such as Christopher Marlowe's "Come live with me and be my love," which is an especially good instance because it is one of the many poems of its sort upon a standard topos, the promise of idyllic happiness in a love life together. Not only a novel, but any work of literature, even a future-focused work, such as this little poem, is possessed when the reader has been through it, or better, when it has progressed through his mind, which is to say when it is a thing of the past in the reader's own history. *"M'introduire dans ton histoire,"* Mallarmé begins his distraught love poem.

In this sense, the glow of all literary enjoyment is retrospective rather than anticipatory or even participatory. Life as such can be enjoyed while it is being lived. So can a football game be enjoyed while it is being played. A literary work, too, is enjoyed while it is being read (or seen or heard, in the case of a play), but it is most fully enjoyed, as life and football hardly are, when it has been completed. This is because, unlike life or a football game, a literary work has a plot (more or less obtrusive, more or less obfuscated) which makes it a unit, a whole. Readers are tempted to peek at the closing pages of a story to see how it "comes out." The plot focuses the work in its climax and denouement: a literary work has an interior posteriority, a posterior slant from the beginning. The story hangs back into time from its conclusion. This organizational posteriority we can call interior retrospectivity.

To this interior retrospectivity or posteriority of literature, to its being in one way or another plotted, the academic study of literature in the West—and elsewhere, too—had in the past added another retrospectivity, an exterior one, in that for centuries academic study of literature had included in its purview only the literature of classical antiquity to the exclusion of more recent and, a fortiori, of contemporary works. Works of literature were not only retrospective interiorly; they also came out of the distant past, and in this sense were exteriorly retrospective.

The feeling for literature as a matter of nostalgic recollections about a well-known shared past, recollections called up before a fireplace with a flagon of ale and a hot poker, a feeling cultivated as paradigmatic by older litterateurs such as Sir Arthur Quiller-Couch, was one of the things which set on edge the teeth of F. R. Leavis and, with less querulous, more boisterous reactions, the teeth of Ezra Pound, thereby helping to call into being the once New Criticism. This New Criticism took form as vernacular literature claimed the attention of the universities, and it thought programmatically of serious literature not as a distillation out of the past, but as an organization of human experience, which could be attempted and achieved variously, at any period at all, past or present or future.[9]

This exterior retrospectivity, the association of literature with the remote past, had been in great part a heritage from the old oral culture of mankind, where narrative and other verbal art forms tended to be concerned with the past—"tell us a story of the days of old"—because of the need for an oral culture to keep verbalizing its past in order to not have it slip completely out of consciousness. The relatively high, though not exclusive, concentration on literature concerned with the present or near-present, which is one of the characteristics of the New Criticism and of the age for which it spoke and still speaks,[10] marks a major shift in consciousness away from some last survivals of oral psychic structures.

This shift in consciousness is shown by the fact that the age of the New Criticism registered not only the abandonment of "exterior retrospectivity" but a certain abandonment of "interior retrospectivity" as well. Interior retrospectivity, we have seen, is connected with plot: a story plotted in standard or linear fashion is rather conspicuously organized from its ending, for the ending controls the selection of earlier incidents. But this kind of story has appreciably been downgraded in recent decades, which have undertaken in one way or another con-

9. See Walter J. Ong, *The Barbarian Within* (New York: Macmillan, 1962), Ch. 10, "The Vernacular Matrix of the New Criticism."
    10. See Chapter 8 above.

spicuously to minimize plot, burying it in infinite conplexities (as in Joyce's *Ulysses* or *Finnegans Wake*), tangling it back into itself (as in Alain Robbe-Grillet's *La Jalousie* or *Marienbad* or in Julio Cortázar's *Rayuela*), or even pretending to eliminate it, as in countless anecdoctal short stories that seem to start nowhere and end nowhere.

But the plot is most often not really eliminated by these tactics; only obvious plot is. Many of the most effective works that seem to attenuate or obfuscate what can be styled standard or linear plot still hang from their endings, although in tortuous ways, and indeed tend to breath a nostalgia—as in Joyce or Robbe-Grillet—that makes them more "posterior" or retrospective for readers than many or most other works.

Narrative and Retrospectivity

It is natural to treat the retrospectivity of literature as focused somehow in storytelling or narrative, to which we can for our purposes here assimilate drama, which presents a tale, though it lacks explicit narrative voice. The warrant for focusing literature on narrative is simply that narrative enjoys a kind of paramountcy among literary forms, and indeed among the oral forms which preceded literature and out of which literature grew.[11] In some sense, the urge to "tell a story" is the paradigmatic urge which results in getting literary creation onto paper. Even a lyric poem in a way is an attempt to "tell a story," the story of the author's reaction to something. A child's earliest experience of protracted verbal art forms is normally experience of stories. If he or she has experience of briefer verbal art forms— mnemonic verses or nursery rhymes, for example—these themselves after a while are likely to generate stories in which they can be set in order to explain what they "mean," much as early man generated myth as his primal explanation of the universe, to represent why things are the way they are.

In this sense, narrative is the primal way in which the

11. See Robert Scholes and Robert Kellogg, *The Nature of Narrative* (New York: Oxford University Press, 1966).

human lifeworld is organized verbally and intellectually. All science itself is grounded somehow in narrative history: the phenomenon or experiment has first to be observed step-by-step and "written up." In other words, all knowledge is grounded in experience; experience is strung out in time; time sequence calls for narrative.

The roots of narrative are sunk in retrospectivity, where they run off in all directions in great tangles. Even a story purported to be cast in a future age is normally told in a past tense: "I went there in 1984" rather than "I will go there in 1984." This posteriority of an imagined future is so much taken for granted that it appears banal to call attention to it.

The reason for casting the narrative future in the cadre of the past is not far to seek. The future as such is not in fact strung out sequentially as the past is. Contingencies, which constitute the human future, do not have fixed antecedents. They are "if's" in the context of other "if's". The human future as such is at loose ends, and a narrative needs connections. Contingencies provide no story line, but branch out like computer charts. A narrative, even about the future, must therefore set up the future as a quasi-real concatenation of free acts, which can be really connected only if viewed as over with—which is to say, as past. Even stringing together a series of connected events in clearly marked future tenses does not produce an effect much different from narration in the past tense: "She will go to her bedchamber. A frog will be sitting on her bed. He will beg her for a kiss. She will bestow the kiss on him, and he will become a handsome prince and carry her off to his mountain kingdom." Such narrative is still structured back from the last of the future events, the kingdom come.

Tricks can be played of course, with this basic orientation to the past, as they are played in the case of Merlin in T. H. White's *The Once and Future King*. But such tours de force are interesting largely because they are *bizarreries,* distorting the basic retrospective orientation of narrative, which paradigmatically begins, "Once upon a time there was. . . ." There is no normal way of framing a story, "Once upon a time there will be. . . ." Although a statement such as this may be equivalently a dare, and someone may immediately compose and publish a story which does begin "Once upon a time there will be . . ." such a story will spark interest precisely because it is, or will be, abnormal—which is not to say that it is, or will be, uninteresting or artistically unsound.

Even comedy, which typically ends by facing into the future— "ever after"—does so with curious retrospectivity. At the "ever after" end of a comedy—and I am speaking of the inclusive genre, not just of the dramatic comedy—one might expect a statement that the characters *will* now lead a happy life. But that is not the way the texts typically read. They say, "they lived happily ever after," or the equivalent. Why the past tense, "lived"? And why the "after" which refers to the future as lodged in the past? We are still looking back to see these happy-ever-after-people. Even the future of narrative is a rear-vision mirror.

The Retrospectivity of Plot

We have noted earlier that plot itself binds narrative to retrospectivity. Further reflections on this effect of plot will prove helpful. I am speaking here of standard or "classical" linear plot—rise to climax, reversal (recognition), falling action, denouement—though in a given case these elements may be delivered in a sequence somewhat different from this, for example, through flashbacks. As noted earlier, for some time now such standard plotting has been in certain disfavor, but it is still with us, for what has replaced the linear-plotted narrative is not simply unplotted stories, but deplotted stories, not stories which have no plot but stories which in one way or another advertise that they have no plot. That is to say, they have an antiplot, something which is not a plot but is defined by reference to plot. Plot is very much still with us, only now displayed under wraps.

The linear or standard plot is programed to be structurally

retrospective, bound to the past, by the very fact that typically it involves recognition, a kind of return movement to the past, as Coleridge has noted,[12] a reknowing toward the end in definitive fashion what was earlier, at the plot's beginning, sensed only in some obscure way. This reknowing is re-cognition. At the end of a plotted story, the reader says to himself or herself, "Ahah! Looking back I see now how all this was present in germ anteriorly, given the setting, the characters, and their decisions and other actions, which were themselves somewhat present from the start."

Such re-cognition is not the same as Aristotle's *anagnōrisis* (usually translated, recognition), in which a character within a story gains knowledge previously withheld and thereby triggers the reversal or *peripeteia* in the movement of the plot. But the two of them are related. The *anagnōrisis* whereby the character gains previously withheld knowledge is a kind of model of re-cognition whereby the reader (or playgoer) gains knowledge previously not possessed. One retrospectivity mirrors the other. For this reason, a good many stories and plays, as has earlier been hinted, can be viewed as plays not just about their ostensible subject matter but also about narrative plot itself.

This is the case with Sophocles' *Oedipus Rex,* for example. In any standardly plotted play or narrative, the introduction sets up a conflict which is in effect an enigmatic prediction of what is to come. The situation in Act I of *King Lear* hints, confusingly and uncertainly, at the way the play will end. The standard plot, however, does not treat expressly and in so many words prediction and fulfillment. It enacts them. As do other standardly plotted plays, *Oedipus Rex* enacts prediction and fulfillment, but it also talks explicitly about them as such. In *Oedipus Rex,* the Sphinx has made an explicit, enigmatic prediction about Oedipus' future which the play works toward fulfilling, though in unexpected ways. Prediction and fulfillment

12. Letter to Cottle, 1815, in *Collected Letters of Samuel Taylor Coleridge,* ed. Earl Leslie Griggs (Oxford: Oxford University Press, 1956–), IV, 545.

thus become this play's subject matter as well as its mode of proceeding. *Oedipus Rex* takes as its explicit subject the prediction-fulfillment which is the underlying, implicit principle of standard dramatic plot generally, for, as we have seen, in dramatic plot the conclusion is made to appear somehow fitted to the beginning. The way the conclusion fits the beginning varies, of course. The conclusion may register what was unconsciously expected, given the beginning, or what was "unexpected," that is to say, the outcome that was feared and unconsciously rejected as a possibility. After its occurrence, the "unexpected" somehow fits well in a well constructed plot.

Plot is paradoxical. On the one hand, it makes a story seem real and gives it its psychological appeal or bite. The plot of *Oedipus Rex* fits everyone's psychological structures so well that Freud could psychoanalyze real human beings and interpret their problems in terms of what is fittingly called the "Oedipus complex." On the other hand, plot is what differentiates art from real life. Plotting is highly artificial, a contrived arrangement. To match the end of a series of events in a human being's life to the beginning, or, more accurately, the beginning to the end, in a standard narrative plot, a narrator or playwright has to be exquisitely and ruthlessly selective. He or she treats only what fits his or her feel for "structure," that is, for plot in the sense in which we have been using this term. This differentiates fiction from real life, which never has a plot, for real life is generally spotty, stringy, and always "dense": it includes all the myriads of things and events, "too numerous to be enumerated," as James Joyce puts it, that the narrator must leave out to make his story, in which everything bears on the final recognition. Our real lives are cognized, not re-cognized; known, not reknown.

Plot and Cyclic Pattern

The retrospective exigencies of plot help explain the drift into cyclic patterns which marks the time sense of a great deal of narrative. I have discussed this drift elsewhere, and the ways in which it inhibits assimilation by serious poetry and serious literature of the present-day sense of an open-system, noncyclic, evolutionary universe.[13] Here we need only note the way in which cyclic patterns enforce retrospectivity. Plot means movement. A circle is described by moving away from a starting point, but, unlike a straight line, formed by moving simply farther and farther away from the starting point, a line describing a circle begins its relentless return to its starting point at the very instant it starts to move away from it. A circle is a paradigm of all repetition, from its start bent toward the past. "In my beginning is my end" is eminently true of the circle or cycle.

The instances of cyclical patterns in literature and art are beyond all counting—the classic one, that of myth of the seasons, works in various ways from as far back in history or prehistory as we can go, through Yeat's poetry and vertiginious theorizing in *A Vision,* and on to present-day creations such as Anthony Powell's just completed work, *A Dance to the Music of Time,* with its four volumes, *Spring, Summer, Autumn,* and *Winter,* each with three parts corresponding to the three months of each season. The most famous recent instance of cyclical pattern is doubtlessly Joyce's *Finnegans Wake,* which has the added advantage for our present purposes of being, even more than is *Oedipus Rex,* a self-conscious model of literature itself.

Finnegans Wake faces backward into itself. It is an uroboros, the mythical serpent with its tail in its own mouth. The last sentence of *Finnegans Wake* trails off incomplete because the reader is to feed it back into the first sentence of the work: in one of the most beautifully sad and profoundly nostalgic passages in all literature, Joyce has the River Liffey, and all life with her, slipping back into the sea—"it's old and old it's sad and old it's sad and weary I go back to you, my cold father, my cold mad father, my cold mad feary father . . . I rush, my only, into your arms. . . . Save me from those therrble prongs!"—only to rise softly from the sea again in vapor and

13. Walter J. Ong, *In the Human Grain* (New York: Macmillan, 1967), pp. 99–126.

to come down once more as rain to begin her journey over again forever and ever. The journey will be renewed, but renewal here means not the future, not new newness, but old newness, repetition of the past. When you put *Finnegans Wake* aside, what dwells with you is not the future but an overwhelming pastness, and its sweet sadness. With "moyles and moyles" of deliberation behind it, deliberation which was strictly aesthetic in the Kierkegaardian sense of this term, Joyce's work dramatizes in its very textual shape, in its uroboric structure, the "deep posteriority," or retrospective flavor of literature generally.

Its retrospectivity is what gives *Finnegans Wake* its overpowering impact on the unconscious. For the unconscious is retrospective, tied to what has been, ontogenetically and phylogenetically. Its archetypal images carry us back to the beginnings of existence, not to where existence is going. For the reader who brings to it adequate erudition and feeling for the language, I know of no other passage in literature which reaches into all corners of the unconscious, as well as into many areas of consciousness, more deftly or deeply or more hauntingly than the last pages of *Finnegans Wake,* or that presents to the reader more exquisite or nostalgic beauty. In my beginning is my end. This is not the same as to say, in my end is my beginning—the latter is a statement not of fatalism but of hope.

Orality and Retrospectivity

Much of what I have said about the retrospectivity of literary narrative applies likewise to oral genres. In oral performance, too, narrative is about the past, and in some ways even more explicitly and intently and urgently than in literary art.[14] The paradigmatic situation out of which narrative arises in an oral culture is caught in the invitation, "Tell us a story of the days of old." In literate cultures, such a story may well be a luxury.

14. See G. A. Groningen, *In the Grip of the Past: Essay on an Aspect of Greek Thought* (Leiden: Brill, 1953).

In an oral culture, it is a matter of life and death. Without such stories, the culture would disappear, the personality structures in which it consists and which constitute it would disintegrate. Narrative about the past encapsulates most of the lore of an oral culture; that is to say, it stores the culture's verbalized knowledge.

Nevertheless, in one way verbal genres of an oral culture are quite evidently less tied to the past than are words in script or print. For the so-called "work" of oral art, the instance of the genre, is always live performance. It is really not a "work," but an action. There is no narrative set down in the past once and for all, to survive in the present as a monument. The oral story actually exists only when it is being performed.

Potentially, of course, a story that has been told orally exists in living memory. But living memory is by no means the same thing as a fixed text, as St. Augustine and, before him, Plato were well aware. For one thing, living memory of a lengthy narrative in an oral culture, as we know from field work, and resulting recordings, is never verbatim.[15] The only lengthy

15. See the documentation in Ong, *The Presence of the Word,* p. 32. The Vedic hymns are often instanced as an example of verbatim memory in an oral culture. In *The Singer of Tales,* p. 280, n. 9, citing Bogatyrev and Jakobson, Lord comments on the case of the Vedic hymns to question in what sense they could have been oral. I have never seen or heard a statement asserting their verbatim preservation under totally oral conditions which takes into account what we know about oral recitation since the work of Parry and Lord.

It does appear that oral poets do and did at times make some efforts to commit verses to verbatim memory more calculated than recent students of oral tradition have sometimes implied such efforts might be. But success here and, perhaps, even objectives do not at all correspond to those of writing cultures. In a paper, "Oral Poetry: Some Linguistic and Typological Considerations," in Benjamin A. Stolz and Richard S. Shannon, eds., *Oral Literature and the Formula* (Ann Arbor, Mich.: Center for the Coordination of Ancient and Modern Studies, 1976), pp. 73–106, Paul Kiparsky cites (pp. 99–100) the usual instance of the Vedic hymns, but his only references affirming their verbatim memorization are to two works, one published in 1906 and the other in 1927, when features distinctive of literate cultures were regularly and unconsciously imputed to what we can now call primary orality (orality untouched by any knowledge of writing). In the discussion following Professor Kiparsky's paper, Jeffrey Opland notes that oral poets with whom he has worked in Africa do make an effort at times

verbalization ever effectively recuperable verbatim is one which has been displaced from the living world of sound by being fixed artificially in space by writing. To think of memory as essentially verbatim is to resort to an unreal model for memory fostered by literacy and its practice of transcribing texts. In the New Testament, still exquisitely oral by comparison with texts coming out of latter-day vigorously programed literacy, even the words of institution of the Eucharist do not appear exactly the same in any two places. In purely oral memory, formulas and themes are more or less fixed, the stable elements in the storage and retrieval process. But they are always assembled in the present, and each time in a different way.

Compared to these relationships of orality to pastness or "posteriority," the relationships of literature to such "posteriority" are more complex. In oral performance the past lives at the surface of the present. In written performance it both lives there and enjoys a reflective, historical existence of its own. T. S. Eliot's poem *The Wasteland* is exquisitely contemporary and incorporates snatches of past literature into itself as live bits of contemporary reading and reflective experience but also as located in specific periods of the past. The way in which material anterior to the *Iliad* or the *Odyssey* is incorporated into these poems leaves such material hardly any discernible historical

---

to commit verses to memory. To show the seriousness of their effort he reports that "any poet in the community will repeat the poem which is in my limited testing at least sixty percent in correlation with other versions." This is hardly even an approximation of what "verbatim" means in a chirographic culture. The fact that it attests to a concerted effort on the part of the poets and that it represents a remarkable achievement shows how far apart orality and literacy are.

From Lord's work (*The Singer of Tales,* pp. 26–29) we know that illiterate (which does not mean unskilled or unsophisticated) oral performers will assert and believe that verbatim repetition is achieved, "line for line and word for word," when sound tapes attest with absolute certainty that such is not the case at all. Indeed, Lord finds it is never the case: variation is the universal rule. Moreover, even so standard a recent source as the article "Sanskrit Language and Literature," second section, "Literature," by H. Julius Eggeling and John Allan, in the *Encyclopaedia Britannica* (1965) cites the fluidity of the Vedic texts, the variability of the oral tradition, the various stages of the poems over the centuries, etc.

base of its own to stand on. *Beowulf,* it appears, is an example of intermediate work. It seems to have a touch of historicity. That is to say, there is some kind of literary, and indeed Christian, influence at work here.

Textuality and Plot

One further connection or series of connections remains to be noted. It is that between the retrospectivity occasioned by textuality and the retrospectivity encouraged by plot. Text and plot are in fact intimately connected. Writing makes possible plotting that is tighter than oral performance can manage. Lengthy oral plot is always more or less episodic, and not by conscious design but simply out of necessity. The work of Lord and Havelock has shown that it is virtually, if not indeed absolutely, impossible for the oral poet (or prose narrator) fully to control the narrative sequence, and indeed that poems of the length of the *Iliad* and the *Odyssey* had probably never been performed as wholes, but only in more or less separate episodes, so long as the culture was purely oral—a situation paralleled today in oral narrative among the Nyanga people in eastern Zaire. When moderately long sequences of episodes are strung together by narrators in primary oral cultures, it is inevitable that what literates would style major lapses in control of temporal sequences would occur, such as that concerning the scar of Odysseus discussed by Erich Auerbach in *Mimesis.*[16]

The good oral narrator was not the one who avoided flash-backs, for no one could do this: he was the one who could

16. See Lord, *The Singer of Tales,* pp. 124–138, 153; Havelock, *Preface to Plato,* pp. 125, 133, 185–186; Daniel Biebuyck and Kahombo C. Mateene, eds., *The Mwindo Epic: From the Banyanga* (Berkeley: University of California Press, 1969), p. 14; Erich Auerbach, *Mimesis: The Representation of Reality in Western Literature* (Princeton, N.J.: Princeton University Press, 1953), pp. 1–20. When Candi Rureke was asked to do the narrative now published as *The Mwindo Epic,* he insisted that no one had ever before put all these stories about Mwindo into a whole within a continuous span of days (it took him twelve successive days). Other narrators were not even interested in trying, but the new idea of taping excited Mr. Rureke and produced the necessary outburst of energy—just as the new idea of writing out the stories of the Trojan War presumably excited a poet such as Homer,

make flashbacks work well. Starting by a plunge *in media res* was hardly a free choice. The poet found himself doing it willy-nilly. A later literate age putting into writing long narratives deriving from oral tradition would of course find it natural, even though no longer necessary, to preserve their episodic organization and flashbacks.

Closer plotting demands writing. The first closely plotted genre that formed in Western classical antiquity was the Greek drama, which, paradoxically, although it was presented orally, was the first genre in which the verbal product was completely controlled by writing. Plays were produced from texts. Some of Euripides' we know were performed for the first time after his death. This fact alone proves the textuality of ancient Greek drama, as does also the verbatim joint recitation of passages by a chorus, as well as contemporary testimony.

The alliance of plotting with writing and print is even more strikingly brought out by the fact that prose narrative nowhere develops the close plotting which the drama had developed until not only writing but print itself had been deeply interiorized in the psyche. Until the rise of the novel in the Romantic age, say with Jane Austen, prose narrative all remained more or less episodic. Such are the ancient Greek romances, medieval romances, lengthy Renaissance narrative, and later narrative through Fielding. The prose writer had a hard time getting out of his sensibility the idea that he was "telling" a story orally. The addresses to the "dear reader" which punctuate even nineteenth-century novels show how self-conscious the narrator had to be to adjust to the fact that it was really isolated readers, not an oral audience, to whom he or she was addressing himself or herself. A fully tight plot, where carefully advertised recognition scenes determine the movement of the entire narrative, as in a detective story, can only develop in the age of Edgar Allan Poe.

The detailed connections here remain somewhat obscure, for, I believe, no one has fully worked them out. But the fact is that retrospectivity deriving from the physical textuality of a story is needed in order to establish the full interior retrospectivity of the plot. The author has to be able to put something down, leave it there, and return to it when it is necessary to get the closely plotted story organized. This is not to deny that, having once learned how to do this with the help of writing, it may well be possible for an individual author to compose fairly complex stories without actual chirographic control, or only with partial chirographic control. Still, there are limits.

Dickens is a case in point. Dickens often wrote his novels with reduced chirographic control—serially, so that the anterior parts of the stories appeared in print before Dickens had written the succeeding parts. The stories are often highly episodic, but not so much as typical oral performance. Dickens' situation differed from that of the oral rhapsodist on several counts. First, he had had experience of prose narrative, his own and others, with full chirographic control, that is, with the opportunity for revision anywhere in the story at any time during the composition. Secondly, although in serial writing and publication he never had his complete text in front of him in a revisable state— what was printed was printed and had to fit the coming installments the way it was—he did at least have an exact record of what he had told in the story. One can imagine how much more episodic *Nicholas Nickleby*, for example, might have been had Dickens not had his printed fascicles of earlier installments to consult as he moved ahead with the new installments, but only recollections of their oral renditions.

In sum, the posteriority of textuality and the posteriority intrinsic to standard, linear plot in lengthy narrative grow out of the same soil, for without text there is in lengthy narrative no full-blown, linear plot, structured back from its climactic end.

The Fecundity of Writing and Print

The largely unconscious association of writing and print with retrospectivity, the past, and death is by no means exclusive of an association, more largely conscious, of these same media with life, and not merely life as perdurance, in the sense discussed earlier here, but with life as fecundity, growth, exuberance.

There is a vast literature and an even vaster general awareness concerning the limitless fecundity of texts. Where would culture be without writing? The accumulation of information, the growth of understanding, the network of human awareness that now unites mankind in what Pierre Teilhard de Chardin calls the "noosphere," the tremendous surge of consciousness which has brought together the human race across the globe and launched it into space—all this and immeasurably more that constitutes our human lifeworld would be unthinkable without writing practices that are deeply interiorized in the human psyche. The Bible itself, with which we are particularly concerned here, associates writing not only with death but also quite explicitly with redemption, liberation, and exuberant life. The Gospel according to John states at its close (20:31) that "these things are written that you may believe that Jesus is the Christ, the Son of God, and that believing you may have life in his name."

Writing has made possible the vast evolution of consciousness that marks the later stages of human history. Without writing, not only tightly plotted lengthy narrative but also the kind of mental processes which go with the composition of even an encyclopedia article, not to mention more massive scholarly and scientific treatises, would be unthinkable in the fullest sense of this term. Oral cultures cannot organize information in this sequentiality. Writing has made possible not only development of science and technology as well as of the humanities (that is, the study of language, history, philosophy, theology, and other subjects having to do with man not as a physical being or an organism, but with man as a self-conscious being and thus with the life of the mind and with freedom); it has also made possible the complex relationships between large groups of people which a fully populated planet demands.

The thought processes of oral cultures are complex and beautiful, and they are never quite foregone by chirographic cultures but they have quite a different movement from those typical of chirographic cultures: oral noetic processes, as has already been pointed out, are typically formulaic and conservative of wholes, not analytic and dissecting. Without the mental processes implemented by writing and print, it is impossible even to discover that there are such things as oral cultures. The word reduced to an inscribed surface, silenced, then resurrected, has a potential, new fecundities, even regarding our relationship to the oral word, which are forever denied to the purely oral word. The word must die and be resurrected if it is to come into its own.

What this means is that what is true in other areas of existence is also curiously true in the case of the human word. Death is fecund. We must die to one stage of our existence in order to achieve the next. The child entering school for the first time weeps, mourns, because he or she senses that the old life with mother, the security of the home, is gone forever. Without the mourning, the sadness, the death, there could be no growth. At a graduation, a marriage, the entering of the novitiate (from *novus,* new) of a religious order (I remember this well), there is sadness, there are tears, and there is death to the old, but this for the sake of the bracing newness—without such death, life is stagnated. "Those wedding bells are breaking up that old gang of mine," the popular song ran. It was a good thing they were. The gang did not have much future. Death in these cases is not only sad, it is also strengthening, invigorating. It has no merit in itself, but it means everything: it is the only gate to something new. "Unless the grain of wheat die."

Those reared in a highly literate culture, where literate habits of thought are acquired shortly after infancy, commonly have little if any memory of entry into writing as a cutting loose from oral thought processes, as a kind of death. For those dominated through adolescence by the functional orality of subcultures in our American cities or some of our rural districts, the situation is quite different. They feel writing as a threat, a destruction of their psychic world, however desirable writing may be. Without proper encouragement to enter into this death, persons from such subcultures grow into adulthood without entering into, much less mastering, the analytic thinking processes which can be interiorized only by grappling with the written word.

Once it has entered into the death of the text, the word becomes in countless ways more versatile than the purely vocal, living word. It can be freed from the surface, resurrected, variously. It can be put into more combinations because it can be retrieved from the past, immediate or remote, and inserted into any number of times and places and thus be combined with other words in a maze of patterns unknown to oral cultures. An oral culture, as has been seen, can establish only limited linearity or sequence, temporal or analytic. Genealogies, boring to literates, are a favorite oral art from across the globe because they have proved a ready way of doing conspicuously what oral cultures have great difficulties in doing at all, namely, lining up a sizable assortment of discreet elements.

The fecundity of the text, however, is realizable only through its connections with the oral world. In this sense, text as text is essentially dead. For texts are there to produce words, which are irreducibly sounds, realized orally either in externalized utterance or in the interior imagination. The most elaborate computer program, which is simultaneously a vastly simplified and a vastly complicated text, becomes meaningful only at the point when a human being can link it to words, which are ultimately sounds. The huge computer banks put men on the moon, but only because of the teams of human beings constantly checking out everything in the universe of words which hold together their consciousness in today's noosphere.

The reestablishment of the written or printed word in the oral world means that the word must somehow be restored to the mouth, the oral cavities and apparatus where the word originated. This restoration is minimized, though real, in highly technologized print cultures. Technologized print cultures foster rapid reading, in which words are formed chiefly in the imagination and often sketchily. They regard movement of the lips in reading as retrograde or childish. The case was different in the highly oral cultures in which the biblical texts came into being, where reading was less deeply interiorized, that is to say, where reading called for a more conscious effort, was considered a greater achievement, and was less a determinant of psychic structures and personality, still basically oral in organization.

In such highly oral cultures, it was not sufficient for the reader simply to imagine the sounds of the words being read. Books in such a culture do not "contain" something called "material." They speak or say words.[17] The written words had to be mouthed aloud, in their full being, restored to and made to live in the oral cavities in which they came into existence. In *La Manducation de la parole,* a posthumous collection of two of his works, one previously published and one not, the late distinguished specialist in biblical and other Middle East orality, past and present, Père Marcel Jousse, S.J., treats beautifully what he calls the "eating of the word in oral cultures, its being passed from mouth to mouth."[18] This "eating of the word" gives a new dimension and force to imaginary incidents such as the eating of the little scroll in Revelation 10:9–10, which otherwise may appear merely quaint or bizarre to technological man.

Those who know highly oral cultures will recognize what Jousse means. I recall an instance from my own experience in the Arab world. After a talk I had given to a group of Moslem intellectual and cultural leaders at the residence of the United States Ambassador in Rabat in the spring of 1975, one of the Moslem guests was holding forth on the subject of my talk, which in fact had to do with the differences between oral cultures and typographically controlled cultures. He was punctuating his remarks with quotations from the Koran, which he knew by heart in Arabic and was rendering impromptu into French, the language in which I had spoken and in which the discussion

---

17. Walter J. Ong, *Ramus, Method, and the Decay of Dialogue* (Cambridge, Mass.: Harvard University Press, 1958), pp. 307–318. See also Chapter 6 above.

18. Marcel Jousse, *La Manducation de la parole* (Paris: Gallimard, 1975), pp. 45–54.

was being conducted. As he shaped each quotation into French, the other Moslems present excitedly mouthed the passage in subdued voices in Arabic. Their compulsive chiming in struck me as so natural that it appeared inevitable. I recalled that the word "Koran" means "recitation." The ear and the mouth, with the rest of the associated vocalizing apparatus here worked simultaneously in making the word spoken by another one's own. The uttered (that is "outered"), oral word in such a culture is almost palpable. It provides the base and substance of thought. The spoken word is not assimilated passively, but chewed on, eaten, mouthed by the hearers themselves when they fully participate in listening and in the thinking that goes with the listening.

This was the basis of the old-style school recitation that dominated academic education in the West from antiquity until only a few generations ago and that still dominates academic education in much of the world.[19] Such recitation is inevitably killed off by the literacy which academic education ultimately establishes in a deeply interiorized form. In the oral setting, the fascination with the discovery of the hitherto unknown which marks technologized print cultures is less operative: here it is more satisfying to avoid novelties and to listen to what you know and can recite, so that you can mouth, taste, savor knowledge. Oral culture manifests here, as in so many other places, its ultra-conservatism, its drive and need to remain with what it has, to downgrade what is novel as inconsequential—in short, its commitment to repetition, which, despite certain shortcomings, can be a beautifully human thing.

Life, Death, and the Word of God

Within the perspectives elaborated here in order to situate a text as text in relation to death and life, what can be said about the Bible as text? For, as has been noted initially in this study,

19. See Walter J. Ong, "Agonistic Structures in Academia: Past to Present," *Interchange* (Toronto), 5 (1974), 1–12.

the Bible as such exists as text and only as a text, despite its manifold and tangled oral roots. The psychodynamics of orality have to be taken into account as never before and concurrently the deep-structured contrast between textuality and orality has to be attended to more explicitly. In the case of the Bible, even more than in the cases of other texts, we do not commonly think of writing and print as connected with retrospectivity and with death and with restoration to a new life, as the present perspectives invite us to do. The connections here do not leap to the eye. Conscious acknowledgment of their presence may meet with resistance, for what we are dealing with are connections operating well below the ordinary threshold of consciousness, in the unconscious or subconscious realms of the psyche.

The Bible as a text has certain unique characteristics which can be examined here under two related heads: first, the futurity of the Bible, its nonpreterite cast, and second, the special status of textuality, despite its kinship with death, established by the Christian doctrine of the incarnation of the Word of God. Questions here can be considered basically with reference to the Bible as a whole. Much more could be said, and obviously would need to be said, with reference to its individual parts.

The futurity of the biblical text has been pointed out by James Nohrnberg in the article initially cited here. As quoted earlier, Nohrnberg notes, "When a story ends, it ends *ever after,* just as it began *once upon a time.*"[20] The Bible is not like a story in this sense. It is not something that "crosses into time and out of it at aligned points. . . . The Bible does not want to end ever after, however clear it is that the canon itself is closed." Nohrnberg thus makes clear his point that the Bible is hardly a member of the class "literature" but presents a rival kind of organization, so that treating the Bible simply as "literature" misses what the Bible proposes itself to be,[21] or, one might add, it misses what literature is, or it misses both. These statements need to be made

20. Nohrnberg, "On Literature and the Bible," *Centrum,* 2, No. 2 (1974), 29.
21. Ibid., p. 5.

with full awareness of the tendency in modern literature, discussed earlier in this chapter and in Chapter 11 below, to blur the edge between art and life, but they are still basically true, for the blurring itself is art.

Nohrnberg's case can be argued on certain more explicit grounds which he skirts but does not undertake to explore. For the Bible actually ends with an explicit cast into the future, the explicit opposite of "ever after." The last words of the Book of Revelation and thus of the Christian Bible are explicitly, "Come, Lord Jesus! The grace of our Lord Jesus Christ be with all. Amen."[22] The gesturing into the future here is not restricted to the close of the Bible. This close is climactic, for future gesturing characterizes the whole New Testament and, as Nohrnberg again has shown, is also in line with the pervasive prophetic tone and the future-oriented messianism of the Old. Paul closes his First Letter to the Corinthians (16:22) with the same expression put urgently into Aramaic, *"Maranatha,"* "Our Lord, come" (the translation more probable than the credal "Our Lord has come").

It is true that Jesus, the Word, has already come. But what the New Testament kerygma announces is not simply a repetition of the first coming. The text does not read, "Come back," but simply "Come." The new coming is not by any means a mere repetition of the first. It will not be like the first. No uroboros here. This the Bible itself makes clear. The second coming will be "on the clouds of heaven," in judgment. And there are only two comings: the first, which prepares for the last, and the last, which is neither to repeat the first nor to finish off the first but rather to confirm and transmute the first and with it, everything, into the fullness of life.

In a recent article,[23] Karl Rahner considers the problem for

22. When Nohrnberg treats the "last words of the Bible" as "creating an expectation that keeps the Bible theoretically open," (ibid., p. 27), he appears to be thinking of these words generically as biblical text without attending to their explicit meaning.

23. "The Death of Jesus and the Closing of Revelation," *Theology Digest,* 23 (1975), 320–329.

modern man when it is said that "all of revelation" is present by the end of the apostolic age. "All of revelation" can mean either of two things: all I am going to tell you or all there is to say. Rahner opts for the second meaning, as I certainly would, too. In the Church mankind has been given by God all there is to say because God has given man his Son, who is his Word, in the Church. As St. John of the Cross long ago noted (see his *Ascent of Mount Carmel,* 2.22.5), once you have Jesus Christ you have all of revelation. There is nothing more to say, nothing to add to *the* Word. All you have to do, once the Father has given his Word, is to learn better and better what he as a Person incarnate "means." The Christian knows that the Word "means" or refers to the Father and that coming better to know the Word and Father is an ongoing work throughout all of history, personal and communal, always pointed into the future because the truth of the Father through the Son in the Holy Spirit is inexhaustible. All we know suggests that we should learn more.

The Bible, including the text itself, is caught up in this living economy of the Word. The story of the Bible is not finished nor is it meant to be. Jesus Christ has come and He is still to come, and His coming in Nazareth was in order that he might come again. But his second coming is not to be a cyclic action, not uroboric, not "posterior" or retrospective, not calculated to close a literary plot. There is a great difference between a story which starts, "Once upon a time," and one which ends, "Come, Lord Jesus!" The one is beautiful with the nostalgic, often heart-rending beauty associated with remembrance of what was and is no more. The other is urgent, for it is life. The futurity of the Bible's text, as Nohrnberg has suggested,[24] typically inhibits or at least works against closure of plot, the underlying cyclic pull of normal narrative, which still asserts itself despite the recent efforts to open literature to life and real time discussed earlier in this chapter and more at length in Chapter 11 below.

Erich Auerbach has made something of the same point in his

24. "On Literature and the Bible," *Centrum,* 2, No. 2 (1974), 25–27.

essay, earlier mentioned, on "Odysseus' Scar," calling attention to the biblical indifference to filling in details which would make plot work out more neatly, as contrasted with the normal Greek narrative concern for such detail.[25] Books of the Bible most like closed-plot narratives, notably Tobit and Esther, have been among the parts of the Bible most under attack as noncanonical. They can strike the reader, perhaps unconsciously, as somehow anomalous: too compact, too self-contained, too "literary." Similarly, the almost happy-ever-after ending tacked onto Job (42:7–17) to round out the work, to make its ending more conspicuously fit its beginning, with Job wealthy once more, has troubled scholars deeply. By contrast, another book about misfortunes, Jonah, presents no problem. It is compactly put together but open-ended: what eventually happened to Jonah after his last show of indignant resentment is left untreated, as a matter of little concern.

The Bible's basically historical cast, contrasted by Auerbach with Homer's basically fictional structures, of course accounts in part for the relative lack of closure in its narratives. Real life, as noted earlier here, is not plotted and, while history can be given something like a plot by proper selectivity, and generally is so designed, it cannot honestly be plotted for "recognition" quite like fiction—however the possibility of such plotting may tempt the historian. Indeed, lack of interest in closure is one of the features that show the Bible as a whole to be radically historical, though in various ways in its various parts.

Futurity and relative indifference to narrative plotting can be assigned to the biblical text without discomfort to believers. The same is not true of involvement of the biblical text with death. To associate God's word in the Bible with death rather than purely with life appears at first blush scandalous, grossly irreverent, or at the very least bizarre. Yet the association is there among believers, unreflectively perhaps but conspicuously, in the common conception of the Christian Bible as consisting of the Old Testament and the New Testament.

25. Auerbach, *Mimesis*, pp. 1–20.

A testament or will of course provides for the future, assures life, but does so by relating to death. A will not only commonly goes into effect following someone's death, but also exhibits a textual fixity conceived of, unconsciously or subconsciously if not consciously, in terms of the fixity of death. The last decision has been made and can never be altered. "Put it in writing," for writing is frozen, stock-still, an immobile witness. A testament is an agreement providing stabilization for life and growth because it has passed through death.

An oral antecedent of the written agreement is the covenant, which, in the Bible as elsewhere, is an assurance of continued sustenance, continued life, but an assurance fundamentally, if variously, also associated with death. God's covenant with Noah (Genesis 9:8–17) was made in the aftermath of the disaster of the flood, which not only caused all but universal death but also was itself terminal—the rainbow promised "never again." Death was dead, at least death on such a catastrophic scale. God's covenant with Abraham was entered into as a smoking oven and a fiery torch passed between the halves of the animal carcasses that (except for the tiny turtle dove and young pigeon) Abraham had split (Genesis 15:19–20) in a covenanting ceremony of a sort also reported elsewhere in the Bible (Jeremiah 34:18). As in sacrifices generally, the blood shed here might well have symbolized life, but the biblical description here makes no mention of blood, but only of the dead carcasses (from which all blood, in accordance with Hebrew practice, had presumably been drained). Life for the future is here assured by passage through death.

The connection of a testament with death has to be put together with what we have been calling the futurity of the Bible, its facing away from death into life. At this point it appears helpful to consider the entry of the Word of God into history in terms of the contrast between orality and chirography, for these are not merely two parallel tracks transporting the same message as though it were some kind of commodity (which a message is not), but, as should be apparent from much in the present volume, two different modes of appropriating existence.

When the Christian thinks of the Word made flesh, in accordance with the indications in the Bible, he or she thinks of the Word of God by analogy with our own human spoken word, not our own written word. The Father utters the Word, the Son. Nowhere do we find that he writes him. The Word of God become flesh in Jesus Christ is thus conceived of as what God the Father says to man, utters or "outers" to humankind, a Word who is also a living Person, the Son, distinct from and yet one with the Father, and now become man, entered into human history. *Eo verbum quo filius,* the theological logion goes: He is word by reason of that which makes him Son. God the Father is revealed in the Person of the Word, but also in the words the Word speaks and in the actions of the Word, which are in effect words, for whatever the Word is and does is a manifestation of the Father. "The words that I speak to you I speak not on my own authority. But the Father dwelling in me, it is he who does the works" (John 14:10).

Had the incarnation of the Word been an event in a purely oral culture, the words that he spoke and his life itself would have entered into communal memory and not into the Gospels. The support system for this memory—the oral equivalent of the books in the Bible other than the Gospels—would have been only other communal memory. Now, the entry of the Word into history did in fact take place in a largely oral setting. Jesus Christ, the Word of God incarnate, left no writing of his own, despite his evident literacy (Luke 4:16–25). To have left his proclamation of the Kingdom in writing would, it appears, at least have somewhat obscured the fact that he is the Word of his Father in a sense that refers to our spoken words, not to written words. The nascent Church was left with the orally recallable knowledge of his oral teaching. Out of oral recollection of his oral teaching came the Gospels, produced, according to common Christian doctrine, under the inspiration of the Holy Spirit. The earlier support system for his teaching, the preparation for it in the consciousness of the Hebrews, had also an oral base, more so in some books of the Old Testament than in others, but in all of them to some extent. This support system, the Old Testament, had by Jesus' time been put into writing, and very shortly after his death and resurrection the texts of the Gospels and the rest of the New Testament sprang into being, and the canon of the Old Testament also took relatively firm and final shape.

To the text of the Bible which has resulted, the Church has always given an immediate, unmediated kind of authority. Whatever explanation and interpretation the text may at one time or another require, the life of the Bible is in the biblical text, not in its oral antecedents and much less in later explanations or interpretations, however indispensable these may be. The result of this entry of the words of the Word into a text—for the Christian Bible centers in the Gospels, which are basically collections of the spoken words of the incarnate Word—is quite different from what it would have been had the Word become incarnate in a purely oral culture, where his words and actions would have entered immediately only into communal memory. The incarnation of the Word was primarily an event in the physical world, the event reported in the Gospels. The Word was made flesh in the actual physical world around us. But in the vital relationship with the text that followed in the wake of the physical incarnation, the incarnate Word entered into the evolution of the psychological world that dovetails into the physical. Entering not only into the orally retrievable communal memory but also with a special immediacy into the written text as well, the divine Word established itself in the life and evolution of man's mind and consciousness.

The text into which the Word entered is, in the senses earlier discussed, like all texts, something fixed and of itself dead. The access it has to life is through the present. A text, in the light of the reflections here, is no simple thing. It is not just a visual equivalent of speech, for there is no visual equivalent of speech, but only a set of visual patterns relatable to speech. In the text the Word is established in an artificial and always dated—which is to say historical—relationship to himself and to other actuality.

Demythologizing the text is a minor problem. The larger problem, toward which demythologizing can work, is to give the text present life, to complete the text today in actual discourse—for which, among other things, asceticism is required. For without present life, a text has no meaning. Like all texts, the Bible must be interpreted. It must be interpreted in terms of an intimate knowledge of the past where it came into being, but of the past as related to the present. Purely antiquarian knowledge is of itself useless. Like any text, the biblical text must be given meaning by being completed in actual discourse now.

The only access the biblical text has to life is through the present. Here, in the present, and only here, it can produce at any moment real words, can be resurrected from the page into real speech, sounding within the real human lifeworld either aloud or in imagination. But these words in the text read today sound at a distance from the original setting of the text onto a writing surface. To relate to present discourse, they require hermeneutic, interpretation, in Paul Ricoeur's sense of the term developed out of Wilhelm Dilthey.[26]

If interpretation means, as it does in the sense I employ and in Ricoeur's sense, the appropriation of a text, its completion in actual discourse now, its insertion into the present—which can involve the use of other texts, written or printed commentaries, but which, to avoid infinite regression, must ultimately connect with present oral utterances—to say that interpretation of the Bible is for the Christian more urgent than the interpretation of other texts is a commonplace. For the Christian believes that the word of God is given in order to be interiorized, appropriated by men and women of all times and places. The Bible does not merely allow interpretation, as other texts do, but invites interpretation and even commands it. Given such urgency, we can also be aware of certain problems of biblical interpretation for the Christian, which are, if not new, at least formulable in new ways within the perspectives here suggested.

26. Paul Ricoeur, "What Is a Text? Explanation and Interpretation," pp. 135–150 in Rasmussen, *Mythic-Symbolic Language*.

First, we have seen, composition in writing, or even setting down in writing something actually said orally, is not the same as oral speech, nor is it simply a parallel operation, for it involves utterance in a different way with time, with past, present, and future, and relates writer and reader differently from the way oral speech relates speaker and listener. Secondly, a reader is not the same as a listener, nor a writer the same as a speaker. The reader is absent from the writing of a text, and may be anyone from anywhere, the writer absent from the reading of a text, whereas speaker and hearer are fully determined persons normally present to one another quite consciously in vocal exchange. (Questions regarding the relationship of television and sound tapes to oral presence are discussed in the last chapter of the present book.) Texts relate to other texts, and this relationship establishes what we know as literature, which, because of the provenience of texts out of the past, is always a thing of the past.

Such statements as these, giving special status to text which is quite different from the status of oral utterance, tend to be resented by Christians when they are applied to the Bible. This appears to be so first because of the presence of the Word, incarnate in Jesus Christ, through history. The Bible has regularly seemed to the Christian to be much simpler than all we have said here: it is God speaking to man, here and now. And so it is, of course. However, to say this is not to do away with questions, but to create them. Secondly, the biblical text is understood somehow by the Church as being addressed to all ages. The relationship of the word of God in the text of the Bible, which as text is dead, and the Word of God incarnate in Jesus Christ, who lives now and forever—"*Maranatha;* come, Lord Jesus"— is here in play, and this relationship has never been adequately defined or explored in the perspectives available to us now and suggested here. These perspectives can frame the following concluding questions.

How far is the Bible as Bible to be regarded as actually composed in writing and how far as a record of speech insofar as it is considered God's revelation to mankind? This knotty question refers variously to various parts of the Bible. Moreover, as the present study hopes to have suggested, it is psychologically, linguistically, culturally, and existentially an exceedingly complex question. It refers not merely to temporal sequence: Is revelation to be thought of as earlier or later, before or after textuality? More significantly, it refers to the kind of message conveyed: How far is the biblical message the more participatory message of pure orality and how far is it imbued with the analytic, explanatory possibilities implemented by writing and indeed enforced by writing?

What are the faith implications of the divergent psychodynamics of the two processes, the oral and the chirographic? How can the reader of the Bible today be assimilated to a listener? Or should he or she be so assimilated? This problem is not met by reading the text out loud. It is still a text, out of the past, calling for interpretation. And it is common experience that, given a text in hand, while the scriptures are being read to the congregation aloud at a liturgical service, the normal able-bodied American will, almost without fail, bury his or her head in the text as though no one were reading aloud at all. We prefer visual to aural assimilation. How far does the reading of the Bible today call for reestablishing relationship between the text and reader distinctive of the highly oral culture of the biblical age, when writing was far less interiorized in the psyche than it normally is today in highly technologized cultures?

What is the role of the Church as perpetuator of the dialogue in the Holy Spirit with the Father through the living incarnate Word which gives the biblical text the life of faith at all times? Is the text of the Bible a commentary on this ecclesial dialogue, or the dialogue a commentary on the text? What is the role of the Church in resurrecting the dead letter into living speech, so that the reader, whether an individual or a congregation, is in effect truly a listener? *Fides ex auditu.* If the ecclesial dialogue through the living Word of God in Jesus Christ is the essential element in Christian hermeneutic, how is the exegesis furnished out of biblical scholarship to be appropriated into this hermeneutic? What kind of control of the times in which a text is later read is presupposed by the Bible's prophetic and futurist cast?

These questions, in one way or another, are all old. They have undergone earlier formulations, successively patristic (largely oral, for writing was not deeply interiorized), medieval (highly literate but with very active residual orality), and Renaissance (typographic). But the framework in which they are presented here is, I believe, restructured in accord with our newly reflective awareness of the technological transformations of the word in past and present.

Finally, to sum it all up, given that the resurrection of Jesus Christ is like nothing else in all creation, and that the interpretation of any text in the present, the insertion of any text into present discourse, the reentry of any text into the oral world is a kind of resurrection, is the Christian to think of the individual's and the community's here-and-now appropriation of the word in the Bible as a resurrection suggesting that of Jesus? Given that writing is not just a visual equivalent of speech and that there is a psychological progression from orality to a literate culture, how necessary was it that the Good News of the death, resurrection, and ascension of the Lord itself die and be buried in a text in order to come to a later, resurrected life throughout history?

10

From Mimesis to Irony: Writing and Print as Integuments of Voice

Vision, Content, and Voice

The present study grew out of an assignment to consider the subject "Response to Vision: Judging the Value of Literary Content." This is a vast subject. In one or another guise, questions concerning the value of literary content have woven their way through most of twentieth-century Western poetics and literary theory, from the Russian Formalism of the first third of this century through the succeeding Prague Structuralism, the American New Criticism of the second third of the century and its British connections, and the French Formalism running from Ferdinand de Saussure, with late detours through Claude Lévi-Strauss, down to Tzvetan Todorov, Michel Foucault, Jacques Derrida, Roland Barthes, and others, to intersect with the hermeneutic of Paul Ricoeur. Inevitably, over the years the avenues of discussion have often become intricate mazes, not always made more negotiable by specially contrived, sometimes fanciful, concepts and terms posted along the route.

Instead of working into or within or out of this maze, I propose to skirt it, without losing sight of it, and to discuss the value of literary content against the background of the spoken word, in which literature has its pristine and its permanent roots. My reflections will be sketchy, for in taking up the problem of judging literary content, I am taking up more than I or anyone else can possibly handle comprehensively even in treating the subject at far greater length than is possible here.

Literature consists of words, at times with some admixture of other elements. It is impossible to have real words without a real speaker or writer and without a real-life, existential situation in which speaker or writer performs. A story has aesthetic distance, but it always is told or written at a given place in a given moment of history. These axioms can provide one way to frame a discussion of the value of literary content, and they are the ones I shall use to frame these reflections.

I shall not undertake to define here the exact meaning of "literary content." The term "content" shows reliance on a spatial model for literature. Literature is taken to be like a box or other container, with something "in" it. All models are inadequate, and this is perhaps more inadequate than most. It is a relatively new model, dependent on the strong feeling for words as localized units encouraged by print and on modes of conceptualization useful for Newtonian physics. The model was developed largely under vernacular auspices. Short of some enterprising circumlocution, Latin had provided no way to think of literature or other utterance as having "content." Literature had not "contained" but simply "said" something. Nevertheless, despite the problems with the concept, we have enough tacit agreement about what the term "content" means to permit us to forego further discussion here, allowing the rest of this paper to clarify in more detail as need be what "literary content" comes to.

The term "vision" in our thematic title shows a similar inclination to reduce verbalization to spatial equivalents, to reduce sound to sight. Again, the term is not without meaning. Perhaps it is even overmeaningful, for it indicates not only, to a degree, what we are talking about but also, implicitly, where we ourselves are who are doing the talking. We are standing back, away, from literature. We have objectified it visually (with some help from the tactile). Literature "contains" a "vision," so it seems. Sight distances its objects. Eyeball-to-eyeball or eyeball-to-object vision is impossible. A vision is an experience of something at a certain distance, something from which we stand off, something out there or over there.

Literature was not always like this. And the oral performance out of which literature grows, and to which literature is permanently related and indeed attached, was like this hardly at all. In an oral culture, which of course has no literature, the oral performance out of which literature grows is not distanced from either performer or audience in the way in which literature is. I should like, therefore, to go back to the point in history, or the points in histories—for literature accrues to and grows out of oral performance somewhat differently in each culture and period—and to consider our subjects at a period when verbal utterance could not so adequately be conceived in terms of "vision" or "content" and when, indeed, it was never literature at all. In the resulting perspectives—note the visualist term, "perspectives," for in my twentieth-century posture, I am standing back too—the sense of our present subject can perhaps be better interpreted.

Participatory Poetics

About any work of literature, it is legitimate to ask who is saying what to whom. To treat any work exhaustively, this question must always ultimately be asked. Without addressing oneself to this question, it would appear impossible to judge the value of any utterance, and literature is utterance, however contrived or complicated, and however externally inaudible. The question of who is saying what to whom can call for responses at any number of levels: at the level of the narrative persona telling a story, for example, or at the level of the other individual whose story the narrator may be retailing (for example, Marlow's story as retailed by the narrative voice in *Heart of Darkness*), or at the level of the various interlocutors in the direct discourse exchanges in a story. Ultimately, beneath it all, there is always the level of the real storyteller—Joseph Conrad himself in *Heart of Darkness*—the real person who rigs the narrative persona and who we cannot pretend is not there, for he is. Without him there would be no story at all. He is telling the story because he, Joseph Conrad, wishes to say something in one or more of the many ways storytellers say something. He wishes to say it for reasons growing out of his real life—aesthetic reasons, no doubt, at least in part, and, perhaps we can hope, even totally, but aesthetic in the particular ways available to him. The motivation and aims of this real person may not be entirely clear to him or her—it is a rare moment when motivation and aims for doing anything are totally clear to anyone—but they are not entirely inaccessible either to one who may wish to study the situation.

The interrelationships that I have just referred to in terms of levels can be thought of more accurately, because less diagrammatically, less artificially, more directly, as voices within voices, or voices within voices within voices within voices.[1] The echoing of voice within voice, as I hope to make clear, has come to its present involuted complexity as the result of writing. Writing has made possible literature, in the basic sense of more or less self-conscious imaginative verbalization of the sorts produced by composing in writing. (Not all written texts are "literature" in this basic sense, and no purely oral composition as such can be "literature.") Works of literature, works composed in writing, can no longer be studied seriously simply in themselves without cognizance of the fact that literature has a vast prehistory in highly self-conscious oral verbalization, which works quite differently from composition in writing. Literature came into existence not immediately with writing but only some time after the invention of writing (which was first devised for practical, account-

1. For a brief and careful discussion of "double-voiced" discourse and other involuted forms, see Mixail Baxtin, "Discourse Typology in Prose," in *Readings in Russian Poetics: Formalist and Structuralist Views,* ed. Ladislav Matejka and Krystyna Pomorska (Cambridge, Mass.: MIT Press, 1971), pp. 176–196. Some other related studies will be found in this same volume as also in the work of J. R. Searle, John R. Austin, and others. Baxtin gives some attention to oral discourse reported in writing, but not to oral cultures as such. I am indebted to Professor Wolfgang Karrer for calling my attention to this article by Baxtin and also to him and to Professor Clarence H. Miller, both of Saint Louis University, for other suggestions affecting this present chapter.

keeping purposes), but when literature did come into existence, it did so only as an adaptation and, later, transformation of highly developed antecedent oral performance, which had had nothing to do with writing at all. The question, then, Who is saying what to whom? has to be asked first with reference to primary oral cultures, cultures with no knowledge of writing, and, more specifically about their formal public oral performances, the kind of oral performances which enter most immediately into the development of literature some time after writing had been devised. (Writing, as just noted, had first been devised not at all for what we should style literary purposes, but for practical, chiefly economic, itemizing purposes. It was adapted later to more imaginative work.)

In a sense, in public oral performance—such as, for example, the classical Greek epics in Homer's own preliterate ninth-century world, or the formal oral narratives recited in Central African villages today or the performances of the West African *griot*— everyone is saying everything to everybody through the mouth of the poet or other narrative performer. The poetic of oral cultures is participatory. Speaker, audience, and subject form a kind of continuum. Eric Havelock has noted in his *Preface to Plato* that out of the first hundred lines of the *Iliad* about fifty simply recall or memorialize acts, attitudes, judgments, and procedures typical of Homeric Hellenes in such a way that report and didactic message coincide to create the total agreement, the identification of knower with known and of speaker with audience typical of the frame of mind in primary oral cultures: "This is the way in which the society does normally behave (or does not) and at the same time the way in which we, its members, who form the poet's audience, are encouraged to behave."[2] In certain African villages, the formal narratives, never told except "between the two suns," that is, in the always twelve-hour-long equatorial night when much of the village socializing goes on, are introduced by the narrator with the question, "Take the story." The audience

2. Eric A. Havelock, *Preface to Plato* (Cambridge, Mass.: Belknap Press of Harvard University Press, 1963), p. 87.

respond, "Tell your story." The narrator comes back with, "And what is the story?" The audience, "The story is the corrector."[3] The story has it the way it is and the way it ought to be. Everyone knows the way the story itself is to be told, although, paradoxically, it is never told in exactly the same style by two different narrators nor in exactly the same words by the same narrator on different occasions. Each performance calls forth a somewhat different interaction between narrator and audience.[4]

An oral performance is always a live interaction between a speaker and his audience. It is necessarily participatory at least to the extent that the way the audience reacts determines to a degree the way the speaker performs, and vice versa. A *griot* singing the praises of a goldsmith in a Mande village in West Africa because he has been hired by a woman customer who wants the goldsmith to speed up manufacture of her golden hair ornament, as reported by Camara Laye in *L'Enfant noir*,[5] is going to perform somewhat differently from a *griot* singing to entertain an entire village, although they both deal in the same themes (of which praise is one of the commonest) and formulas. The *griot* serving as a part of the smithy team will react both to his woman client's concerns and to his living subject's own more or less responsive vanity. Poetry has direct cash value in oral cultures at times. It is common in many African villages for young boys to whistle in drum talk the praises of prominent villagers in the hope of receiving tips.[6] Otherwise they might

3. Mufuta Kabemba, "Littérature orale et authenticité," *Jiwe: Organe idéologique, culturel, et scientifique du Comité Sectionnaire MPR/UNAZA* (Lubumbashi, Zaire), No. 2 (1973), p. 27.

4. Albert B. Lord, *The Singer of Tales*, Harvard Studies in Comparative Literature, 24 (Cambridge, Mass.: Harvard University Press, 1960), pp. 13–29. On the creative quality of the interaction between narrator and audience, see Ngal Mbwil a Mpaang, "L'Artiste africain: Tradition, critique, et liberté créatrice," a paper presented at the Colloque sur la Critique Littéraire en Afrique, Yaoundé, Cameroun, April 1973 (unpublished, mimeographed copy in my possession, received from Professor Ngal).

5. In Dakar in the spring of 1974, M. Laye assured me that incidents in *L'Enfant noir* are in fact very close to or identical with those of his own childhood. His father was a metalsmith, and one of great virtuosity.

6. John F. Carrington, *La Voix des tambours* (Kinshasa: Centre Protestant d'Editions et de Diffusion, 1974), p. 102.

whistle a less pleasant story. Trick or treat on Mount Parnassus.

In an oral culture, public oral performance, the paradigmatic oral antecedent of literature, presents us in effect with a situation in which the public oral performer typically is speaking for everyone to everyone about what every adult already knows, and asking no questions. Although the situation is a special formalized one, and although the language is generally, and perhaps always everywhere, not quite normal speech but a special variant of the vernacular (as was Homeric Greek), a once-upon-a-time language like the special idiom used for children's fairy stories even in today's technological cultures, nevertheless the voice speaking in the formal oral narrative is not so distinct from the voice of the ordinary villager going about his or her ordinary business as the voice of literature would have to be when literature came into being. The oral Greek epic poet was very much part of the workaday world, simultaneously entertainer, chronicler and historian, recorder of genealogies and deeds, cheer leader, ethician, philosopher, and schoolmaster. The ideal of "pure" poetry—an idea destined to become effective only with the Romantic Movement, which in the late eighteenth century marked the full interiorization of print—is impossible in this milieu. All discourse, even the most poetic, is intended to be and is understood to be rhetorical, involved purposefully in the real-life world, where men and women and children live and eat and grow and talk about existential concerns, and come to practical decisions. Not only was the epic poet involved in real-life concerns, but real-life concerns were akin to epic. Ordinary talk and practical thought processes consisted largely of the same proverbs, exempla, epithets, and formulas of all sorts which the epic poet or narrator stitched into his more elaborate and exquisite art forms in his somewhat variant language. The oration, in many if not all oral cultures, is the other major verbal art form besides narrative. More directly than other discourse, the oration is typically concerned with practical decision making. And it, too, is constituted largely of similar formulary elements.

The poetic doctrine of mimesis, as will later be seen, has a natural affinity for this oral world, out of which it grows, a world of agreement, the world Socrates was to blast apart by substituting for imitation or repetition the asking of questions. Socrates, as Eric Havelock has shown, belonged to the age in Greek culture when the effects of the alphabet on thought were finally being felt, and when the old oral world could no longer go on quite as before.

Writing, Print, and Separation

After the invention of writing, and much more after the invention of print, the question of who is saying what to whom becomes confusingly and sometimes devastatingly complicated. The writer's audience is always a fiction, as I have undertaken to show in Chapter 2 above. For addressing a person or persons not present (otherwise why write?) as though they were present (the use of real words is possible only when interlocutors are present to one another in a living here-and-now) is not a natural state of affairs, but an artificial, contrived, fictionalized arrangement. Author and reader both have to find roles to play—even, or especially, when they may both be the same person, as in the case of the diary. For no one really talks to himself or herself in protracted discourse, and to which self is one talking? Oneself as one really is now? (You never talk at length to this self.) Or oneself as one thinks one is? Or wants to be? Or hopes others think one is? Or to oneself as one now imagines one will be twenty years from now? What games are being played here? What roles? It is little wonder that only some six thousand years after the invention of writing does anything like the modern diary appear.[7]

Who is saying what to whom in any written work? The party at either end of the dialogue may not even be there. A given individual may be dead and buried when an urgent, personal letter is being penned to him by an unaware correspondent. Or the sender may be dead when a letter from him is delivered to his

7. See Peter Boerner, *Tagebuch* (Stuttgart: Metzlersche Verlagsbuchhandlung, 1969), pp. 37–58.

addressee. Or both sender and addressee may be dead by the time the letter arrives at the locale to which it is sent. Such absences are complicated endlessly in the case of printed literature floated off by the author to completely unknown readers.

What any writer has written lives in a way, yet in such a way that it makes no difference whatsoever regarding what the work says whether the author is physically alive or dead. An oral performance can in no way be a monument of this sort. Every written work is its author's own epitaph. In the literate, typographic culture which shapes our consciousness we normally pay no attention to such submerged truths, although they have recently been brought to the level of conscious reflection by structuralists or phenomenologists interested in text as texts, such as Jacques Derrida or Paul Ricoeur. They are in themselves banal and self-evident truths, but they sound bizarre because our highly literate culture finds it helpful to regard writing, a thoroughly artificial and essentially defective contrivance, as a quite natural activity, although few truly educated persons would any longer go so far as John Wilkins, who in 1668 maintained that, despite the fact that historically oral speech did precede writing, language by nature is essentially something written and that it is on the written language that the oral language is founded.[8]

The author's obligatory absence from literature sets the stage for distancing the work of literature in ways unknown and indeed unrealizable for the verbal creations of primary oral cultures. As the distancing is accomplished by literature, the verbal creation comes more and more to be regarded as an object—after all, "it" is there in the form of marks on a surface not only when the author is dead but even if everybody is. Ultimately, twentieth-century criticism at its extreme would insist that the object is all that counts—the author and the contemporary readers whose lifeworld and whose language he shares will make no difference any more. The author never knew his contemporary readers any-

8. John Wilkins, *An Essay Toward a Real Character and a Philosophical Language* (London: Sa. Gellibrand and John Martin, 1668), p. 385.

how, except for perhaps an infinitesimal fraction of them, any more than he knew his posthumous readers. The verbal object would become so much an object that in a sense it does not even say anything. "Concrete poetry," which often simply cannot be pronounced at all, could become a kind of absolute ideal. "A poem should be palpable, and mute / As a globed fruit," Archibald MacLeish could prescribe in his new *Ars Poetica* (1926) for a whole generation of readers. "A poem should not mean / But be." Of course, if such a prescription is taken at face value as a meaningful prescription or hermeneutic, it disqualifies as a poem the poem in which it occurs.

But compulsion to take this extreme position—a position which I by no means want to ridicule, since it does incarnate a certain truth—grew only gradually. We can see that it was truly a compulsion, and an inevitable one, if we note some of the stages in the transition from orality through writing into print.

Print maximized the conversion, or the pretended conversion, of the living, evanescent sound of words into the quasi-permanence of visual space. The conversion began with writing, and particularly alphabetic writing, for the alphabet converts sound into space with an efficiency quite unknown to other writing systems (which may have different, competing advantages). But the objectifying potential inherent in writing is not fully realized until print. The reasons for this I have tried to spell out elsewhere in detail, and I can only summarize them here. In brief, print intensifies the commitment of sound to space which writing, and most intensively alphabetic writing, initiates. Typography makes words out of preexisting objects (types) as one makes houses out of bricks: it hooks up the words in machines and stamps out on hundreds or thousands of surfaces exactly the same spatial arrangement of words—constituting the first assembly line; and it facilitates indexing to locate physical places where specified knowledge can be retrieved through the eyes.

Under the resulting circumstances, who is saying what to whom? At first, the situation after writing is much like that in an oral culture. What is put down in writing is in effect oral performance. The first age of writing is the age of scribes, writers of more or less orally conceived discourse. The author addresses himself to imagined listeners at an imagined oral performance of his, which is simply transcribed onto a writing surface. The next age, arrived at gradually of course, is the age of true authors, in today's ordinary sense of author, a person who composes in writing and, later, for print. At this point, the writing surface enters into the thought processes, just as the computer has entered into thought processes today. The new technology does not merely help answer old questions: it makes it possible to conceive of new, different kinds of questions. As compared to the scribe, the author no longer imagines recitation or direct oral address at all, but only the transaction with the paper and the putative, always absent, reader in whatever role this reader can be cast. Although oral residue persists in patterns of thought and expression not only for millennia after writing but also for centuries even after the invention of letterpress alphabetic print,[9] the new literary, authorial patterns would pretty definitively have won out by the end of the eighteenth century. George Eliot or Charles Dickens or Gerard Manley Hopkins or William Faulkner would not imagine themselves while they were writing as reciting their texts to an audience, even though Dickens gave readings from his works, Hopkins urged that his poetry be read aloud, and Faulkner wrote a prose that achieves beautiful literary effects by echoing specifically oral discourse.

As has been noted earlier, public verbal performance in an oral culture is participatory and essentially integrative. Speaker and audience and subject matter are raveled together in a kind of whole which, as Havelock has shown, constituted one of the major problems faced by Plato, who, without explicitly identifying earlier Greek culture as oral in the way in which we can see it today, passionately wanted to move this culture to a new stage characterized by a drastic separation of the knower from the

9. See Walter J. Ong, *Rhetoric, Romance, and Technology* (Ithaca, N.Y.: Cornell University Press, 1971), Ch. 2, "Oral Residue in Tudor Prose Style," and Walter J. Ong, *The Presence of the Word* (New Haven: Yale University Press, 1967), pp. 53–76.

known, the analytic stage.[10] Plato wanted cleavage, and cleavage
was what writing, and, later and more effectively, print could
furnish. Writing and print distance the utterer of discourse from
the hearer, and both from the word, which appears in writing
and print as an object or thing. The result was that, when the
effects of writing and print matured, when typography was interiorized in the Western psyche definitively at the moment in
Western history known as the Romantic Movement, the question,
Who is saying what to whom? raised exceedingly complex issues.

Mimesis

The issues are, in fact, far too complex to be all gathered
together here. But we can get an idea of what they are by looking
at some relationships between mimesis and irony. In literary
history and theory, mimesis and irony stand in complementary
relationship. As mimesis loses ground in poetic and other aesthetic
theory and performance, irony gains ground. The exchange of
territory between mimesis and irony becomes an issue, again, at
the time of the Romantic Movement.

Mimesis no doubt has its own permanent intrinsic value in
poetic theory, but it also accords particularly well with the psychology of an oral world, where, as has been seen, speaker and
audience and subject matter form a close unit and where, even in
the case of aesthetic performances, all three remain in or very
close to the existential human lifeworld. Theories of mimesis,
whether articulated or merely implied, preserve the felt unity between art and natural life: art obviously differs in some way
from nature, but it differs from nature precisely in trying to be
like nature—which is comforting, because this means there is
hardly any difference at all. Mimetic theory is both diaeretic and
integrative. The greater art is, the more it is like nature, and the
less troublesome is the question about what art is. Good art is no
problem; only bad art is, and bad art should be abolished. In its
internal dynamics, imitation is amiably self-destructive: if the
imitation is totally successful, the product is indistinguishable

10. Havelock, *Preface to Plato,* pp. 197–233.

from nature. The implicit aim of this theory is thus to have nothing distinct from nature, to have only the real thing. In mimetic theory art is most evident when you cannot find it. *Ars celare artem.* Essentially, mimetic theories of art explain nothing because they do not explain why imitation as such is desirable: but they are invaluable, for they provide an initiation into the mystery of art and of human existence, and into the paradoxes, that is, the asymmetrically opposed but not contradictory pairs of truths, in which all depth thinking is grounded.

Mimetic theories have complex origins,[11] and you do not have to belong to any particular culture to be aware that art, at least at times or frequently, imitates nature. Yet there is a special feature in the deep structure of oral cultures which can make mimetic theories congenial to such cultures: the entire oral noetic world relies heavily, even fundamentally, on copying not just nature but oral utterance itself in its management of knowledge. Oral cultures preserve their articulated knowledge by constantly repeating the fixed sayings and formulas—including epithets, standard parallelisms and oppositions, kennings, set phrases, and all sorts of other mnemonic or recall devices in which their knowledge is couched. Oral noetics enforce the copying of human productions as well as of nature. Copying becomes an overwhelming and preemptive state of mind. Even storytelling, which would seem to derive necessarily from external events as such occurring in unpredictable sequences calling for unique statement—for is it not the unpredictability which makes history history and makes a story interesting?—is managed in oral cultures chiefly by stringing together preexistent, imitable formulary elements—in however intricately managed patterns. Mimetic ideas of art are based on acceptance of copying as a primary human enterprise. And oral cultures build their whole world of knowledge largely on copying in speech what has been said before.

11. In the literature on mimesis, which is vast, a major entry is still Erich Auerbach's classic work, *Mimesis: The Representation of Reality in Western Literature,* trans. Willard Trask (Princeton, N.J.: Princeton University Press, 1937). See also John D. Boyd, *The Function of Mimesis and Its Decline* (Cambridge, Mass.: Harvard University Press, 1968).

Mnemonic patterns, patterns of repetition, copyings, are not added to the thought of oral cultures. They are what the thought consists in. Since we know only what we can recall, an oral culture must think readily recallable thoughts, mnemonically cast thoughts, or it might as well not be thinking, for it will never be able to retrieve what it has once thought. Unless it thinks in mnemonic patterns, an oral culture is only daydreaming: verbalization that passes through consciousness in nonmnemonic patterns tends to drift away. Education which is oral or residually oral thus trains pupils in copying, in mastering clichés—which writing and print would downgrade and even attempt to outlaw. These mnemonic processes of oral cultures have been treated in detail in earlier chapters. The point here is that the need for constant mnemonic activity does more than develop memory. It creates what can be called a mimetic culture, a culture of imitation, a state of mind that values copying—over-values it, later ages would judge. The old education for patterned recall was one of the features of oral culture that Plato rebelled against in excluding poets from his Republic. Poets were essentially repeaters. Plato wanted to establish analytic thinking in place of their endless mimicking of what had already been said.

All matters of deep human import, however, are paradoxical. Plato's doctrine here is doubly so. First, although, as we now know, writing was what made possible the keenly analytic thinking developed by Socrates, Plato, Aristotle, and subsequent philosophers,[12] Plato expresses distrust of writing (in the Seventh Letter and *Phaedrus* 274). Second, although his analytic venturesomeness moves away from mimetic orality by virtue of its alliance with writing, Plato's philosophy of ideas itself remains basically a mimetic approach. Indeed, it is the most mimetic of mimetic approaches: everything that man contacts is essentially a copy. No one has ever contacted the original, the Platonic *idea*, which gives the copies whatever validity they have.

Partly because of this paradox in his philosophy of ideas, Plato

12. Havelock, *Preface to Plato*, pp. 3–60, and *passim*.

lost the battle to outlaw mimetic learning, even of the old oral poetic sort. Through the sixteenth and seventeenth centuries of the Christian era and even later, two millennia after Plato, schoolboys such as William Shakespeare and John Milton were still being programmatically drilled in imitating the Latin classics. Though from the beginning of the Middle Ages on, academic education in the West grew progressively more and more attentive to writing and, later, to print, becoming more and more profoundly literate than classical antiquity had ever been, even well after the Middle Ages writing was felt still to be, not a self-contained enterprise, but largely a means for recycling materials out of and back into the oral world. Mimesis continued to rule theories of poetry and education until, roughly, the Romantic Movement. In the *Essay on Criticism* Alexander Pope was prescribing still for his own age. The business of the eighteenth-century poet, as of his predecessors, was to deal with "What oft was thought, but ne'er so well expressed." And, of course, in saying this, or writing it, Pope was wittily exemplifying his own prescription, for this prescription itself has been mouthed by hundreds before, only not so well: Pope's line provides our preferred formulation today.

Irony

It is a commonplace that mimetic theories of art take a turn for the worse with the Romantic Age (as it should be a commonplace also that in one way or another mimetic theories, however etiolated, will always be around, and are needed). With the onset of the Romantic Age, doctrines of "creativity" tend to crowd out mimetic theory. To produce art, the artist does not imitate nature but simply "creates," producing his work *ex nihilo*. M. H. Abrams has caught the dialectic exquisitely in his book title *The Mirror and the Lamp*: art no longer reflects nature, but illuminates nature with its own artistic lights. Coleridge's doctrine of the "imagination" as distinct from "fancy" or fantasy contains the germ of this theory: it is not what the imagination represents but rather the fusion it effects, its own interior and independent life principle, that constitutes the work of art as such. Here in germ is the doctrine that "A poem should not mean / But be." This doctrine is pivotal in a variety of ways in all modern criticism, from Russian Formalism, Prague Structuralism, American and British New Criticism (including the aesthetics of Bloomsbury distilled in the ethics of G. E. Moore) on through French Formalism and Structuralism, all of which build on the distance of art from life. The doctrine has a thousand avatars, each generated out of the inadequacies of its predecessors and each more exquisite than the last. *Mais, plus ça change, plus c'est la même chose.*

In the gross pattern of development from antiquity to the present, as doctrines of mimesis fade from the academic and intellectual scene, concern with irony mounts, This fact deserves attention that it has not received in the perspectives set up here. The displacement of mimesis by irony as a focus of critical attention advertises further the diaeretic or divisive effects of writing and print. I do not by any means wish to suggest that the psychological effects of writing and print are the sole causes of this subtle displacement of mimesis or of all the other related developments noted here, but rather that writing and print enter into these developments and—I will go this far—are related to and illuminate almost every aspect of the developments if not as cause or effect at least as connected phenomena. Writing and print show their divisive character in one way by making feasible and attractive the multiple layers of irony in creative writing and the resulting critical fascination with irony in literature and critical discussion today.

Irony is almost as old as speech itself. Perhaps it is in some way even inherent in speech, surfacing incipiently in every question cuing in an expected answer of yes or no with its contradictory: Isn't it? (Answer: It is.) *N'est-ce pas? Nonne?* He didn't, did he? (Answer: He didn't.) But, as will be seen, in the past irony has commanded very little explicit critical attention, whereas today it can be and often is an obsession, displacing even metaphor as the favorite old bone for criticism to gnaw on. The unreliable narrator, who, as Wayne Booth has shown,[13] is far more operative in fiction today than ever in the past, is one of the chief producers of massive ironic effects, for unreliability is of the essence of irony: the obvious sense is not to be trusted.

Irony has become a focus of concern today for creative writers and critics alike as the person who produces an utterance has been more and more effectively distanced from the person who takes in the utterance. This distancing has been effected by writing and, much more, by print.

Irony in its most ordinary sense today—the conveying of a truth by asserting its opposite—attracted widespread attention as a major literary device or phenomenon only after the invention of print. An *eirōn* in classical Greek was a dissembler, one who said less than he thought, and consequently a deceptive rascal, the opposite of a frank, candid person. "Irony," being an *eirōn*, was something repulsive. However, Plato presented Socrates as an *eirōn*, perhaps the most effective *eirōn* known to the ancient Greeks—and this usage probably upgraded the term, although not enough to save Socrates from execution. Cicero and Quintilian remain concerned, however, about the negative tonality of *eironia* or *ironia*, although among the senses which Quintilian already finds in the term is the modern, seemingly not too threatening, sense of conveying a truth by asserting its opposite.[14]

Irony in this sense is not unknown in artistic verbal narrative and other verbalization in oral cultures. But its use there is severely limited. Oral cultures appropriate knowledge ceremonially and formulaicly, in ways discussed here above in Chapter 4, and their verbalization remains basically conservative and in principle directly accountable to hearers. Verbal attacks in oral cultures, where such attacks are exceedingly frequent, are normally direct and ostentatiously hostile. Their standard form is the

13. *The Rhetoric of Fiction* (Chicago: University of Chicago Press, 1961), pp. 339–398.

14. John B. McKee, *Literary Irony and the Literary Audience: Studies in the Victimization of the Reader in Augustan Fiction* (Amsterdam: Rodopi, N.V., 1974), pp. 89–93, gives a helpful summary history of the term "irony" drawn from the endless literature on the subject.

ceremonially taunting name-calling or fliting that is common, it seems, in most if not indeed absolutely all oral cultures. Of course, oral folk are no more virtuous than are the literate. Unreliability there may well be in the verbal performance of many speakers in the world of primary (preliterate) orality but unreliability is not vaunted in this world as a major rhetorical device. Oral performance cannot readily achieve the distance from life which complex irony demands. Oral cultures want participation, not questions. It is informative that even the highly literate orality of television cannot command the irony common in much serious fiction today, such as, for example, that of Vladimir Nabokov.

To a degree oral cultures permit certain standard ironies, of the sort Wayne Booth would include under "stable irony," irony pretty well labeled as such.[15] Such occur in the *Iliad* and the *Odyssey*, though not in sufficient number to warrant the listing of "irony" in the index to Lord's *The Singer of Tales* or to Havelock's *Preface to Plato*. The riddle, common in oral cultures, is a stable ironic form: a question seeming to defy answering, but readily answered with a fixed formula. The clever trickster of folklore across the globe—the African rabbit or tortoise or spider, the American Indian coyote, and of course Odysseus himself—uses irony, but of a relatively obvious sort: the clever trickster is the primitive, reliably unreliable narrator. A recent multifaceted presentation of a still living folktale from Senegal, outside the European tradition, *El Hadj Bouc,* presented as told in original Fulfulde (Fulani, Peul) with a French text *en face* and with accompanying Wolof and Serer versions, shows the sort of straightforward irony which folklorists recognize as typical of oral cultures as such, not just those of the West: expressions of predatory animals (the Hyena or the Lion) politely telling their victim (the Buck Goat) how welcome he is (to be eaten).[16] The tale is pre-

15. Wayne C. Booth, *A Rhetoric of Irony* (Chicago: University of Chicago Press, 1974), pp. 1–31.

16. Amadou A. Diaw, Cheikh Tidiane N'Diaye, *et al.,* eds., *Demb ak Tey: Cahiers du mythe* (Centre d'Etude de Civilisations, Dakar, Senegal), No. 1 [1974], *El Hadj Bouc* (Dakar: Les Nouvelles Editions Africains, [1974]).

sented by its editors as a typical sample to encourage further collection of folk stories. It expresses social satire, and the reader
might discern irony of a sort in the ways in which the different
animals symbolize the various levels of society. But throughout
there is no deliberately unresolved ambiguity, no mistaking what
is being openly praised, namely, intelligence over brute strength
or over other crude power. The narrator's way of looking at the
world is essentially clear.

The increased serviceability of irony in Socrates' world was
certainly due to the effects of writing on the consciousness of the
ancient Greeks. As has been noted earlier, Havelock has shown
how the interiorization of writing, realized in Plato's day some
three hundred years after the Greek alphabet had come into
being, had brought about a change in Greek mental processes by
effecting a "separation of knower from the known" and the
"recognition of the known as object,"[17] such as oral cultures do
not exhibit. Earlier Greek *paideia* had sought to insure that
pupils identified with Greek cultural types (such as Achilles,
Odysseus, Nestor). Committing the epics to memory assimilated
the schoolboy to the culture, guaranteed that the young Greek
boys were "with it." As Havelock has explained in detail, such
education for participation has to be eliminated, or at least minimized, if pupils are to achieve the distancing of themselves from
subject matter which abstract analysis requires. The problem of
ancient Greek culture in moving from a participatory oral
paideia, which used writing only incidentally, to one where
writing shaped the thought processes is still real and urgent today
in developing countries and in the oral inner-city black culture
and white hill-country culture of the United States: either one
moves, at least to some degree, out of the participatory oral
lifestyle (without necessarily closing the door to all reentry) or
one cannot enter the mainstream of objectivist cultures implemented by literacy. The choice between total immersion and
objective understanding cannot be forced, but it has to be made,

17. Havelock, *Preface to Plato,* pp. 197–233.

implicitly or explicitly. Havelock does not discuss irony as such, but it is evident that irony demands a distancing from subject matter similar to that demanded for analytic thought. The ironist is known to be cold-blooded, more like a Platonic idealist than a warm-blooded participant in life.

The light load of irony carried by oral genres quickly gains weight in genres controlled by writing. The first of these in the West is, paradoxically, the Greek theater, which, despite its oral presentation, is completely dependent on a text, composed by the dramatist in writing. In the Greek theater, in both comedy and tragedy, irony quickly becomes dense, until in Euripides' *The Bacchae* it is all but impenetrable. Dionysus' supercilious sophistication is ironically downgraded, and Pentheus' complementary righteousness is also. The old men Tiresias and Cadmus treat themselves, as well as others, ironically. Only Agave appears to escape ironic downgrading: her personal tragedy is pitifully real. And, as in much writing today, because of the multilayered irony, what the ultimate values inherent in the play are, is not easy to say, though it is not impossible, either. Who is worse off, Dionysus or Pentheus? There is much to argue against both of them. And the reference of the play to the Athenian political scene around the time of Euripides' death (the play was first staged posthumously) is a further ironic story all in itself.

The ironic heritage of literacy, developed also in other chirographic forms of antiquity such as the satire and the epigram, was passed on in the West through many medieval literary genres—one thinks of Chaucer's *Troilus and Criseyde* or certain of his *Canterbury Tales*—and it was strengthened immeasurably in the Renaissance after the appearance of print. Erasmus' *Encomium Moriae* is at least as dense ironically as *The Bacchae*. Rabelais is somewhat less so perhaps because of his frequent involvement in pretypographic oral techniques of boisterousness and outrage, which he spoofs but remains deeply committed to. *Don Quixote*, on the other hand, a work infinitely more self-consciously involved in typography than any earlier work, stands as a specimen of multilayered irony worked out through the most self-conscious interaction between author and printed text that the world had yet seen.

Irony built up its presence through the eighteenth century. In their high-spirited and savage satirization of the printed book as an object, Swift, in *The Battle of the Books* (1697, published 1704), and Sterne, in *Tristram Shandy* (1760–67) advertised and expanded the typographic distances between writer and reader and thus the possibilities of ironic indirection: at points, Sterne turns his book over to the reader, telling the reader to write it himself and leaving blank pages for him to work on. The interchange of living interlocutors has completely broken down here. The full-blown novel exploited indirection further: beneath the story of more or less ordinary people (for print had made dysfunctional the heroic, "heavy" figures whereby an oral culture had managed its noetic economy), the typical novel such as George Eliot's or Stendhal's characteristically hints at or bluntly protests the fraudulence of the surface of life, suggesting a deeper, ironic truth beneath. The modern novel puts in its appearance with the Romantic Movement in the late 1700s, when, with the full interiorization of print, the spacing out of art and life and of author and reader in a way culminates.

From this point on, transactions of the author with the printed text as an object become more and more an arm's-length struggle as they become more self-consciously strenuous—as in Henry James's stories and speculations, or even more in Mallarmé's *Un coup de dés,* where the white space on the printed page plays against the aural elements of the poem, or in E. E. Cummings' Poem No. 176, where the disintegrating and then reassembled printed words act out visually the explosion of a grasshopper into his jagging flight and his sudden reconstitution upon alighting. There is no way to read this last poem aloud, although consummate silent reading skill is needed to assimilate it.

Regarding irony in the electronic age, the age of what I have elsewhere called secondary orality, I can offer here only brief comment, for to say more would open explicitly questions calling for too detailed treatment. Since a new medium of communication always reinforces at first the characteristic tendencies in the old, the age of electronic orality has seen the layers of irony in literature increased and intensified in their interrelations. Note that it is the old medium, not the new, that is reinforced: what has become more ironic is literature, not the electronic media generally. Electronic tapes furnish Samuel Beckett with the wherewithal for the irony in his literary work, *Krapp's Last Tape*. How many voices within voices are to be found in Pound's *Cantos*, which have been shown to be coefficients of an electronic culture?[18] It appears in fact impossible for television or even radio ever to support in themselves the multi-leveled irony of printed works. Television's high oral coefficient conditions it to be a participatory medium: audiences are shown pictures of the studio audience with whom they are supposed to identify, joining in their taped laughs. Radio is participatory too, with its phone-in programs and other audience-studio interplay. This new secondary orality, however, so strikingly like primary orality in its bent for participation, is also totally unlike the primary orality of mankind in that its participatory qualities are self-consciously planned and fully supervised. Somehow, all members of the studio audiences from whom volunteers on give-away programs are selected arrive clothed in the high-contrast or psychedelic styles which color television demands. Nothing is left to chance in the world of secondary orality, not even chance itself, for the producer is obliged to present a program which is not only spontaneous but conspicuously so. The only way to succeed is to plan your spontaneity carefully and circumstantially. Otherwise how can you be sure it's spontaneous? And you have to be sure. A seriously ironic mood would disintegrate this totally masked total control, so "stable" irony or irony pretty well labeled as such is all that television can normally tolerate.

The movies, another major medium of the electronic age, would seem to confuse the issues here because, unlike radio or

18. See Max Nänny, *Ezra Pound: Poetics for an Electric Age* (Bern: Franke Verlag, 1973).

television (when television is not just showing movies, doing what is not its own distinctive thing), movies can at times be quite ironic. But in several ways cinematic irony corroborates what has just been said. For the clue to the ironic potential in movies seems to be their visualism, which keeps them nonparticipatory in its relationship to voice. By comparison with the oral coefficient in radio and television (talk shows and the like), the oral coefficient in movies is minimal. What counts most is the sequence of visual events rather than any vocal exchange as such.

Voice, which is represented only in soundless code on the printed page, becomes even more utterly silent in stories told by cinema. A movie has in effect a narrator without a narrative voice. Let us see what this means. A verbal narrative, a story told or read, has a narrator who articulates sequences of events, determining by his words what the audience is to attend to in the narration, item after item, moving the audience's attention around independently of real time and space: "The engineer put his hand on the throttle and a rattling spasm moved down the train all the way to the caboose. Indoors, a half mile down the road, the living room glowed red. Memories welled up in her mind as she stoked the fire. The day at school when. . . . " In the live theater, although the playwright of course determines the sequence of scenes and of words and actions, no narrator normally articulates a story line at all. The only vocal exchanges are between the characters on the stage, and events are strung together in the quasi-real time and space in which these characters exist and operate. Like live theater, a movie normally has no narrator either, articulating a story line, telling the audience in words what to think of next. But it is unlike live theater in that, without words, inarticulately, the movie director has it in his power to do what the narrator of a story does and what a playwright normally cannot do. The director can establish sequences utterly independent of the quasi-real time and space in which his characters must act, a sequence existing only within the director's mind, and often including units with no characters at all: first a close-up of a face, then immediately a view of a leafy country road miles away, next a sled in a snowstorm, then Victoria Falls superimposed on the Mohave Desert. Such sequences normally cannot figure in live theater but they can in articulated narrative (and they can, and most often do, in dreams). Movies are thus more like novels (and dreams) than like plays: there is always a narrator in a movie, as in a story, who can direct attention to sequences which are independent of the time and space in which his characters perform; only in place of saying something, this storyteller provides visual sequences. He says not a word. The movie, that is to say, has a narrator without a narrative voice.

In writing and print, the narrator is distanced because his voice is not alive, but visually mummified for visual-aural re-processing. In the movies, the narrator is distanced because his "voice," the line of presentation he is following, is not even a mummy: it is not there at all as words, which are ultimately always sounds. Vision has taken over completely from voice. The question of who is saying what to whom becomes not merely complicated, but wraith-like as well. Irony can of course result. Nevertheless, the height of irony in the movies can probably never reach that possible in print, such as that in a Henry James story or in *Finnegans Wake*. A movie, for example, of *The Aspern Papers* could hardly manage all the nuances of tone that sound through James's text. Irony depends on tones as well as on distances. The ironic devaluation of photography in a well-done movie such as *Blow-Up* is devastating and deeply philosophical but the irony is thematic rather than tonal: for complexity of ironic involutions it can hardly compare with, let us say, twenty selected pages of Stendhal's or Conrad's or Joyce's text.

Rhetoric, Print, and "Pure" Poetry

The place of rhetoric in Western culture as an academic institutionalization of pristine orality should by now be well known. Beginning with the Sophists and Aristotle's *Art of Rhetoric,* writing had been used to codify and improve the preliterate skill in public speaking, in Greek, *technē rhētorikē*. Although this essentially oral art of rhetoric was adapted in some degree to the teaching of writing, the adaptation was hardly a reflective process at all and it was in effect minimal. So long as rhetoric remained dominant in the teaching of the use of language, the oral residue in writing and print cultures remained massive, and the assumption prevailed, implicit and vague but forceful, that the paradigm for all expression was in some way the classical oration.[19]

Rhetoric kept alive the old oral culture's participatory noetics. For rhetoric was eminently practical: basically, it had to do with moving real audiences to real decisions in the existential world. Orations were to be planned but not written (at least not until after they had been given): each one was shaped in delivery by speaker-audience interaction. An oration was a performance, not a declamation of a text—such declamation was to come as an approved institution only with the "elocution" movement in the eighteenth and nineteenth centuries, when the histrionic techniques for making a written text sound like extempore speech were imported from the theater to the pulpit and platform.[20]

The old rhetorically dominated world was basically intolerant of poetry except as a variant of rhetoric. Not only the rhetoricians but also early poets themselves tended to think of poetry in this way. The speaker-audience-subject relationship, as we have seen, was monolithic, and aesthetic subject matter was inseparable from the lived world. Even narrative poetry was made up largely of versified speeches, metrical orations airing issues hardly detachable from real-life situations. Here was where poetry remained for the most part, in Western culture generally and especially in academia, until romanticism ultimately overpowered the rhetorical world in the latter half of the eighteenth century. So long as orality was in the ascendancy, even though it was an orality kept alive by writing, poetry was more or less involved in the ordinary business of living. It was not allowed to withdraw from the human lifeworld into a text.

The Romantic Movement marked the beginning of the end of

19. Ong, *Rhetoric, Romance, and Technology*, pp. 27–33, 64.
20. See Wilbur Samuel Howell, *Eighteenth-Century British Logic and Rhetoric* (Princeton, N.J.: Princeton University Press, 1971), pp. 145–256.

rhetoric as a major academic and cultural force in the West. The Romantic Age took form with the maturing of knowledge storage and retrieval processes made possible by print. These processes had produced a store of readily retrievable knowledge greater than had ever before been possible. Print had effectively reduced sound to surface, hearing to vision. Despite the fact that it was verbally constituted and ultimately tied to the oral world, the store of knowledge accumulated in print was no longer managed by repetitive, oral techniques, but by visual means, through print, tables of contents, and indices. Knowledge was tied not to spoken words but to texts. This separated knowledge from the lived world. It could be "parked" outside consciousness. It became more than ever before an object, a thing. Inevitably, the new economy affected ideas of poetry. A poem, too, was now clearly a text. It, too, was separated from the lived world. As print was more and more deeply assimilated into consciousness, it became more and more feasible and attractive to think of the poem as having its own peculiar poetic life, organized from within. Earlier poems had perhaps had something of a life of their own, but not much, and what they had could not feasibly be considered separate from the rest of existence. With the new state of noetic affairs, it was eventually feasible so to think of the poem, as separate from "life" with its own "content" and "values." And it was increasingly feasible to write poems whose direct connection with the lived human lifeworld was more and more tenuous. The grounds for surrealism were being laid. At this point, the germ of the doctrine of "pure" poetry appears and begins to grow. The germ is nurtured by the visualist objectivism fostered by print.

At the same time, the doctrine of mimesis atrophies and concern with irony intensifies. For the insistently repetitious, imitative, antidivisive noetic economy of pristine oral cultures was finished, and with it the close identification of author, audience, and material which marks the unquestioning, aggregative noetic economy of the old oral world. The new world is split a thousand ways, and irony enters into its own as never before. Whether

literary values and lived human values are the same or not becomes a question. Whereas the old oral world had to be saved
from itself by Platonic dialectic, a diaeretic or divisive technique,
the new world will have as its converse problem the search for
means of integration to preserve it from total fragmentation. This
problem shaped the romantic enterprise, although romanticism
hardly solved the problem. Romanticism, in these perspectives, is
the development which finally and definitively phases out the
old participatory oral economy in favor of the nonparticipatory
noetic economy of print.

Who Is Saying What to Whom?

These reflections have been far-ranging and sketchy, but they
make it possible to return over new routes to our original question, Who is saying what to whom? as this relates to values and
content in literature today.

Obviously, the answers to the question must be varied. They
come in a complex continuum. Lots of people today are saying
lots of things to lots of other people and to themselves, and the
other people and they themselves are blended or separated in a
variety of ways. At one end of the continuum are the electronic
sound media, and the literature that is spin-off from these media,
such as the lyrics of Bob Dylan and Simon and Garfunkel, to
cite some examples which must strike the new now generation
as at least Pleistocene. Here we are in the world of secondary
orality, as it may be called, superficially identical with that of
primary orality but in depth utterly contrary, planned and self-
conscious where primary orality is unplanned and unselfcon-
scious, totally dependent on writing and print for its existence
(try to imagine a television network operated by complete illiterates, unable to read sets of instructions, not to mention tele-
prompters), whereas primary orality was not only innocent of
writing and print but vulnerable to these media and ultimately
destroyed by them. But the aura of spontaneity and participation
clings to television like a shroud, carefully pinned into position
to be sure that the artificiality does not show. Here mimesis

rules, but often in reverse. For the rock bands and other color television shows determine the high contrast clothes that real people will wear on the streets, and the script writers and news-casters and commentators tell the real people, who live in the real world, what is really going on or should be going on in their real lives.

At the other end of the spectrum are writers such as Vladimir Nabokov, whose multifaceted ironies teach, move, and delight, and also leave us asking many questions, as well as the still less reliable narrative voices treated in *The Rhetoric of Fiction* by Wayne Booth, who finds some writers pretending that not taking a position is the best possible position to take.[21]

In between, there is almost everything, except the unselfcon-sciously participatory and integrative, but essentially limited and fragile, world of oral verbal performance before literature began. For this world can never be recaptured by literates except in retrospect, as a mock-up made of pieces remodeled from the writing and print cultures which succeeded it. But the world of primary orality cannot be understood either except in retrospect, for it had no way of reflecting on itself. The oral world is open to reflection only from this end of history. It is at least likely that in some way a child in technological society today passes through a stage something like that of the old oral culture. Ontogeny recapitulates phylogeny. But the stage is only some-thing like the old, for it remains a child's stage and cannot be protracted into adulthood. The old oral world was not a world of children but of adults, who had children of their own.

In the adult world of literature today, writer and reader are distanced from one another by a thousand conventions, and tied to one another by them too, at a distance. The writer is distanced from himself, as the emergence of the modern diary as a literary form shows. An oral culture that achieves this distancing has already destroyed itself.

The content of literature is distanced, too. We have become

21. Booth, *The Rhetoric of Fiction* (Chicago: University of Chicago Press, 1961), pp. 340–374.

objects to ourselves. Here lies a danger. Machines can take over—not in the sense that they will direct human society, an idea which is nonsense if not paranoid, but in the sense that we may, and often do, regard ourselves as machines, taking a mechanical device as a model for the human being. This is unfortunately a commonplace occurrence in certain psychologies and in genetic planning.

Does what has been said then suggest that writing and print are corrupting? Not necessarily. Not more so than ordinary oral speech. But it does suggest that they are not entirely purifying either, that there is no particular sacredness attaching to the press, that, since writing and print are essentially fabrications, they are always in need of repair, not self-corrective. It would be going too far, I believe, to say that writing and print enforce schizophrenia. But it is a fact that they dissociate the reader from actuality to a degree at the same time that they can make him or her more responsive, indirectly and reflexively, to actuality. To achieve understanding, human beings need distance as well as proximity. Despite and in part because of their diaeretic effects, writing and print remain basically good, and indeed essential if one wants to be learned, for literacy is the necessary ground of all learning as learning contrasts with "lore," which is learning's oral antecedent. Learning enforces cleavage. This is true. And cleavage is not evil. Living organisms grow by cleavage of their cells. However, if learning enforces cleavage, it also calls for integration, even though learning cannot bring about integration but can only serve the forces that do. The same is true of writing and print, which of themselves have no therapeutic, and a fortiori no redemptive value, although to achieve certain goods they may at times be indispensable. The resulting problem of identifying and cultivating the true forces of integration remains one of our major literary and social problems today.

In view of the fragmentation within and around literature, is it possible for the author not to take a stand, possible for him or her to dissociate his or her writing from the real, lived world in such a way as neither to affirm nor to deny any real human goods in this lived human lifeworld? Can literature really take on a life of its own? The answer is evidently no. The most abstract subjects hook up at one point or another with real life, and generally at many points. Formal logic as a discipline grew not out of analysis of some Cartesian solipsistic assertion, but out of the analysis of dispute, of the interaction of two human beings locked in verbal and intellectual contest. Abstract logic is a spin-off from real rhetoric. The terms in mathematical definitions or axioms can never be fully defined, but at one point or another must be resolved on grounds other than those of formal mathematics, grounds where persons have some general agreement regarding the meaning of words in real life, as the foundations of mathematics make evident. Nothing in literature means anything apart from our lived lives and the good and evil in real life. No word or group of words has meaning apart from its insertion into an existential, historical, lived context.

This is not to say that the words in literature mean in the same way as those in an executive order, for the modes of involvement in poetry and in real life are diverse and manifold. Nor is it to say that the values expressed in literature can be derived from ingenuous readings. Literature may be almost as complex as life itself, and both are growing more and more complex in many ways. However, both repay thought. They also demand thought. To say that the author can take no stand at all in his writing is as mindless and as irresponsible as to say that he is always writing moralized fables.

Finally, what do the foregoing reflections suggest regarding the possibility of "pure" literature in which the literary content would simply constitute its own world? They suggest that perhaps no serious thinker is even interested in this possibility anymore. Marxist critics, for example, have never even allowed the question. And the new orality of our age, incarnate in television, appears inhibitory to ideas of "pure" art, for it upgrades, however artificially, participation and the blurring of the lines between art and life. Despite the high incidence of irony as a literary technique and as a critical preoccupation, there are signs—of which this paper is one—that we are increasingly critical of irony as a basic strategy in literature and art, and critical of other distancing strategies as well, although I hope that we will always remain aware that aesthetic distance is essential to art and that the art-nature distinction is as real and necessary as it is elusive. If this distinction is not clear in primary oral cultures, as I have tried to show it is not, this is one of the weaknesses of such cultures, for they have their own weaknesses, too, as literate and electronic cultures have theirs. But if we must distinguish art and nature—as we must—we must also remember that the relationship between art and nature is a dialectical one, and that each is involved in the other. This leaves the quest for an ultimately "pure" literature disabled for good. Such a quest for "pure" literature, I hope it is by now clear, is or was a historical phenomenon belonging to a certain stage in the development of knowledge and the evolution of consciousness.

IV

PRESENT AND FUTURE

11

Voice and the Opening of Closed Systems

Closure, Openness, and the Word

Studies in this book have treated the history of the word often, though not entirely, in terms of sequestration, interposition, diaeresis or division, alienation, and closed fields or systems. The history of the word since its encounter and interaction with technology when the first writing systems were devised some six thousand years ago has been largely a matter of such separations and systems. By comparison with oral speech, writing is itself a closed system: a written text exists on its own, physically separate from any speaker or hearer, as no real spoken word can exist. Print creates a world even more spectacularly contained: every *a* in a font of type is exactly like every other; every copy of an edition matches every other.

Closure is not the only result of writing and print, for writing and print also open and liberate. They give access not only to information otherwise inaccessible but also make possible new thought processes. Moreover, they also give rise to and interact with their own dialectical opposites. Today, it appears, we live in a culture or in cultures very much drawn to openness and in particular to open-system models for conceptual representations. This openness can be connected with our new kind of orality, the secondary orality of our electronic age, which both resembles and contrasts with primary or preliterate orality. This new kind of orality, secondary orality, has its own openness, but is itself dependent upon writing and print. As has been seen in Chapter

3, writing and print inevitably make possible the world which transforms them. If they still retain their diaeretic, closed-field thrust, they do so differently from before, within a dialectically opposed, more open, noetic economy which is nevertheless dependent on them and their closures.

A system in actuality is always only relatively closed: a group of interrelated elements which interact with one another in a pattern which is relatively stable and relatively free or resistant to outside interference. Paul A. Weiss puts it this way: "Pragmatically defined, a system is a rather circumscribed complex of relatively bounded phenomena, which, within those bounds, retains a relatively stationary pattern or structure in space or sequential configuration in time in spite of a high degree of variability in the details of distribution and interrelations among its constituent units of lower order."[1] The "rather" and the "relatively" are essential, as Professor Weiss here and elsewhere makes clear, and as others have made equally clear.

A completely closed system, physical or biological or psychological or noetic, is impossible. We have become increasingly sensitive to this fact today, both with regard to language and with regard to existence as a whole. We live in an age which quite widely favors open-system thinking, at least in principle, with some of the same fervor with which earlier chirographic and typographic cultures championed closed-system thinking. At least, this is true in the Free World, for the state of consciousness in the Communist countries and in many others still inhibits any wide use of many open-system models which the Free World finds nonthreatening.

1. See Paul A. Weiss, "The Living System: Determinism Stratified," in *The Alpbach Symposium 1968: Beyond Reductionism—New Perspectives in Life Sciences,* ed. Arthur Koestler and J. R. Smythies (New York: Macmillan, 1967), pp. 3–55; the definition here quoted is on pp. 11–12. For a sweeping overview of the whole matter of systems, see Anthony Wilden, *System and Structure: Essays in Communication and Exchange* (London: Tavistock Publications, 1972); for social implications, see Dante Germino and Klaus Van Beyme, eds., *The Open Society in Theory and Practice* (The Hague: Martinus Nijhoff, 1976), in which seventeen political theorists from nine countries treat the question of openness.

The reasons for change to an open-system mentality are complex, and in assessing the cultural developments associated with the change it is often difficult to distinguish cause from effect. Interconnections are bewildering. Here an attempt will be made to give a brief account of some of the interconnections by examining the present inclination or drive to open-system models throughout society, especially in the West but also to some extent across the world, in terms of the technological history of the word. It should be emphasized that what is said here is only a part of all that could be said to describe and try to account for the current benign attitude toward open systems. This account is not meant to be reductionist. It is not intended to reduce all explanations of today's open-system mentality to the technological history of the word. Rather, the account is relationist. It suggests that many other causes, and perhaps even all other causes, of the open-system mind set are related, complexly but intimately, to the technological history of the word.

Structuralism: Openness or Closure?

Discussion of the current open-system mind-set cannot avoid adverting to structuralist thinking. The protean term or concept "structuralism" designates an agglomerate of issues within which a good deal of the struggle between closed-system and open-system thinking is taking place today. The spread of this concept into the most varied areas of thought shows how pervasive the openness-closure struggle is in the evolution of human consciousness: there is structuralism in linguistics (notably in the study of grammar, generative and transformational), in anthropology and other behavioral sciences, in literary and textual analysis from that of the *Tel Quel* group in France to that of biblical scholarship (where, however, structuralism is a latecomer), in history (where it is also a latecomer), in philosophy of various sorts, particularly that concerned with noetics, signification, and hermeneutics, in psychology (where *Gestalt* theorizing indirectly adumbrated present structuralist concerns), and so on and on and on.

Structuralist theorizing is so vast that a thorough-going treatment of it here would be utterly distracting were it even possible.[2] What is most relevant here is the structuralist preoccupation with language. Because language registers and helps constitute the central ordering activities of the psyche, and thereby offers the first serious invitation to effect closure, structuralism in linguistics has been a primary focus or disseminating point for all structuralism insofar as structuralism can be identified as a unified movement or, better, a unified problematic mind-set. In linguistics, structuralism has two polarities. First, there is grammar-derived structuralism, that emanating from the age-old interests of grammarians and their chronic uneasiness at their abiding inability to complete their abstract science. This kind of structuralism has its great modern source in the highly original work of Ferdinand de Saussure (1857–1913). Second, there is the structuralism emanating from linguistic anthropologists such as Claude Lévi-Strauss, who studies the "concrete" classificatory structures of the "savage" mind (better called, I believe, the radically oral mind).

From the beginning, and increasingly over the years, structuralist thinking evinces an incredible sophistication and admirably patient circumstantiality, but at the same time can be beset with an annoying naïveté. It elaborates psychic and other constructs of incredible complexity, all the more impressive because before the structuralists state them they exist in their complexity for

2. Works guiding the reader into structuralist issues and bibliography would include Wilden, *System and Structure,* which ranges widely through all sorts of structuralism and systems analysis; Claude Lévi-Strauss, *The Savage Mind,* translated from the French, *La Pensée sauvage* (Chicago: University of Chicago Press, 1966), and various other works by the same author; Jean Piaget, *Structuralism,* translated and edited by Chaninah Maschler (New York: Basic Books, 1970); Jonathan Culler, *Structuralist Poetics: Structuralism, Linguistics and the Study of Literature* (Ithaca, N.Y.: Cornell University Press, 1975), in which the author argues (p. 253) that structuralism cannot escape from ideology or provide its own foundations any more than competing analyses can; and Edward O. Wilson, *Sociobiology: The New Synthesis* (Cambridge, Mass.: Belknap Press of Harvard University Press, 1975), a massive work which is not directly structuralist but which plots some of the varied anthropological and biological terrain over which structuralism works.

the most part only in the subconscious or unconscious realms of the psyche. But the very comprehensiveness of the goals which give structuralism its drive—the drive, for example, to isolate and state absolutely all the rules of generative grammar so that a computer can be programed to speak English or Twi at least as well as a ten-year-old native speaker—soon make it transparently clear that a closed system is impossible, as Goedel's theorem and other considerations also make clear independently. Structuralism has provided wonderful new insights into a multiplicity of things because of its passion to organize all existence in structures. But by the same token it has made evident, as more and more structuralists like to proclaim, that you cannot reduce language or anything else to a closed system, despite the fact that without using some provisional closed-system models we cannot understand anything, including language or existence itself, even as poorly as we do.

Thus, while structuralism on the one hand seems object-like (a "structure" as such is conceived of as somehow visibly or tangibly apprehensible, at least by analogy), a kind of "thing," and thus inhuman, it proves on the other hand to be very human after all by sharing the tragedy of all mortal existence, chronic incompleteness—which, thanks in part to structuralism, we can understand more specifically as both synchronic and diachronic incompleteness.

With reference to the concerns of the present work, we can note that the structuralist enterprise has frequently been plagued by its chirographic and typographic bias, that is, by its failure by and large to consider language primarily as it really is, as sound. Even when attending to spoken language as such, structuralist speculation has frequently treated language and noetic processes, sometimes crudely but more often subtly and unconsciously, as though their primary habitat were the inscribed surface covered by writing and print, whereas their primary and permanent habitat is the world of sound, to which writing and print ultimately refer. Structuralism has said little about differences between oral and written discourse and has seldom adverted to the fact that texts must be recycled back through sound to have meaning. What is needed is a knowledge of the phenomenology of orality, including an understanding of the psychodynamics of oral noetics and of some of the ways in which chirographic and typographic thought processes and discourse have grown out of and away from oral noetics. To this understanding the way has been opened by Milman Parry, Albert B. Lord, and Eric A. Havelock and those who have variously qualified or nuanced their findings. Of these now classic findings, however, most structuralist literature shows no awareness at all.

The Blurring of Art and Nature

Whatever the role of structuralism in advertising current openness-closure crises, consciousness has evidently shifted in recent times to favor open-system paradigms in many areas of verbalization, at least in the West. Shifts toward openness are evident in various kinds of literature. It has become fashionable to dissolve the bounds and controls of literary works. Chapter 9 has discussed one of the forms this fashion has taken, namely the obscuring or dissolution of plot, which typically differentiates fiction from nature or "life." Your life or mine can be given a "plot" of a fictional sort, if at all, only by leaving out almost everything that has happened to us and concentrating on a single line or single lines of events which make a "story": a play-by-play account of every single occurrence in life is no "plot" at all.

Other openings of recent literature into more or less real life are too manifold to catalogue here. Among those that suggest themselves would be breakthroughs of the sort in Baudelaire's line picked up in T. S. Eliot's *The Wasteland*, "You! hypocrite lecteur!—mon semblable,—mon frère!" or the narrative structure of Camus' *La Chute*, in which the narrator directly addresses the reader, apparently reacts to the reader's implied responses, and involves the reader in his own complicity and guilt—all this in ways far more direct than Victorian novelists had in mind with their "dear reader" apostrophes. A similar disposition to blur fiction and real life shows very widely in the recent obsession with confessional writing not only in fiction, which has a narrator, but even in drama, which does not, as in Tennessee Williams' *The Glass Menagerie* or Arthur Miller's *After the Fall.*

The line between fiction and nonfictional existence is not the only border broken through in the literary world today. Much critical discussion deliberately attacks earlier conventional attitudes which separate reader and writer. Thus Roland Barthes complains of "the pitiless divorce which the literary institution maintains between the producer of the text and its user, between its owner and its customer, between its author and its reader," and pleads for a "readerly" text in which the reader himself or herself is creative.[3] Barthes's basic meaning appears to rest on a simple enough truth: whoever reads a text has to interpret it, relate it to the lived world of the reader, which means that he or she will bring out elements in the text otherwise obscured. Any statement (including this one) has implications which are really there but which only time and varied contexts can surface. This is true even of the spoken word, and a fortiori of a text, for memory of the spoken word is normally limited whereas a text can have readers from now to the day of judgment, a potentially infinite number of contexts. Readers have always interacted with texts, but the present excitement about the interaction felt by Barthes and others in the literary-structuralist milieu in France and the United States reveals the neo-oral cast of contemporary literature. The excitement is shared by philosophically sophisticated fiction writers such as William Gass.[4]

Barthes's creative readers interacting with texts are curiously reminiscent of the audiences at verbal performances in primary

3. Roland Barthes, *S/Z,* trans. Richard Miller (New York: Hill & Wang, 1974), p. 4; cf. ibid., pp. 5–18.

4. See the informative article, which treats also other breakdowns of the once usual borders between fiction and nonfictional existence, by Gore Vidal, "American Plastic: The Matter of Fiction," *New York Review of Books,* July 15, 1976, pp. 31–39. I am indebted to Professor Albert J. Montesi of Saint Louis University for calling my attention to this article.

oral cultures (cultures before the advent of writing, as against secondary oral cultures, such as our own, where the orality of the mass media is dependent on writing). In primary oral cultures the epic poet or other narrator actually shapes any given rendition of his narrative to the living response of the audience.[5] It would be a mistake to equate the present situation with the otherwise vastly different situation of primary oral cultures, but in both situations open-system interactions are prized, and the closed-system paradigms encouraged by writing and print are in certain ways inoperative.

Contemporary theater provides further examples of opened closure. Here no longer is the play always the closed system it once was, cut off cleanly, as a formally constituted play, from existential life, the world of "work." For Aristotle, a play had a beginning, a middle, and an end (*Poetics* 1450b). The beginning marks the cut-off from real existence, when the actor Aristodemus becomes the *dramatis persona* Creon; at the end, in a similar cut between art and nature, Creon vanishes and the actor becomes the real-self Aristodemus again. In between, in the "middle," something, organized in the plot, happens to Creon, who at the end of Act 5 is in a state quite different from that at the beginning of Act 1. A good bit of recent drama destroys this histrionic package or closed system. Jack Gelber's

5. See Max Lüthi, "Aspects of the Märchen and the Legend," *Folklore Genres,* ed. Dan Ben-Amos (Austin: University of Texas Press, 1976), pp. 17–33, for a discussion of the way in which the audience takes part in the creation of variants of an oral tale. Neither the old "spontaneous creation" theory of Jacob Grimm and others nor the later chain-of-individual-artists theory accounts for the actuality, in which the individual artist and a particular audience interact to make every performance, even of basically the same story, a new creation. Details of this interaction are worked out by Ngal Mbwil a Mpaang, "L'Artiste africain: tradition, critique, et liberté créatrice," mimeographed text of a conference paper received from the author April 19, 1974, in Lubumbashi, Zaire, and now in my possession. Professor Ngal, Chairman of the Department of French Studies at the Université Nationale du Zaire at Lubumbashi, shows how the creativity of the African oral narrator comes into play differently in each and every performance as the narrator brings into being in each and every performance a different interaction between his culture and its content, the particular audience before him, and himself, to produce each time a uniquely shaped narrative out of the traditional lore.

The Connection opens with the curtain up and the people on the stage set appearing not at all like actors—indeed, from time to time glaring hostilely at the audience in evident resentment.[6] The "author" is introduced to the audience, to whom the actors are also introduced by the "producer" after he stops the action, and the "author" and actors get into an argument. One of the characters panhandles from the audience during the intermission. This kind of "living theater" of course is reminiscent of Pirandello's *Six Characters in Search of an Author,* and, long before that, of Calderón's *La vida es sueño,* for the "life is a dream" topos is an old way of transposing art and life. But Calderón and Pirandello keep their action formally dramatic, however involuted. The actors become concerned with what they are doing as dramatic creation, not with what the audience is doing. The dramatic transaction with the live theater audience is another thing, distinctive of contemporary pieces such as Gelber's. Some of Gelber's actor-panhandlers receive a larger take from the real audience, some a smaller. LeRoi Jones's *Dutchman* is another instance in point, virtually a direct—if symbolically transformed—assault on a white audience's behavior in real life.

One thinks also of the old dramatic aside as a crossover between dramatic fiction and real life. But the aside is normally written into the text of the play. It is a part of the actor's act, although anomalous. The actor steps out into an extracontextual arena. But he does not directly assault the audience, as with the hostile glares in Gelber's play. Moreover, asides were sporadic and minor. In much modern theater, the mood producing the crossovers between dramatic fiction and nondramatic existence pervades the whole play, and insistently. "Everybody wants to get into the act," the old trooper Jimmy Durante used to rasp.

6. The contemporary plays discussed here and some other relevant ones, in various ways "open-system," are treated in Bernard F. Dukore, "The Noncommercial Theater in New York," pp. 155–167 in Alan S. Downer, ed., *The American Theater Today* (New York: Basic Books, 1967). See also Oscar G. Brockett, *Perspectives on Contemporary Theatre* (Baton Rouge: Louisiana State University Press, 1971), pp. 142–151, and *passim.*

His bemused complaint was precocious. In *The Connection* and similar work, everybody is in the act willy-nilly.

Other early instances of blurred edges between literature and life can be adduced. The play-within-the-play makes the encompassing play within which it is set seem, by contrast, to be real life. Still, in earlier periods, the borderline between the play-within-the-play (for example, *The Murder of Gonzago* in *Hamlet*) and the encompassing play itself (*Hamlet*) was likely to be kept clear, even when, as in *Hamlet,* the play-within-the-play was deliberately equipped with open references to the "real" life of the encompassing play. Today, the interface between the play-within-the-play and the encompassing play is likely to be more studiously blurred. In Tom Stoppard's *Rosencrantz and Guildenstern Are Dead,* an inside-out version of *Hamlet,* this interface is much more confused than in Shakespeare's original *Hamlet.* And Stoppard's *Jumpers* is a still more strenuous exercise in the jumping of borders for audiences addicted to such things.

Further earlier instances of blurred edges between fiction and existence might be More's *Utopia* (1516), where real and fictitious characters figure side-by-side in the same narrative, or *Don Quixote* (1605, 1615), the incredibly precocious work registering the effects of the new invention of typography on narrative: in the second part of this work, Cervantes has his characters affected by the readers' reactions to the first part. But in their time such works were tours de force. Today the state of mind which once produced such tours de force has become a pervasive obsession.

In a certain sense, of course, art and nature, play and work, dramatic action and real action, have never been in fact entirely closed off from one another, for they are modes of life dialectically related, mutually definitive, both matching and contrasting as explained in Chapter 10. Art is what is not nature; nature stops where art begins. And yet art is like nature. The best plays are those most like real life (in any of a bewildering variety of ways). Or conversely, nature is like art, at least for human beings. A human being enters into the human lifeworld by role-playing; a child learns to walk and talk, as a teacher learns to teach or a swimmer to swim, by playing at it until he or she is actually doing it. In sports, the best players are the professionals for whom the play is work, while in real life, the best workers are those for whom the work is like play, a kind of game, a free outpouring.[7] This dialectical relationship of life (work) and art (play), however, had not inhibited an earlier tendency to think of art, or more particularly the work of art, as a closed system. This tendency, as Chapter 8 has tried to show, marked the distinctively literate aesthetics of the New Criticism, particularly in the United States, and the equally literate aesthetics of G. E. Moore and the Bloomsbury Group in England, with which the New Criticism is in part connected. Today the tendency is weakened by opposed and highly competitive drives.

Television as Open System

The most spectacular and intrusive of the recent technological transformations of the word, television, manifests perhaps most clearly, and certainly most massively and deeply, the breaking up of the closed systems associated with the verbal art forms generated by writing and print. Television blurs the fictional with the real on a scale previously inconceivable. It does so not through deliberate choices made by executives, directors, writers, technicians, performers, or viewers, but rather of its very nature. The "tube of plenty" has generated an other-than-real world which is not quite life but more than fiction.[8]

Both visually and aurally (sound is of the essence of television), the instrument takes a real presence from the place where it is real and present and represents it in other localities where it is neither real nor truly present. This representation is not a

7. See Walter J. Ong, Preface, pp. ix–xiv, in Hugo Rahner, *Man at Play*, trans. Brian Battershaw and Edward Quinn (New York: Herder and Herder, 1967).

8. For a good overview of the history of television, see Erik Barnouw, *Tube of Plenty: The Evolution of American Television* (New York: Oxford University Press, 1975).

report. The football game you view on television is going on, its outcome unrealized as yet, and thus unknown. Reports are essentially ex post facto. Not all television presentations are simultaneous with reality, but, in a way, all television presentations seem to be; the fact that the instrument is capable of such presentations defines its impact.

Before television no human psyche had experienced visually and aurally events actually going on in the real present but in an extraneous locale. Various signs (smoke, bonfires) could give crude reports. Radio could do better, providing detailed oral accounts of distant events. But an oral account is always in essence a report: however recent, the event described is over with. The speaker knew the *fait accompli* before the hearer did. Television is different. The voice on a live television sports broadcast lags behind the audience's perceptions. Jack Ruby was viewed by millions while he was actually murdering Lee Harvey Oswald in Dallas. But he was murdering him in Dallas, not in hundreds of thousands of homes into which the killing was artificially projected as it took place. This intrusion creates a new unreality of presence, grotesquely assertive in the case of such tragic violence. The event in Dallas and the synchronized nonevent in living rooms across the country corresponded in time, though not even remotely in human context. More routinely but no less really than the Ruby-Oswald killing, such conditions obtain in a live television presentation of scheduled events, such as football games. Living in the ambience of such nonpresent present events has reorganized human consciousness, which is to say, the individual's own sense of presence in and to himself and in and to the world around him.

The individual's sense of presence to himself and others is not always rendered grotesque by television, as it was in the case of the Ruby-Oswald killing. It can be a healing and strengthening sense, too. Television coverage of the funeral ceremonies and related matters made the entire United States into a community in a new and healing way as the country mourned collectively the assassination of President Kennedy in 1963. Something similar happened at the national mourning for the assassination of Dr. Martin Luther King. In both these cases the collective self-presence, the sense of community, came into being around live events. More recently, a similar collective healing and strengthening has been experienced through the television presentation of Alex Haley's *Roots,* where the events were not live. Although the story was basically historical (with many fictional elements) and in this sense real, it was played by actors and its historical (and fictional) events belonged to the past. But the participatory sense conveyed by television, plus the fact that the events were symbolically momentous in national history, again created a sense of community. It has become a commonplace to remark about *Roots* that nothing like the same effect would have been achieved had the story been put out as a movie, so that the experience of viewing it could not have been shared, as it was on television, by millions simultaneously, blacks and whites and others. As in the John F. Kennedy and Martin Luther King tragedies, the audience could sense its own vast unity.

The audience in television is, however, a puzzling actuality on the whole. The writer's audience, it has been said earlier in this book, is always a fiction. So is the television "audience" in its own way: it is never present, though performers and audience alike pretend that it is. And it is never a unitary group as the audience in a theater is. The problems are particularly evident when television is presenting not live events but some sort of "show," something "staged," such as drama, vaudeville, give-away programs, discussions, or interviews.

Taping or performing before a live audience does not eliminate the paradox but only enhances and complicates it. For instead of merely one audience, the performer is now dealing with two. The "live" audience in the studio is not the real audience at all. It serves as a substitute for the audience of those watching the TV screens who are by implication not "live" but somehow "real." But these watchers are not a real audience at all either in the sense that they are not present to the performers—which is why the studio audience is set up. Nevertheless, the nonpresent viewers are in effect more real as audience than the seemingly "real" studio audience, for the studio audience appears as part of the show on the television screen for the non-present audience, and thus disqualifies itself as an audience by becoming part of the show. To complicate interrelations further, laughs of this televised studio audience or even laughs from old tapes encourage and add substance to the real laughs of the nonpresent real audience. Open systems with a vengeance. A tangle of apertures. The effect is again reminiscent of the trans-actions between reader and fictional narrative in *Don Quixote,* but *Don Quixote* is much less open.

Introversions and extroversions and convolutions are limitless here. At the Encuentro Mundial de Comunicación in Acapulco in October 1974, as a hall of some six hundred persons listened to and saw live panelists engaged in discussion on the dais before them, television cameras in the rear of the hall picked up the panelists and projected them onto a huge sixteen-by-twenty-foot screen (my own calculations on the spot) suspended above the panelists' heads. The audience was thus encouraged to view not the live panelists but the television projection of the live panel-ists, more assertive in its assault on the senses than the live panelists it was presenting.

At times the cameras would enlarge their field and pick up the entire hall, including, besides the panelists, members of the audience (the backs of heads and shoulders) as well as the huge screen itself, which was, with everything else, projected onto itself. At this point the audience found itself on the equivalent of a one-way electronic hall of mirrors. On the huge screen appeared images of the panelists, audience, and the screen itself as a part of the hall's equipment. On this smaller screen thus projected onto the larger screen appear the same elements as upon the larger screen: panelists, audience, and screen again, which once more was reproduced with panel, audience, and screen, still smaller, and so on, until too tiny to discern. To the question I put to the panel, "What is the purpose, conscious or unconscious, of this curious exercise in introversion or narcissism, and of the blending of image and actuality?" no direct answer in depth was available. This Encuentro Mundial de Comunicación was a world-wide meeting of the media greats, got together by the major Mexican television chain Televisa. The impression one got was that you do these things because the medium makes it possible to do these things. This is what television essentially is: interplay between actuality and image. The more such interplay, the more the medium is true to itself.

The in-and-out relationship of television as an art form with its audience in the real world is maximized with videotape, whereby a taped past performance can be played back into the present and merged on another videotape with a live perform-ance so that the composite can be presented on monitors to the live performers who, as part of their performance, can view themselves interacting simultaneously with what is real and what is fictitious. This kind of introversion—more complex than the Acapulco phenomenon because it is also diachronic and not merely synchronic—was adumbrated a good many years ago, though in simpler form, by Samuel Beckett in *Krapp's Last Tape*, in which the protagonist enters into a dialogue with his voice taped some years earlier. Such intro-introversion on tele-vision makes it clear that the new medium is not just a new way of purveying what other media purvey in their own ways, but is rather the implementation of a new state of awareness and of a new gaming relationship with both space and time, which of course affects our sense of real time.

A recent book by Paul Ryan, which comes out of extensive experimentation with videotape, treats relationships made pos-sible with videotape by analogy with Klein bottles or "klein-forms" (more elaborate, more introverted Klein bottles).[9] A Klein bottle is a construct, well known in mathematics, made by passing the narrow end of a tapered tube back through the side of the tube and flaring out the narrow tube end to join the other

9. Paul Ryan, *Cybernetics of the Sacred* (Garden City, N.Y.: Anchor Press, Doubleday, 1974); first published as *Birth and Death and Cybernation* (New York: Gordon & Breach, Science Publishers, 1973).

end from the inside. The resulting form is something analogous to a Moebius strip devised in a world of solids. As a Moebius strip is a surface with no other side, a Klein bottle is a container with no bottom. In a Klein bottle or other kleinform, the container is also the contained, and vice versa. The television audience and the television show can likewise contain one another, as we have seen. In elaborated kleinforms, a tube containing part of itself can in turn be contained in another part of itself, or can emerge from itself again and re-enter. In kleinforms, closures are open. The analogy with television, if not total, is nevertheless apt.

The open relationship between television and nontelevised actuality puts a special premium on preserving spontaneity—which in fact for television products mostly means creating spontaneity. All art forms to some degree tend to pass themselves off as in one way or another unprogramed, spontaneously achieved actuality: *ars celare artem*. Art consists in concealing art. The ballet dancer or trapeze artist or figure skater makes his or her movements look completely effortless and natural: paradoxically (and all art is a paradox), you have to work harder to make essentially difficult actions appear easy. The easier you want them to appear, the harder you have to work. But in television the spontaneity cultivated by art is more essential than in other art forms and more complexly artificial.

Drama has always exploited planned spontaneity: since Greek antiquity the text composed in writing has been made by actors to sound, more or less, like spontaneous speech. Still, everyone knows that a play's a play (with the seeming exceptions for "living theater" noted earlier in this chapter). In the classic play-within-a-play, such as in Shakespeare's *A Midsummer Night's Dream,* the lines between fictionalized fiction (the play-within-a-play), mere fiction (the play), and actuality are still relatively easy to draw. Lines are also easy to draw in the play-outside-the-play, such as Francis Beaumont's *The Knight of the Burning Pestle,* where a grocer in the audience insists that his apprentice Ralph have his own idiosyncratic part in the play being staged by a troup of professional players, who then have desperately to keep their own play going in the midst of the melodrama being enacted by Ralph. There is no mistaking here that the grocer and his wife and Ralph are fictional, too, though at a different level than the other characters.

In television the line between the show and actuality is often much more difficult to assess. Besides the cases already noted, give-away shows are a case in point. They must presumably be honestly run, so that the recipients of the prizes cannot be known in advance and thus the receiving of the prizes cannot be rehearsed. The recipients are to be purely parts of the natural world, as against the world of art. However, not any old recipient will really do: the recipient must fit a certain mold, be assimilable to the show through his or her proper grooming. And thus the entire audience is somehow carefully screened, so that whoever from among those in the audience receives a prize is properly attired in effective television garb. The "natural" audience consists exclusively of potential performers. Since the studio audience of this sort is tacitly expected to be representative of all mankind, or at least in the United States, roughly representative of all the country's citizenry, the implication is that everybody in the world dresses in clothes suited to television, and the implication of this implication is that television dress is the natural way to dress.

The implication of such an implication in this art form has a real and immediate effect. Much art has been fed back into the directly lived world, but none more than that of television. Fashion design has often imitated Hollywood movie costumes. But television has projected a walking replay of itself on United States streets. The garish garb fashionable today appears largely as a spin-off from the color-television screen: real life adopts the psychedelic colors and costumes that work best, or are thought to work best, in television fantasia, such as that of Sonny and Cher or of rock musicians, or even in newscasts, where the drab objectivity of "facts" and generally quite "square" personalities come onto the screen in glowing clothes or against contrasting contrived-color backgrounds. Color television does not merely present high-contrast colors: it replicates them in the real lives of its viewers.

The blurring of the edge between art and reality on television as in other art forms, however, is not an innocent achievement. It is not sinister either. But it is dangerous, and tragedy lurks at the interface between unrehearsed actuality and fiction on which this medium is forced to live. With cultivated nonplanning, as is well known, a documentary of a real family in the United States was televised a few years ago, and in the course of the documentary, the family broke up. It would appear that the break-up was earlier on its way, for it is hard to see how a normally cohesive family could have consented to this savage and inhuman invasion of its privacy, but television provided the ultimate format for real-life catastrophe. Still, the break-up comes through in the medium as essentially unpremeditated and unforeseen. It is the essence of television to give all it touches at least some gloss of spontaneity. To this day, the greatest television scandal in the United States has been that of the "Sixty-Four-Thousand-Dollar Question" of a few decades ago, when responses programed as unrehearsed and spontaneous turned out to have been planned in advance. They were programed as unrehearsed and were magically successful as unrehearsed because television favors the unrehearsed show.

Television in the United States is often noted as different from that of other countries because it is commercialized, or more commercialized than elsewhere. What is probably more distinctive of United States television, however, as conversations at international media meetings have suggested to the author, is that in the United States, where the medium is relatively free of the heavy hand of partisan governmental control, the interior dynamics of television have more fully asserted themselves than they have elsewhere. Although social pressures—commercial, religious, educational, ethnic, and other—distinctive of the United States of course shape the United States television phenomena, to know what television as such really is, you will probably do best to study it in the United States because there it registers a wider range of social pressures than elsewhere (though it never registers them quite equally or equitably, of course). Elsewhere, television tells you basically what government wants it to say, to a greater or lesser degree, to the obscuring of its own nature.

Whether television's more full-blown state of existence in the United States is due precisely to commercialization is an interesting question. It may be, and this may indeed indicate that television is in some very deep sense, and even essentially, a commercial medium. It was certainly brought into being by commercial cultures, not by others. It may even ultimately promote or reinforce commercial culture wherever it becomes prominent. But whatever its alignments with commerce, the open-system qualities of the medium, such as those just mentioned, appear more markedly in the United States than anywhere else.

If it is the essence of the present state of consciousness to cultivate open-system models and if television itself essentially promotes such models, being itself essentially open-system (whatever constraints may be put on it from the outside), the strong and widespread feeling that television is in some deep sense the modern medium of communication par excellence can be to a certain extent accounted for. But because of its curious, and by no means understood, ways of intertwining unreality with reality, the alignments and cultural implications of television remain a tangle of unsolved mysteries.

Openness and Ecological Concern

The attraction of open-system paradigms which is discernable today in literature as well as in the mass media as typified in television has come to a head in the concern with ecology which permeates present-day consciousness generally. The massive research on biologically open systems or ecosystems, and related sociological work, can be seen impressively displayed and interpreted in Edward O. Wilson's recent *Sociobiology,* a large quarto volume, profusely illustrated, which was so suited to a wide range of thinking that it became a classic as soon as it was published.[10] Ecological concern is a new state of consciousness, the ultimate in open-system awareness. Its thrust is the dialectical opposite of the isolating thrust of writing and print.

The roots of ecological concern are extensive and deep in history, for, before ecology became a significant biological and social issue, "openness" to being was already a germinal concept in philosophy, as in that of Martin Heidegger, whose symptomatic *Sein und Zeit*, which first appeared in 1927, treats "openness" frequently and at length.[11] Heidegger's kind of philosophical questions resonated through consciousness, for they themselves echoed earlier obscure questions generated in and around the evolutionary thinking culminating in Darwin's work, which had shown how species themselves, earlier thought of as the closed-system bases of life and taken to be major elements in philosophical thinking, are not fixed but develop through natural selection brought about by open interaction between individuals and environment. The new philosophical attention to openness appears not unrelated to the opening of previously isolated human groups to one another fostered by electronic communications media, telephone, radio, and ultimately television. Man's feeling for his lifeworld was changing, less defensively closed.

All systems, as has already been noted, are in one way or another open, and thus the openness of biological systems around which ecology centers is not really unique. Everything in the cosmos, physical, biological, intellectual, or other, is involved in one way or another with everything else. As noted in Chapter 1, even mathematics, which popularly is thought to be a closed system or group of systems is in fact open.

But if all systems are open, the openness is most evident in the case of living beings. Insofar as a living being is like a system— for one can argue that a living being is both like and unlike a system—it (or in higher forms of life he or she) is an open system. A living being needs at every moment something outside

---

10. Cambridge, Mass.: Belknap Press of Harvard University Press, 1975.
11. Martin Heidegger, *Being and Time*, trans. John Macquarrie and Edward Robinson (New York: Harper & Row, 1962), *passim*.

itself to interact with in order to live. Life is openness. A totally isolated living being immediately dies.[12]

Only an open-system paradigm represents the living individual in the way in which it must live, that is, in context, inextricably related to the other, the outside, the "environment." The environment acts on the living individual so that the individual responds and thereby changes the environment, which acts differently upon the individual so that the individual must then respond to it differently, too. The different responses thereby further change the environment, which thus evokes a new response—and so on, with or without the achievement of a greater or lesser, more or less stable, equilibrium.

The openness of living things is most spectacularly evident in man. Through his respiratory, transpiratory, and digestive organs as well as through his senses, man interacts, as do lower forms of animal life, with a great deal of the world around him. But man's interaction goes infinitely further. Through his intellect, man is open to absolutely everything, though he may have trouble making contact with it all, and indeed will always be far from such an ultimate achievement. Man is the most open system we know of. For he is most alive because of his freedom, and in a fundamental though limited sense (for man's freedom has constraints, physical, biological, psychological, and moral), he is so open that he eludes the very idea of system itself.

The concern with ecology at the present moment of consciousness grows out of attention to man and the human lifeworld. It focuses on the openness of the most open systems, human beings, and thus brings to a head all other concerns with openness.

Ecological concern, however, has had a curious history in the media and in the communal consciousness of the United States and the West generally. In the Life Nature Library volume *Ecology,* by Peter Farb and the editors of Time-Life Books, pub-

12. The literature on the living being as a system and as more than a system is enormous. A good introduction to the subject as it relates to this present discussion is the paper by Paul A. Weiss, "The Living System: Determinism Stratified," referred to above in n. 1.

lished in 1963, Prince Bernhard of the Netherlands, President of World Wildlife Fund, could predict in his Introduction that "Ecology, in the next ten or twenty years, may well become the most popular of sciences—a household word to those masses who are ignorant of both the word and its meaning."[13] He was right. For reasons which were neither immediately articulated nor fully articulable, in the late 1960s the mass media—press, radio, and television—quite suddenly began to fill themselves and the rest of the world with talk and writing about ecology and ecosystems and environment, as though no one had ever thought of such issues before. The pattern can be seen by noting the dates of most books under these subject headings in the card catalog of any large library: the flood has broken loose in the past ten years. In fact, however, intense concern about ecology and environment had existed for decades and even generations earlier in specialized scientific and scholarly circles. Prince Bernhard and Time-Life Books brought down to earth existing high-level thinking.

The mass media live largely off their ability to sense and respond to shifting unconscious psychic pressures.[14] At this point, they sensed and added force to a groundswell of popular "interest" in this matter of hitherto rather exclusively high-level concern. That is to say, the mass media sensed and encouraged a widespread desire on the part of millions to become consciously informed about something previously known only vaguely. The news media entered into and fostered a process of "conscientiza-

13. New York: Time-Life Books, 1963; revised 1969, p. [7].
14. In a fascinating article, "Writing News and Telling Stories," *Daedalus,* Spring 1975, issued as *Proceedings of the American Academy of Arts and Sciences,* 104, No. 2, 175–194, Robert Darnton has shown some of the fallacies in the belief that newspaper writers are influenced dominantly by an image they presumably have of the "general public" and its presumably well known desires. Newspaper writers in fact write largely for each other, registering the powerful pressures from within their own peer groups. The article suggests, though it does not undertake to examine, the complex unconscious and subconscious web that connects a newspaper writer, his competitors, his editors and other editors, and whatever any and all of these believe the "public" is or may be, and how it ought to be treated by giving the projected story one or another kind of design.

tion," whether or not they thought of their activity in such terms. Ecological thinking moved by way of the media from the unconscious into public consciousness.

Needless to say, opting for open systems was seldom deliberate and was not always entirely altruistic. Sometimes the option for a purportedly open system was in fact an option for a closed system in disguise. This was not infrequently the case where "environment" was the focus of discussion. In the mass media, this term "environment" appears to have been favored over "ecology" or "ecosystem," which sound more preciously scientific. Environment is surroundings, what is round about. Surroundings of what and of whom? The most obvious and easiest answer is *me* (or *us*). The concept is center-focused. The concept "environment" can stem from and thus encourage a certain narcissism, the projection of the universe of which I am the center. Such an ego-centered world is hardly as open as, at first blush, preoccupation with "environment" might suggest. Instead of sharing with others, it can in fact entail manipulation of others. "Environment" can be centripetal as well as centrifugal.

Its centripetal possibilities suggest why "environment" could have a strong narcissistic appeal when it surfaced in the media. In the years preceding the explosion of environmental concern, the media, in the United States especially, had been preoccupied with the insistently sticky, divisive, and spectacularly open-system problems of racism and the Vietnam War, and to some extent abortion (this issue came to a head slightly later). From such problems environmental concern could provide welcome relief. About the importance of environmental thinking everyone could agree in principle. (Or at least everyone in the technologically developed nations could agree, for the developing nations have a different environmental problem, underexploitation rather than overexploitation). And environmental concern could quite plausibly and comfortingly displace antiracism and anti-Vietnam War activity by appearing to be equally open-system. Only it so happened that environmental concern could also be, though it certainly was not always, a subtle way of achieving narcissistic comfort—which means that it might not necessarily be so open after all, but rather might be simply a disguised self-centeredness. Antiracist and antiwar groups were aware that environmental concerns about peace between man and nature could serve as a welcome and comfortable distraction from problems of securing peace between human beings, and some spoke against "ecological hysteria" which could draw off attention from more pressing social matters—thus Richard Neuhaus in his book *In Defense of People: Ecology and the Seduction of Radicalism* (1971).

But no matter how it may have been at times deceptively appropriated, the open-system paradigm was favored by the stage that consciousness had reached in the late 1960s, and in a great many places pretty well around the world. "Interaction" had become almost an irrefutably good word, even when, as might well happen, it described processes which had been in a given case bad. At least so far as media symbolism and popular ideology went, barriers were out—racial, national, psychological, theological, male-female, child-adult, student-teacher, student-administrater, and others. Good fences no longer made good neighbors. Even in the armed services, generals and privates, admirals and ordinary seamen, were no longer cut off from one another as they used to be. In the United States, the only wall growing higher was that separating church and state—a late closed-system model not found even in the chirographically programed federal Constitution and in fact out of touch with present actuality.

The closed-system paradigm generated in this case by the courts no longer functioned as it once had among religious groups themselves. Ecumenicism in religious belief has proved irresistible, its subconscious roots too deep for extraction. Significantly, individuals most dedicated to their own faith have often proven themselves most responsive to ecumenical drives. And even more significantly, the Roman Catholic Church, purportedly always the most stalwart advocate of closed-system thinking, since the Second Vatican Council has been a world leader in ecumenicism, an open-system movement. Needless to say, the shift to open-system thinking has disquieted the many who equate truth and security with a closed-system model of whatever sort—social, sociological, political, administrative, scientific, philosophical, religious, or other.

Open-system thinking is interactional, transactional, developmental, process-oriented. Terms such as these have by now operated in the discourse about human activity at almost all levels. The open-system paradigm determines the world view of most of the younger generation. It has deeply affected academic curricula, both for liberal arts and for professional training, introducing interdisciplinary programs, "open" classrooms, "open" discussion, and "open" admissions policies, not to mention courses and institutes on ecology, and on environment as such. How far the fashion for this "openness" approach reflects truly changed needs in the various areas of knowledge one can hardly be sure. What one can be sure of is that the "openness" talk does register an imperative need of those who work in the various areas and of others generally to think about subjects in this certain way. The newly assertive preference for open-system models appears to effect a change in external conditions far less surely than a change in consciousness. There had never been any closed systems anyhow and the basic insights offered by open-system models were at root even banal. The assertion that everything interacts with everything else is hardly news. But for complex reasons, some of which will be suggested below, it has become urgent to exploit this insight.

Earlier Open-System and Closed-System Models

The open-system paradigm which has asserted itself so forcefully in recent years had antecedents of course far back in time, many of them of major consequence in intellectual or cultural history. One can readily instance a few more or less relevant to the matters of the present book. In Western antiquity, Socratic dialogue and Platonic dialectic were consistently open-system. So in another way was the preaching of Jesus and his followers: the Kingdom is good news to be shared, thought of in the para-

bles as a mustard plant growing from a tiny seed (Matthew
13:31–32) or as yeast spreading through dough (Matthew
13:33)—this latter model is caught in the term "catholic"
(*katholikos,* a Greek word adopted also by the Latin Church),
which means not "universal" (that is, "inclusive," "encompassing," and hence by implication to some degree bounding) but
rather, in its Greek etymology, *kata* + *hōlos,* through-the-whole,
outgoing, expansive. The rhetorical and dialectical methods of
teaching which dominated intellectual activity in the West from
classical antiquity through the eighteenth century perpetuated
something of the Socratic and Platonic paradigms: thought was
always open to attack. Countless other early examples of more
or less open-system models abound. The point here is simply that
significant ones were available and in use.

But early open-system models existed in a climate which
within the past four or five centuries came to favor closure of
thought in significant ways. The tendency to closure had to do
with a state of mind encouraged by print and its way of suggesting that knowledge, and thus indirectly actuality itself, could
somehow be packaged.[15] Though of course there were other
factors at work besides print, it would appear that many if not
most of the other factors can be related dynamically to print. In
System and Structure Anthony Wilden has discussed some of the
ways in which widely dominant Cartesian and Newtonian frames
of reference relied on "closed-system energy models of all reality."[16]

Backtracking, one finds that there are many pre-Cartesian
representatives of closed-system thinking, just as there are many
representatives of open-system thinking who are contemporaries
of Descartes (Wilden instances Pascal, who is also discussed along
with related thinkers by Lucien Goldmann[17]) or who belong to
the later Cartesian age (Wilden instances Rousseau). Perhaps the

15. See Walter J. Ong, *Ramus, Method, and the Decay of Dialogue*
(Cambridge, Mass.: Harvard University Press, 1958), pp. 151–152, 307–318.
16. Wilden, *System and Structure,* pp. 213–217, and *passim.*
17. *The Hidden God: A Study of Tragic Vision in the Pensées of Pascal
and the Tragedies of Racine,* trans. Phillip Thody (New York: Humanities
Press, 1964).

most tight-fisted[18] pre-Cartesian proponent of the closed system, one not mentioned by Wilden, was the French philosopher and educational reformer Pierre de la Ramée or Petrus Ramus, discussed in earlier chapters. Ramus' close-field thinking is absolute and imperious, welling out of unconscious drives for completeness and security, (and thus in some ways regressive to the self-enclosed, infantile stage represented by the uroboros, the serpent with its tail in its mouth—the thumb-sucking infant).[19] It is unencumbered by any profound philosophical speculation, and yet it is supposed to apply to every field of knowledge.[20] Insofar as a strong stress on closed-system thinking marks the beginning of the modern era, Ramus, rather than Descartes, stands at the beginning.

The closed-system paradigm was encouraged by the new science of the sixteenth and seventeenth centuries in its reliance on seemingly closed-system mathematics: the physical universe was assimilated to a closed system, or, rather, a system of systems, each operating on purely mathematical laws. The term *systema* itself, with its implication of closure, became widely current, as it had not been before, and a whole armory of related closed-system terms for fields of knowledge achieved spectacularly wide, almost ubiquitous, currency, particularly in text books: *idea*, *typus* (imprint, outline), *fabrica* (fabric), *corpus* (body), *series* (array), *tabella* (table), *tabula* (chart) *synopsis*, and many more.[21] Frank E. Manuel's brilliant and incisive Fremantle

18. Since at least the time of Zeno of Citium, logic has been compared to the closed fist, rhetoric to the open hand. See Wilbur Samuel Howell, *Logic and Rhetoric in England, 1500–1700* (Princeton, N.J.: Princeton University Press, 1956), pp. 14–15, 33, 51, 141, 208, 315, 365, 374, 377, 378. All of these places in Howell report on citations of Zeno's model by various ancient and Renaissance philosophers. The "clunch fist of logic" was a widely current closed-system model for centuries, though it served also simultaneously as a model for other things, such as power.

19. See Erich Neumann, *The Origins and History of Consciousness,* trans. R. F. C. Hull (New York: Pantheon Books, 1954), pp. 5–38.

20. Ong, *Ramus, Method, and the Decay of Dialogue,* pp. 36–49, 224–269, and *passim.*

21. Walter J. Ong, " 'Idea' Titles in John Milton's Milieu," *Studies in Honor of DeWitt T. Starnes,* ed. Thomas P. Harrington, *et al.* (Austin, Texas: University of Texas Press, 1967), pp. 227–239.

Lectures, *The Religion of Isaac Newton,* show how Newton's fascination with closure began in the realm of physics and carried far beyond. In the latter half of his long life (1642–1727), the discoverer of the laws of gravitation devoted a major part of his energies to theological writing centered on the interpretation of prophecies, undertaking to construct a system of interpretation which exhausted all the possible meanings of the prophetic symbols in the Bible so that "there was nothing left over, no random words still unexplained, no images that were superfluous. The system was closed, complete, and flawless."[22] Newton really thought he could manage the meaning of Ezekiel and of the Book of Revelation this way. Newton's success in physics was for him a limited success, significant largely because it provided a miniature model for his total ambition, which was "to force everything in the heavens and on earth into a grandiose but tight form from which the most minuscule detail could not escape."[23] The German Ramist Ioannes Piscator (1546–1626) had been bitten earlier by a like ambition, as had many other Ramists.[24] Piscator undertook to do a "logical analysis" of each book of the Bible to state explicitly and totally in his analysis exactly what the book was really saying: the rest of the given book, that is, whatever his analysis did not contain, was understood to be pure ornament, to make the content attractive.[25] After Newton, closed-system theology was given another kind of try by Richard Jack in his *Mathematical Principles of Theology, or the Existence of God Geometrically Demonstrated* (London, 1747).

Closed-system paradigms were maximized by Kant. Noumena are untouched by phenomena; practical reason is disjunct from pure reason. Almost incredibly for a person of such intelligence, Kant believed, as noted in Chapter 8, that logic was so much a closed system that nothing new in it had been discovered or could be discovered after Aristotle. The closed-system paradigms favored

22. Oxford: The Clarendon Press, 1974, p. 98.
23. Page 103.
24. Ong, *Ramus, Method, and the Decay of Dialogue,* pp. 295–318.
25. Ong, "Ioannes Piscator: One Man or a Ramist Dichotomy?" *Harvard Library Bulletin,* 8 (1954), 151–162.

by Newtonian physics dominated many views of language, such as those of John Wilkins in *An Essay towards a Real Character and a Philosophical Language* (1668) or Johann Nicolaus Funck (Funckius) who in his six Latin volumes, *De origine Latinae linguae* (1720) and *De pueritia Latinae linguae* (1720) through *De inerti ac decrepita Latinae linguae senectute* (1750), treats the Latin language as a historically closed system which came into integral existence at a certain moment, went through an infancy, adolescence, and maturity and then grew old and prepared to die. The antecedent life of Latin in its preclassical forms and its evolution into the modern Romance languages, though these had been perfectly normal and ordinary linguistic developments, somehow did not fit Funckius' closed-system model.

The closed-system paradigms were peremptorily disqualified in the early twentieth century with the development of quantum theory and with relativity theory, which brought the observer into consideration. But throughout the Western intellectual world closed systems were under particularly vigorous attack, more or less overt, more or less subtle, from the time that the romantic movement gained enough strength to cast suspicion on the claims of extreme rationalism. In keeping with the romantic sensibility, through its dialectical approach to history Hegel's philosophy was more open than Kant's. Darwin's and Wallace's discoveries regarding natural selection and the selection and evolution of species dealt probably the heaviest blow to closed-system models, as has been noted earlier. Not only individual organisms, but the hitherto supposedly fixed species were open, as species, to change through natural selection, powered by individuals' interaction with environment. In the Darwinian world, ecosystems were far more crucial for life in every one of its specific forms than had ever before been proved.

In the currents feeding out of the romantic movement and related evolutionary thinking, countless other instances of open-system paradigms can be found. Among these would be those favored by phenomenology and by intersubjectivity as it has been developed in recent philosophy and psychology. Intersubjectivity is the open-system paradigm directly countering the closed-system paradigm of solipsistic activity which had characterized Cartesian epistemology and the implied epistemology of Ramist logic. In his *Studies in Ethnomethodology* and other works Harold Garfinkel has effected another opening, showing how the communication of abstract reasoning comes about not simply in a closed, abstract world, but only insofar as this reasoning is embedded in tacitly used or implied practical reasoning, which is to say in social behavioral settings.[26]

This sketchy overview or sampling of some of the fortunes of closed-system and open-system paradigms is meant only to be suggestive. It treats of these paradigms sometimes as consciously and articulatedly appropriated (in ecological planning or in "living" theater) and sometimes as simply present and operative without fully reflective, conscious appropriation. Paradigms of this latter source may be embedded in theories (Cartesian epistemology) or simply in ways of life (uncontrolled exploitation of natural resources). They represent what Thomas H. Kuhn means by "paradigms" in *The Structure of Scientific Revolution.*[27]

Interfaces of the Word and Evolution of Consciousness

The place at which independent systems meet and act on one another or communicate with one another is called an interface. The concept "interface," so defined, presents difficulties, for if the systems are independent, how can they be interacting? The difficulties are due not merely to the concept of "interface" itself but more directly to that of "system," and especially that of "independent system," for the independence of a system is in the last analysis always relative independence. In Paul A. Weiss's definition, as we recall, a system is a "rather circumscribed complex" of "relatively bounded phenomena" which retains a "relatively

26. Harold Garfinkel, *Studies in Ethnomethodology* (Englewood Cliffs, N.J.: Prentice-Hall, 1967). See also Aaron V. Cicourel, *Cognitive Sociology* (Harmondsworth, England: Penguin Education, a Division of Penguin Books, 1973), pp. 99–140.

27. Second enlarged ed. (Chicago: University of Chicago Press, 1970).

stationary pattern" despite a "high degree of variability, . . . among its constituent units." The "rather" and "relatively" are deliberate and crucial. In short, no system is ever totally closed, ever totally independent. They all interact with something other than themselves.

This is why, paradoxically, discussion of systems generates discussion not merely of containedness, of closure, but eventually and inexorably the discussion of exchange, of outwardness, and ultimately of communication. The forces at work in any in-depth consideration of systems are caught in the title of the book by Anthony Wilden noted above, *System and Structure: Essays in Communication and Exchange,* and in the anthropological and linguistic as well as biological and mathematical subject matter that the book treats. System and structure directly involve insidedness and imply outsidedness, otherness. And communication and exchange become issues both inside a system (between the elements within the system) and outside a system (communication between systems). In depth, the discussion of systems becomes another avatar of the metaphysical question of the one and the many.

The concept of communication refers basically to our experience of the living world, of interrelations between unitary organisms, particularly sentient organisms. Even to think of messenger RNA as "communicating" within a cell is to stretch the term a bit: RNA does not "communicate" in quite the sense in which two male mockingbirds communicate at the edges of their respective territories, warning each other off. By comparison, RNA simply "registers" and transports a given structure. This does not mean that it is illegitimate to say that RNA "communicates," but only that this sense of "communicate" is adjusted somewhat from the basic sense.

In the world of living, sentient organisms, communication exists at its peak among human beings. The reason is that communication requires closure, or unification and distinctiveness of a being, maximum interiority, organization from within, like that of a system, and openness, or access to whatever is outside the closure. Human beings are both closed and opened to the maximum.

The focus of closure and openness in human beings is human consciousness itself. What is meant by human consciousness here can be understood by treating it at its center, as caught up in the "I" that I utter. The "I" that I utter is open only to me and closed to all outside me. No one else knows what it feels like to be me. I do not know what any other human being experiences when he or she says "I." In a way it would seem to be "like" what I feel when I say "I," but I am aware that every bit of any other person's sense of "I" is totally different from mine. I simply do not know what it feels like to be the other person. Each of us is isolated, sealed off from every other in this way, even husband from wife and wife from husband, father and mother from daughter and son, brother from brother and sister from sister.

Yet it is only such isolated consciousnesses that can truly communicate, that can share, as no brute animal—that cannot say "I"—can share. What we mean by communication at its maximum intensity, its peak, is what goes on between human beings. Paradoxically, communication demands isolation. Unless a being is somehow closed in on itself, self-possessed from within, able to say "I" and to know in the saying that this "I" is completely and indestructibly unique, separate from all else, that there is simply no possibility that any more of the four billion other human beings alive today is also the same "I," there is no sharing to be done, no communication possible. I can share only what I have control of. If I do not lay hold of myself by reflection, do not know the "taste of self, more distinctive than ale or alum" (in Gerard Manley Hopkins' words), I cannot give myself to another or to others. I have nothing to give—for I have no self, no person, to give.

Communication does not have simply to do with oneself, but in fact can concern anything and everything. But it always involves the self, for communication, whatever it is concerned with, is a conscious activity, and the "I" which I speak and which I alone can speak lies at the center of my consciousness. It is the most insistently accessible of all things in my world, the ground and border of all my waking experience of everything, and even of my dream experience. I can do nothing outside its presence, more or less directly adverted to. In this "I," I am totally open and transparent to myself: by comparison, all else is dark and opaque, including even my own body, which is somehow included in the "I" but in some strange ways also feels a bit external to me. "The heavy bear who goes with me," Delmore Schwartz calls the body in his poem of that name.

Yet, though isolated and unique, in one way open only to itself, in another way the "I" is necessarily and essentially open to others, too. For me to have matured into the self-knowledge whereby I can say "I," there had to be other persons around me, each of them, even mother and father, unique and isolated but communicating with me from infancy, coaxing and coaching me into talking and thinking simultaneously, and into the unique interior awareness of myself that none of them, all strangers, had access to.

The strangers not only coaxed and coached me into an awareness of myself but also guided me into an awareness of the rest of actuality around me impinging on myself. They, isolated though they were, helped me, isolated though I was, and am, to open my consciousness to all being. For, as earlier noted in this chapter, the human person is open to other beings not only physically and physiologically but intellectually—and through his intellect, which is part of his consciousness, to anything and everything. There is no particular limit to how much actuality the human consciousness, directly or indirectly, can pull itself into.

Human consciousness is open closure.

The "I" interfaces with everything.

There can be little doubt that our central experience of unity, the foundation of what we mean by oneness, the datum of experience on which we build (with the help of other data, too, of course) our concept of the "one," of unity, is our conscious experience of self that we capture in the saying of "I." Nothing else in our experience is so irrefragable, so palpably indivisible. Whatever our interior multiplicities, somatic, sensory, psychological, noetic, or other—and we do have experiences of these multiplicities—our sense of "I" somehow transcends them. The "I" cannot be split into simpler units. What could it be severed into? This is a central paradox of existence. How can it be that with all my interior divisions and multiplicities—my welter of sensations, feelings, thoughts, my bodily parts outside parts—this "I" is so purely and indissolubly one? Here my sense of self is my immediate experience in my own life of the paradox of the one and the many which has an infinite number of versions, cosmological and metaphysical and other.

Since my concept of unity is so tied up with my sense of self expressed in "I," the "I" serves as a kind of paradigm for the notion of system, a paradigm, that is, in Thomas Kuhn's sense of a model or frame of reference that is not consciously adverted to as a model but that nevertheless determines the way one thinks about things. A system is a multiplicity, somehow one, separate, self-sustaining (up to a point) in a way that at least unconsciously suggests this center of consciousness, this paramount unity, the "I" that I can utter and that in the welter of other experiences impinging on me at any given time (synchronically) or over a period of time (diachronically) provides me with an experience and concept of oneness, and more specifically of oneness despite diversity.

Looked at carefully, a system does indeed resemble the "I" in being in one way closed but in another way not entirely closed at all. Thus the "I" itself can be thought of as a system, in a certain sense. The difference between systems and the unique "I" are, however, manifold. Basically, systems are neither so definitively closed as is the "I" nor so utterly open. A system is not so definitely closed as is the "I" in that it cannot pull itself together inside itself to the extent that it knows from inside itself that it is different from every other being simply because it experiences itself directly for who it is. For a system is not a "who" but a "what"—which is to say it is not open to itself from the inside, but only more or less open to other things outside.

As communication is a concept derived from the world of living things and then extended to nonliving activities, so a system is a concept derived from the mechanical world and then extended to living things. System and communication stand in complementary relationship to one another.

Because essentially it is modeled on nonlife, a system is not so utterly open as is the "I": it is not receptive to all of being. So likewise, human consciousness, centered in the "I," is not strictly a system, only something like a system, or, better, something that systems are like. Human consciousness is the open-and-closed unity that a system can only approach more and more closely without achieving. For the living world, and more specifically the human world, is ultimately the measure of the mechanical, and not vice versa.

The technological world is part of the human world. There is no technology not totally dependent on man, (which is not to say that any technology is totally under conscious control). Technology enters into consciousness more intimately than has commonly been thought, for the technologies of writing and print and electronic devices radically transform the word and the mental processes which are the coefficients of speech and of which speech is the coefficient. These technological "systems" of writing and print and electronic devices interface with one another, as has been explained in Chapters 2 and 3 above. Writing grows out of oral speech, which can never be quite the same after writing is interiorized in the psyche. Writing leads verbalization out of the agora into a world of imagined audiences—a fascinating and demanding and exquisitely productive world. Print grows out of writing and transforms the modes and uses of writing and thus also of oral speech and of thought itself. Electronic devices grow out of writing and print, and also transform writing and print, so that books of an electronic age can be distinguished, by their very organization of thought, from those of earlier ages.

And beneath it all, consciousness, insofar as it can be considered by analogy with a system, interfaces with everything. Human beings still say "I" and each "I" is always unique. Each

"I" is also open, but the world on which consciousness opens today impinges on consciousness in ways different from the ways of earlier ages. More than ever before, the alert individual consciousness feels that it must do more interfacing, that it must be more "open."

There is no reason to believe that the present hospitality to open-system paradigms in the exercises of conscious activity presages a stage of millennial bliss for mankind either in the West or elsewhere in the world. Wrongdoing appears as rampant as ever before, and some of our most open-system mass media are willing to make real-life tragedy a part of entertainment and to be as venal otherwise as human beings have always tended to be. Still, the drive to openness on the whole does appear to be advantageous and to represent progress in a deep sense of this term. The tendency to openness appears to mark a new and more advanced stage in the evolution of consciousness. Closure can be protected and desirable at times, and it is particularly necessary at earlier stages of thought to rule out distractions and achieve control. But programed closed-system thinking, whether in matters of science, history, philosophy, art, politics, or religious faith is ultimately defensive and, although defenses may be always to some degree necessary, to make defensiveness on principle one's dominant mood and program forever is to opt not for life but for death. The great forces in psychic life, the thirst for knowledge, love for others, religious faith, certainly the Christian faith, are not essentially forces favoring closure, but drives to openness. "The truth shall make you free."

Openness does not mean lack of organization, lack of principle, or lack of all resistance. For the human being, at least, it means quite the contrary: the strengthening of organization, principles, and resistance where needed, so that interaction with the outside can be strong and real. Indeed, paradoxically again, openness means strengthening closure itself.

Ultimately, openness calls for strengthening of closure because of the dialectical relationship of the two in consciousness. When one is heightened in a way, the other normally undergoes heightening in another way. The age of "togetherness," of open-system paradigms, of noetic "kleinforms" that open actuality and fiction into and out of one another in amazing ways, is also the age of the isolated individual. But how isolated can the individual be in an age more openly and explicitly concerned about the individual—in literature, psychology, sociology, philosophy, theology, social legislation, and otherwise—than any earlier age has been? Discussion of the "I" such as that just undertaken here would have been impossible a few centuries ago. Consciousness was not yet ready for it. Such discussion is a twentieth-century phenomenon. We can face the isolation or closure of the "I" with equanimity today because society's openness serves as a counterpoise to the individual's isolation and reminds us that such isolation is a foundation for openness. We can all tolerate being very much alone and acknowledging we are alone so long as we are all alone together.

The closure implemented by print was a prelude to the openness of the television age. And since television has not destroyed print but interfaced with it, the closure is in some ways with us still. There are problems and opportunities with both closure and openness, and we all are going to have to live with the problems and opportunities there are, and more.

Index

Abrams, M. H., 223-224, 286-287
Acapulco phenomenon, *see* Encuentro Mundial de Comunicación
Achebe, Chinua, 199
Addison, Joseph, 66, 236
Agonistic structures: in education, 216-217; in existence, 222; of thought, 113, 210, 216-217, 222-229. *See also* "Dozens," the; Fliting
Agricola, Rudolph, 148
Alexandre, Pierre, 93
Alienation, 17-22, 47, 305; languages and, 27-38
Allan, John, 252
Allen, Don Cameron, 153, 169
Alphabet, history of, 128
Alphabetization: casual, 169; phonetic, 170. *See also* Visual retrieval of verbalized knowledge
Alsted, Johann Heinrich, 187
Amerbach, Boniface, 172
Anagnōrisis (recognition), 247
"Anatomy," as title, 175-176
Anthologia (anthology), 179, 238
Aphorisms, 87, 207
Apuleius, 72
Arabic, 28, 31-32
Arabic "dialects," separate spoken languages, 32
Aristotle, 83, 107, 247, 285; logic of, 208, 332-333; *Nicomachean Ethics,* 75; *Physics,* 192; *Poetics,* 312; *Rhetoric,* 86-87, 149, 192,

295; *Topika,* 160; on topoi, 149-150
Art, nature and, 310-322
Article, definite and indefinite, 64-66
Ascham, Roger, 182, 185
Ashworth, E. J., 190
Audience, for writer, 53-81. *See also* Reader as spectator; Writer's "audience"
Auerbach, Erich, 263-264, 284
Augustine of Hippo, St., 76
Austen, Jane, 73, 254
Austin, John L., 54, 275

Bacon, Francis, 168, 236-237
Baldwin, T. W., 148, 152, 182
Banyanga, 253
Barnouw, Erik, 315
Barthes, Roland, 10, 17, 54, 230, 272, 311-312
Baudelaire, Charles, 310
Baxtin, Mixail, 275
Beaumont, Francis, 320-321
Beaurline, L. A., 176
Beck, August, 148
Beckett, Samuel, 293, 319
Bede, St., The Venerable, 90
Beluacus, Jean, 152
Beowulf, 180, 225, 253
Bergson, Henri, 116
Bernard, Augusta, 24
Bible: aural assimilation of, 270; closed-field interpretation, 332; futurity of, 261-262; not litera-

Interfaces of the Word

Designed by R. E. Rosenbaum.
Composed by York Composition Company, Inc.,
in 11 point Intertype Baskerville, 2 points leaded,
with display lines in Monotype and Intertype Baskerville.
Printed letterpress from type by York Composition Company
on Warren's Number 66 text, 50 pound basis.
Bound by John H. Dekker & Sons, Inc.
in Joanna book cloth
and stamped in All Purpose foil.

Library of Congress Cataloging in Publication Data
(For library cataloging purposes only)

Ong, Walter J
    Interfaces of the word.

    Includes bibliographical references and index.
    1. Languages—Philosophy. 2. Consciousness.
    3. Civilization—Philosophy. I. Title.
P106.0499   401   77-3124
ISBN 0-8014-1105-X